S

The Unseen H...
Icarus's Mother, 4-...
Red Cross, Cow...
The Holy Ghostly, Operation Sidewinder, The Mad Dog Blues,
Back Bog Beast Bait, Killer's Head

This first collection of Sam Shepard's plays brings together fourteen of
his legendary plays from the sixties, which established his reputation as
'the major talent of his generation . . . an original, a major force'
(*The Times*).

'Shepard is a protean figure. The weird dreamlike terrains of his plays
sparkle with the insights of a man who has inhabited many worlds . . .
Hoboes, thieves, rock 'n' rollers, Martians, cowboys, moguls, madmen –
Shepard's heroes range as widely as his interests. His plays are
dreamscapes of the American wasteland.' John Lahr

'The true artist starts with his obsessions, then makes them ours as well.
The very young Sam Shepard exploded his obsessions like firecrackers; in
his crazy, brilliant early plays he was escaping his demons.' *Newsweek*

'Stunning in their originality, defiant and inscrutable.' *Esquire*

Sam Shepard was born in 1943 in Fort Sheridan, Illinois. He moved to
New York from California just as the off-off Broadway theatre scene was
emerging. His first short plays were staged in 1963. He came to London
in 1971 (*La Turista* had already been seen at the Theatre Upstairs, 1969),
and his subsequent UK productions include: *The Unseen Hand* (also
Theatre Upstairs, 1973); *Tooth of Crime* (Open Space, 1972; Royal Court,
1974); *Geography of a Horsedreamer*, directed by Shepard, and *Action* (both at
the Theatre Upstairs, 1974); *Curse of the Starving Class* (Royal Court, 1977);
Suicide in B Flat (Open Space, 1977); *Seduced* (Theatre Upstairs, 1980);
Buried Child (Hampstead, 1980); *True West* (National Theatre, 1981); *Fool for
Love* (National Theatre, 1985, which he directed himself in New York); *A
Lie of the Mind* (Royal Court, 1987); *States of Shock* (off-Broadway, 1991;
Salisbury Playhouse, as part of the Royal National Theatre's
'Springboards' season, 1993); and *Simpatico* (Royal Court, 1995). Eleven of
his plays have won 'Obie' awards. His screenplay of Wim Wenders' *Paris,
Texas* won the Gold Palm Award at the 1984 Cannes Film Festival and he
directed his own screenplay, *Far North*, in 1988. In the spring of 1986, he
was admitted to the American Academy of Arts and Letters. A collection
of short stories, *Cruising Paradise*, was published in 1996.

SAM SHEPARD

Plays: 1

The Unseen Hand
The Rock Garden
Chicago
Icarus's Mother
4-H Club
Fourteen Hundred Thousand
Red Cross
Cowboys #2
Forensic & the Navigators
The Holy Ghostly
Operation Sidewinder
The Mad Dog Blues
Back Bog Beast Bait
Killer's Head

with an introduction by the author

Methuen Drama

METHUEN CONTEMPORARY DRAMATISTS

This collection first published in Great Britain 1996
by Methuen Drama
an imprint of Reed International Books Ltd
Michelin House, 81 Fulham Road, London SW3 6RB
and Auckland, Melbourne, Singapore and Toronto

Originally published in hardcover by Bobbs-Merrill, Indianapolis, in 1972,
and in somewhat different form by Urizen, in 1981, and by Bantam Books,
New York, in 1986

Printed and bound in Great Britain by
Cox & Wyman Ltd, Reading, Berkshire

CONTENTS

A CHRONOLOGY
of first performances

	USA	UK
Cowboys	1964	
The Rock Garden	1964	
Up to Thursday	1965	
Dog	1965	
Rocking Chair	1965	
Chicago	1965	1976
Icarus's Mother	1965	1970
4-H Club	1965	
Fourteen Hundred Thousand	1966	
Red Cross	1966	1969
La Turista	1967	1969
Melodrama Play	1967	1967
Forensic & the Navigators	1967	
Cowboy #2	1967	1980
The Holy Ghostly	1969	1973
The Unseen Hand	1969	1973
Operation Sidewinder	1970	
Shaved Splits	1970	
Cowboy Mouth (with Patti Smith)	1971	1971
The Mad Dog Blues	1971	1978
Back Bog Beast Bait	1971	
The Tooth of Crime	1972	1972
Blue Bitch (televised 1972)	1973	1975
Nightwalk (with Megan Terry and Jean-Claude van Itallie)	1973	1973
Little Ocean		1974
Geography of a Horse Dreamer	1974	1974
Action	1975	1974
Killer's Head	1975	1979
Angel City	1976	1983
Suicide in B Flat	1976	1977
The Sad Lament of Pecos Bill on the Eve of Killing His Wife	1976	
Curse of the Starving Class	1976	1977
Inacoma	1977	
Buried Child	1978	1980
Seduced	1978	1980

INTRODUCTION

The strongest impressions I have now of these early plays are the specific times and places where they were written. The plays themselves seem to drift back to me as flimsy ghosts, in the same way a conversation with someone in the distant past is half-remembered. For me, these plays are inseparable from the experience of the time out of which they came. A series of impulsive chronicles representing a chaotic, subjective world. Basically, without apologizing, I can see now that I was learning how to write. I was breaking the ice with myself. Even though some of this work is slightly embarrassing to me now (twenty years later), it's like objecting to a photograph that illuminates an aspect of the "real you" in a moment when you least expect the truth to be recorded. I can remember being dazed with writing, with the discovery of finding I actually had these worlds inside me. These voices. Shapes. Currents of language. Light. All the mysterious elements that cause anyone to make a journey.

I wrote all the time. Everywhere. When I wasn't writing, I was thinking about it or continuing to "write" in my head. I'd have six or seven ideas for plays rolling at once. I couldn't write fast enough to keep up the flow of material running through me. Needless to say, I wasn't very good company. At that time, a major critic from the *New York Times* commented that I wrote "disposable plays," and in some sense he was probably right. But nothing mattered to me then except to get the stuff down on paper. The judgment of it seemed too far after the fact to make any difference.

There was never a sense, in all this, of evolving a style or moving on to a bigger, longer, "more important" form. Each play had a distinct life of its own and seemed totally self-contained within its one-act structure. Partly, this had to do with the immediacy of the off-off-Broadway situation. Anybody could get his or her piece performed, almost any time. If there wasn't a slot open at one of the cafe theaters or in the churches, you could at least pool together some actors and have a reading. You could go into full-scale rehearsals with nothing more than an idea or half a page of written text. It was a playwright's heaven. Experimentation was the lifeblood not only of the playwright but also of actors, directors, and even of producers and critics. The concept of "audience" was diametrically opposed to the commercial marketplace. The only impulse was to make living, vital theater which spoke to the moment. And the moment, back then in the mid-sixties, was seething with a radical shift of the American psyche.

Today, I don't see how these plays make any real sense unless they're put into perspective with that time.

Sam Shepard
New York,
October 1985

to my son Jesse

The Unseen Hand

The Unseen Hand was first produced at the La Mama Experimental Theatre Club on Friday, December 26, 1969, with the following cast:

BLUE MORPHAN:	Beeson Carroll
WILLIE (THE SPACE FREAK):	Lee Kissman
CISCO MORPHAN:	Bernie Warkentin
THE KID:	Sticks Carlton
SYCAMORE MORPHAN:	Victor Eschbach

The production was directed by Jeff Bleckner.

SCENE

Center stage is an old '51 Chevrolet convertible, badly bashed and dented, no tires and the top torn to shreds. On the side of it is written "Kill Azusa" with red spray paint. All around is garbage, tin cans, cardboard boxes, Coca-Cola bottles and other junk. The stage is dark. Sound of a big diesel truck from a distance, then getting louder, then passing with a whoosh. As the sound passes across the stage the beam of the headlights cuts through the dark and passes across the Chevy. Silence. Soft blue moonlight comes up slowly as the sound of another truck repeats, as before, its headlights cutting through the dark. This should be a synchronized tape-light loop which repeats over and over throughout the play—the headlights sweeping past accompanied by the sound of a truck. The lights come up but maintain a full moon kind of light. The whooshing of the trucks and the passing lights keep up. A figure slowly emerges out of the back seat of the Chevy. His name is BLUE MORPHAN. *He has a scraggly beard, black overcoat, blue jeans, cowboy boots and hat and a bottle in his hand. He is slightly drunk and talks to an imaginary driver in the front seat.*

BLUE: Say listen. Did we pass Cucamunga? Didn't we already pass it up? Listen. This here is Azusa. We must a' passed it up. Why don't ya' pull up on the embankment there and let me out? Come on now. Fair's fair. I didn't stab ya' or nothin'. Nobody stole yer wallet, did they? OK. So let me out like I ask ya'. That's it. Atta' boy. OK. Good. If I had me any loose jingle I'd sure lay it on ya' fer gas money but I'd like to get me a cup a' coffee. You know how it is. Thanks, boy.

(He slowly climbs out of the back seat onto the stage, then reaches into the back and pulls out a battered guitar with broken strings.)

If ya' ever happen through Duarte let me know. Gimme a buzz or something. Drop me a line. 'Course ya' don't got the address but that's all right. Just ask 'em fer Blue Morphan. That's me. Anyone. Just ask any old body fer old Blue. They'll tell ya'.

(He pulls out an old dusty suitcase held together with rope and sets it on the ground, then a rifle.)

I ain't been back there fer quite a spell now but they'll be able to direct ya' to the stables all right. Follow the old Union Pacific till ya' come to Fish Creek. Don't pick up no longhairs though. Now I warned ya'. OK. OK. Do what ya' like but I warned ya'.

(He pulls out a broken bicycle, a fishing rod, a lantern, an inner tube, some pipe, a bag full of bolts and other junk. He keeps taking more and more stuff out of the back seat and setting it down on the stage as he talks.)

You been driving long enough by now to tell who to pick up and who to leave lay. But if they got their thumb out you better look 'em over twice. I know. I used to drive a Chevy myself. Good car. Thing is nowadays it ain't so easy to tell the riff-raff from the gentry. Know what I mean. You can get tricked. They can fool ya'. All kinda' fancy over-the-head talk and all along they're workin' for the government same as you. I mean you might not be. Like me fer instance. I'm a free agent. Used to be a time when I'd take an agency job. Go out and bring in a few bushwackers just for the dinero. Usually a little bonus throwed in. But nowadays ya' gotta keep to yerself. They got nerve gas right now that can kill a man in thirty seconds. Yup. A drop a' that on the back of a man's hand and poof! Thirty seconds. That ain't all. They got rabbit fever, parrot fever and other stuff stored up. Used to be, a man would have hisself a misunderstanding and go out and settle it with a six-gun. Now it's all silent, secret. Everything moves like a fever. Don't know when they'll cut ya' down and when they do ya' don't know who done it. Don't mean to get ya' riled though. Too nice a night fer that. Straight, clean highway all the way from here to Tuba City. Shouldn't have no trouble. If yer hungry though there's a Bob's Big Boy right up the road a piece. I don't know if ya' go in fer double-decker cheeseburgers or not but— Listen, tell ya' what, long as yer hungry I'll jest come along with ya' a ways and we'll chow down together. Sure. Good idea. I ain't ate since yesterday mornin' anyhow. Just before ya' picked me up.

(He starts putting all the junk back into the car.)

Sure is nice of ya' to help me out this a way. Don't come across many good old boys these days. Seems like they all got a chip on the shoulder or somethin'. You noticed that? The way they swagger around givin' ya' that look. Like ya' weren't no more than a road apple or somethin' worse. If they'd a known me in my prime it might change their tune. Hadn't a been fer the old hooch here I'd a been in history books by now. Probably am anyhow, under a different name. They never get the name straight. Don't matter too much anyhow. Least it don't hurt my feelings none. 'Course yer too young to remember the Morphan brothers probably. Cisco, Sycamore, and me, Blue. The three of us. 'Course we had us a few more. Not a gang exactly. Not like these teenage hot-rodders with their Mercurys and Hudson Hornets. Leastways we wasn't no menace. The people loved us. The real people I'm talkin' about. The people people. They helped us out in fact. And vica versa. We'd never go rampant on nobody. Say, you oughta' get yer tires checked before ya' go too much further. That left rear one looks a little spongy. Can't be too careful when yer goin' a distance. A car's like a good horse. You take care a' it and it takes care a' you.

(WILLIE, the space freak, enters. He is young and dressed in super future clothes, badly worn and torn. Orange tights, pointed shoes, a vinyl vest with a black shirt that comes up like a hood over the back of his head. His skin is badly burned and blistered with red open sores. His head is shaved and there is a black handprint burned into the top of his skull. At moments he goes into convulsive fits, his whole body shaking. He staggers on stage. BLUE sees him and stops his babble. They stare at each other for a moment.)

I suppose yer lookin' fer a handout or somethin'.

(WILLIE just stares, exhausted, his sides heaving. BLUE climbs back into the back seat and disappears. His voice can still be heard.)

That's the trouble with you kids. Always lookin' fer a handout. There ain't nothin' romantic about panhandlin', sonny. Ye' ain't gonna' run across the holy grail thataway. Anyhow ya' come to the wrong place. This here is Azusa, not New York City.

(BLUE's *head pops up from the back seat. He looks at* WILLIE *still standing there, panting.*)

"A," "Z," "U," "S," "A." "Everything from 'A' to 'Z' in the USA." Azusa. If yer thinking on robbin' me a' my worldly possessions you can take a look for yerself. I been livin' in this Chevy for twenty years now and I ain't come across no diamond rings yet.

(*He disappears back down in the back seat.*)

'Course if ya' just wanna' rest that's a different story. It's a free highway. Yer welcome to stay a spell. The driver's seat's mighty comfortable once ya' get used to the springs.

WILLIE: You Blue Morphan?

(*A pause as* BLUE *slowly rises, his head coming into view.*)

BLUE: What'd you call me?
WILLIE: Is your name Blue Morphan?
BLUE: Look, sonny, nobody knows my name or where I been or where I'm goin'. Now you better trot along.

(*He sinks back down.*)

WILLIE: I've traveled through two galaxies to see you. At least you could hear me out.

(BLUE's *head comes back into view.*)

BLUE: You been hittin' the juice or somethin'? What's yer name, boy?
WILLIE: They call me Willie.
BLUE: Who's they?
WILLIE: The High Commission.
BLUE: What're ya' shakin for? It's a warm night. Here. Have a swig a' this. It'll put a tingle in ya'.

(*He offers* WILLIE *the bottle.*)

WILLIE: No thanks.

BLUE: What, Apple Jack ain't good enough for ya', huh? Suppose you run in fancy circles or somethin'. Just a second, just a second.

(He climbs out of the back seat and goes around to the trunk and opens it. He starts rummaging through junk in the trunk as WILLIE stands there shaking.)

Got a couple a' Navajo blankets here in the back somewheres. Keep 'em special fer when the wind comes up. Sometimes it blows in off the San Joaquin and gets a bit nippy. Ah, here ya' go. This oughta' do it.

(He pulls out a dusty Indian blanket from the trunk and takes it over to WILLIE.*)*

Here ya' go. Here. Well, take it.

(He offers the blanket to WILLIE, *but* WILLIE *just stares at him, shaking and trembling.)*

You sure got yerself a case a' the DTs there, boy. Here. Wrap this around ya'. Come on now.

*(*BLUE *wraps the blanket around* WILLIE's *shoulders, then notices the handprint on his head.)*

What's that ya' got on yer head there? Some new fashion or somethin'?

WILLIE: The brand.

BLUE: Like they do with steers, ya' mean? Who done it to ya'?

WILLIE: The Sorcerers of the High Commission. It's why I've come.

BLUE: You better come over here and sit down. I can't make hide nor hair out a' what yer sayin'. Come on. Have a seat and collect yerself.

(He leads WILLIE *over to the car, opens the front door, and seats him in the driver's seat.* BLUE *climbs up on the front fender and sits.)*

Now what's this here High Commission stuff? Why would they wanna' put a brand on yer head?

WILLIE: I can't see where I'm driving if you're going to sit there.

BLUE: Say, what's yer game, boy? Any fool can see this Chevy ain't got no wheels.

WILLIE: We used to shoot deer and strap them over the hood.

BLUE: Forget the deer. What's this brand business?

WILLIE: I've been zeroed.

BLUE: What's that mean?

WILLIE: Whenever I think beyond a certain circumference of a certain circle there's a hand that squeezes my brain.

BLUE: What hand?

WILLIE: It's been burned in. You can't see it now. All you can see is the scar.

BLUE: And this High Commission fella did this to ya'?

WILLIE: It's not a fella. It's a body. Nobody ever sees it. Just the sorcerers.

BLUE: Who's that?

WILLIE: Black magicians who know the secrets of the Nogo.

BLUE: I'll have to make a left turn on that one, sonny. I'm a simple man. I eat simple. I talk simple and I think simple.

WILLIE: That's why we need you.

BLUE: We?

WILLIE: The prisoners of the Diamond Cult.

BLUE: Just talk. I'll listen.

WILLIE: I am descended from a race of mandrills. Fierce baboons that were forced into human form by the magic of the Nogo. It was decided since we were so agile and efficient at sorting out diamonds for the Silent Ones that we could be taken a step further into human form and tested as though we were still baboons but give results in the tests as though we were humans.

BLUE: What kinda' tests?

WILLIE: Mind warps. Time splits. Electro-laser fields. Dimensional overlays. Spatial projections. Force fields.

BLUE: But you think like a man?

WILLIE: And feel. This was a mistake the sorcerers had not counted on. They wanted an animal to develop that was slightly subhuman, thereby to maintain full control over its psychosomatic functions. The results were something of the opposite. We developed as superhuman entities with capacities for thought and feeling far beyond that of our captors. In order to continue their tests they needed an invention to curtail our natural reasoning processes. They came up with the Unseen Hand, a muscle-contracting syndrome hooked up to the will of the Silent Ones. Whenever our thoughts transcend those of the magicians the Hand squeezes down and forces our minds to contract into nonpreoccupation.

BLUE: What's that like?

WILLIE: Living death. Sometimes when one of us tries to fight the Hand or escape its control, like me, we are punished by excruciating muscle spasms and nightmare visions. Blood pours past my eyes and smoke fills up my brain.

BLUE: What do ya' want me to do about all this? I'm just a juicer on the way out.

WILLIE: You're more than that. The sorcerers and the Silent Ones of the High Commission have lost all touch with human emotion. They exist in almost a purely telepathic intellectual state. That is why they can still exert control over our race. You and your brothers are part of another world, far beyond anything the High Commission has experienced. If you came into Nogoland blazing your six-guns they wouldn't have any idea how to deal with you. All their technology and magic would be a total loss. You would be too real for their experience.

BLUE: Now hold on there, whatever yer name is.

WILLIE: Willie.

BLUE: Yeah. Well, first off, my brothers are dead. Cisco and Sycamore was gunned down in 1886.

WILLIE: It doesn't matter.

BLUE: Well, unless yer counting on bringin' 'em back from the grave it matters a whole lot.

WILLIE: That's exactly what I'm counting on.

(BLUE *jumps down from the fender and grabs the rifle. He points it at* WILLIE.)

BLUE: All right, wiseacre. Outa' the car. Come on or I'll plug ya' right here on the spot.

WILLIE: You can't plug me, Blue. I don't die.

BLUE: Not ever?

WILLIE: Never.

BLUE: Then how come yer so scared to take on them High Commandos yer own self?

WILLIE: Because of the Hand.

(WILLIE *goes into a violent spasm, clutching his head in agony.* BLUE *drops the rifle and goes to* WILLIE. *He pulls him out of the car and sets him on the ground.*)

BLUE: Now stop jumpin' around, yer makin' me nervous. Just settle down. You want the cops to catch us?

(WILLIE *writhes on the ground and screams phrases and words as though warding off some unseen terror.*)

WILLIE: Wind refraction! Cyclone riff! Get off the rim! Off the rim!
BLUE: What's with you, boy?
WILLIE: The latitudinal's got us! Now! Now! Smoke it up! Smoke him! Gyration forty zero two nodes! Two nodes! You got the wrong mode! Wrong! Correction! Correct that! Step! Stop it! Modulate eighty y's west! Keep it west! Don't let up the field rays! Keep it steady on! Harmonic rhythm scheme! Harmony four! Discord! You got it! Aaah! Aaaaaaaah! Let up! Extract! Implode! Bombard the picture! The picture! Image contact! Major! Minor! Loop syndrome! Drone up! Full drone wave! Now! Oooooh! Just about! Just about! Crystallize fragment mirror! Keep it keen! Sharpen that focus! Hypo filament! Didactachrome! Resolve! Resolve! Resolve! Reverb! Fuzz tone! Don't let the feedback in! Feed it back! Keep your back up! Back it up! Reverse foliage meter! Fauna scope. Graphic tableau. Gramophonic display key. All right. All right. Now raise the horizon. Good. Moon. Planets in place. Heliographic perspective. Atmosphere checking cool. Galactic four count. Star meter gazing central focus. Beam to head on sunset. Systol reading ace in. Dystol balance. Treble boost. All systems baffled. Baffled.

(WILLIE *goes unconscious.* CISCO MORPHAN *enters. He wears a serape, jeans, cowboy hat and boots, a bandanna on his head, a rifle and a handgun. He has long black hair and a scraggly beard. He is younger than* BLUE *by about twenty years.*)

CISCO: Blue!

(*He goes to* BLUE *with his arms out.*)

Well, don't ya' recognize me, boy? It's me! Cisco. Yer brother. Yer mean ornery old flesh and blood.

BLUE: Just stand back, mister. I'm gettin' rid a' this right now.

(He throws his bottle behind the car and holds his rifle on CISCO.*)*

CISCO: Still foxy as ever, ain't ya'. Better watch out that thing don't go off by accident. Let a gun go to rustin' like that and ya' never can tell what it's liable to do.

BLUE: It's plenty greased enough to open daylight in the likes of an impostor.

CISCO: Oh. So ya' don't believe it's really me, huh. Let's see. What if I was to show ya' some honest to God proof of the puddin'?

BLUE: Like what, fer instance?

CISCO: Like say a knife scar ya' gave me fer my sixteenth birthday in Tuscaloosa.

BLUE: That'd do just fine.

CISCO: All right. Now you hold yer fire there while I get outa' my poncho.

BLUE: Just hurry it up.

*(*CISCO *sets down his rifle and starts taking off his serape as* BLUE *holds the rifle on him.)*

CISCO: Yeah, I guess yer plenty busy nowadays.

BLUE: How da ya' mean? Keep yer hand away from that pistol.

CISCO: There we go. Now. Take a looksee.

*(*CISCO *takes off his poncho and shows* BLUE *a long scar going from the middle of his back all the way around to his chest.* BLUE *examines it closely.)*

What ya' got to say now? Ain't that the mark ya' give me with yer very own fishing knife?

BLUE: Sure beats the hell outa' me.

CISCO: If yer satisfied why don't ya' do me a favor and lower that buffalo gun.

*(*BLUE *lowers his rifle as* CISCO *puts his poncho back on.)*

BLUE: But you and Sycamore was gunned down in the street right in broad daylight. I was there.

CISCO: You escaped. Sycamore should be comin' up any second now.

BLUE: I don't get it, Cisco. What's goin' on?

CISCO: Seems there's certain unfinished business. This must be the fella here.

BLUE: You know this looney?

CISCO: Let's take a look. He ain't dead, is he?

(CISCO leans over WILLIE and looks at his face.)

BLUE: Damned if I can tell. He just shows up outa' the clear blue and starts to jawin' about outer space and High Commancheros and what all. I can't make it out.

CISCO: He came alone?

BLUE: So far. First him and then you. You know somethin' I don't, Cisco?

CISCO: All I know is that I was summoned up. Me, you, and Sycamore is gonna' be back in action before too long. And this here dude is gonna set us straight on what the score is.

BLUE: What score? I settled up all my debts a long time ago. I hunted down every last one a' them varmints what got you and Sycamore. I'm an old man, Cisco.

CISCO: There's other upstarts seems to be jammin' up the works. Besides, I'll be glad to see a little action for a change. I been hibernatin' for too long now. You got any grub layin' around here somewhere?

BLUE: Best I can do is Campbell's Pork and Beans, Cisco. Have to be cold outa' the can too. Can't make no fires on account a' the Highway Patrol.

CISCO: What's that?

BLUE: The law. Like the old Texas Rangers, 'cept they got cars now.

(BLUE goes to the car and opens the trunk. He rummages around for a can of beans.)

CISCO: Well, looks like you got yerself a nice enough campsite. What's this here rig?

BLUE: Fifty-one Chevy. Don't make 'em like this anymore. Now they got dual headlights, twin exhausts, bucket seats, wraparound windshields and what all. Extra junk to make it look fancy. Don't go no better though.

(CISCO *sits in the driver's seat and turns the steering wheel.*)

CISCO: Must take a hefty team to pull this load. What's it made out of, iron or somethin'?

BLUE: It drives itself, boy. This here is a gasoline, internal combustion six banger. Don't need no team a' horses.

(*He pulls out a can of beans and walks around to* CISCO.)

CISCO: I'll be damned. And this here is what ya' guide it with, I'll bet.

BLUE: You got it. Here. There's a can opener in the glove compartment.

CISCO: What's that?

BLUE: That little door over there. Ya' just push the button and she flaps open.

CISCO: I'll be damned. Keep gloves in there, do ya'?

(*He opens the glove compartment and takes out a can opener and some other junk.*)

BLUE: Here, ya' better let me handle it for ya'.

(BLUE *takes the can and the can opener and opens the can of beans.*)

CISCO: How fast can ya' go with one a these here?

BLUE: Some of 'em'll do over a hundred mile an hour.

CISCO: What's that mean, Blue?

BLUE: That means in an hour's time if you keep yer boot stomped down on that pedal you'll have covered a hundred mile a' territory.

CISCO: Whooeee! Sure beats hell out of a quarter horse, don't it?

BLUE: You better believe it.

CISCO: What's these buttons for?

(*He pulls a button and the headlights go on.*)

BLUE: Don't pull that! Push that back in. You want the fuzz down on our necks?

(CISCO *pushes the button back in and the lights go out.*)

I just get the damn battery charged so's I can listen to a little radio and you wanna go and run the damn thing down again. Here's yer beans.

(*He hands* CISCO *the can of beans.*)

CISCO: Thanks, boy. How come yer so scared a' the law all of a sudden?

BLUE: It ain't so sudden as all that. I'm goin' on a hundred and twenty years old now. Thanks to modern medicine.

CISCO: That a fact? Sure kept yerself fit, Blue.

BLUE: Well, you live on the lam like I have for a while and you gotta keep yer wits about ya'.

CISCO: What's this radio thing yer talking about?

BLUE: That second knob on yer right. Just turn it a click. It's already set up for Moon Channel.

(CISCO *turns the radio on. Rock and roll or news or any random radio station comes on soft. It should be a real radio and not a tape.*)

CISCO: I'll be damned.

BLUE: Just keep it soft.

CISCO: Where's it comin' from, Blue?

BLUE: Up there. They got a station up there now.

(*He points to the moon.*)

CISCO: The moon? Yer pullin' my leg.

BLUE: Things've changed since you was last here, boy.

CISCO: How'd they get up there?

BLUE: Rocket ship. Damnedest thing ya' ever did see. Taller than a twenty-story office building.

CISCO: How'd they get back?

BLUE: Come right down plop in the ocean. Some of 'em stay up there, though. Don't know what they all do. I've heard tell they travel to Mars and Venus, different planets like that.

CISCO: All in a rocket ship thing?

BLUE: Yep.

CISCO: Don't they like it down here no more?

BLUE: The earth's gettin' cramped, boy. There's lots more people now. They're lookin' for new territory to spread out to. I hear tell they've sent prisoners up there too. 'Stead a' sendin' 'em to jail. They don't hang no one no more. Just strand 'em high and dry on a planet somewheres in space. Probably where this critter come from.

CISCO: Wonder what's keepin' Sycamore.

BLUE: What makes ya' so sure he's comin'?

CISCO: Has to. Same as me. He's been summoned up.

BLUE: How's that work?

CISCO: Some voice wakes ya' up. I don't know. Just like you been sleepin' or somethin'. 'Fore you know it yer movin' and walkin' and talkin' just like always. Hard to get used to at first. Anyhow I'm glad I'm back.

BLUE: Me too, boy. Sure gets lonely on yer own all the time.

CISCO: Well, before you know it we'll be back together just like old times. Robbin', rapin' and killin'.

BLUE: Yeah boy!

(A drunken high-school cheerleader kid comes on yelling. He has a blond crewcut and a long cheerleader's sweater with a huge "A" printed on it. He holds a huge megaphone to his lips. His pants are pulled down around his ankles. His legs are red and bleeding and look as though they've been whipped with a belt. He has white tennis shoes on. He yells through the megaphone to an unseen gang of a rival high school in the distance behind the audience. He doesn't notice BLUE and CISCO.)

KID: You motherfuckers are dead! You're as good as dead! Just wait till Friday night! We're going to wipe your asses off the map! There won't even be an Arcadia High left! You think you're all so fuckin' bitchin' just 'cause your daddies are rich! Just 'cause your old man gives you a fuckin' full-blown Corvette for Christmas and a credit card! You think your girls are so tough-looking! They're fucking dogs! I wouldn't fuck an Arcadia girl if she bled out her asshole! You punk faggots shouldn't even be in the same league as us! The Rio Hondo belongs to us! You're gonna' go fucking scoreless Friday night and I'm gonna' be right there cheering and seeing it all happen! Then we're gonna' burn your fucking grandstand to the ground! Right to the fucking ground! Then we're gonna' burn a huge "A" for Azusa right in the middle of your fucking field. Right on the fifty-yard line!

(He wheels around and faces BLUE *and* CISCO.)

What're you looking at? You think it's funny or something? What the fuck are you looking at? You wanna' make something out of it? You wanna' put your money where your mouth is? Come on! Come on! Try me! You think I'm funny-looking? Come on!

BLUE: I don't know, Cisco. This used to be a quiet little highway.

KID: What'd you say, old man? What'd you say? I'll kill you if you say one more word! I'll fucking kill you!

CISCO: Better watch that kinda' tongue, boy. This here's my brother Blue yer talkin' at.

KID: What're you, some hippie creep? I can smell you all the way over here! I'll kill you too! I'll kill both of you!

CISCO: Better pull yer pants up and head home, boy.

KID: Don't tell me what to do, you commie faggot! I'll fucking kill you!

(He takes a leap toward CISCO. CISCO *draws his pistol lightning fast. The kid stops still.)*

CISCO: Now look, boy. I ain't in the habit of shootin' down unarmed infants, but yer startin' to grate on me. Now git home before this thing goes off.

(The KID *crumples to the ground sobbing.)*

KID: I can't! It's too late now. They grabbed me. Right after the rally. They got me and took me up Lookout Point and whipped me with a belt. They tried to paint my balls black but I wouldn't let them. I fought. I kicked. They stuck a Tampax up me. Right up me. I tried to stop them. I yelled. There were some cars. A couple cars. Girls making out with the fullback and the quarterback. But they turned their lights on and left. They could've helped. At least they could've helped me. I cheered for them plenty of times. Plenty of games. The least they could've done—just because I couldn't make second string. I could've played Junior Varsity but I decided to be a cheerleader instead. They could've helped me. The least they could've done.

CISCO: OK. OK. Why don't ya' just go home now and sleep it off.

KID: I can't! It's too late. My old man'll beat the shit out of me. It's after two. He won't let me use the car for a month. I can't go home. Let me stay here. Please. Let me. Please.

BLUE: Might as well. What's one more looney.

CISCO: We got business to set straight here, Blue.

BLUE: He won't get in the way. Let him stay.

CISCO: All right. But keep to yerself over in the corner there.

KID: Thanks.

(The KID stands up and moves upstage left.)

CISCO: And pull yer pants up, fer Christ's sake.

KID: It stings too bad.

CISCO: All right.

(The KID throws down his megaphone and starts stomping on it violently.)

KID: I'm never going to lead another cheer! Never! Not for them or any-body else! Never! Never! Never! Never! Never! Never! Never! Never! Never!

BLUE: Atta boy. Get it outa' yer system.

KID: I'll just stay over near the drainage ditch there. I won't get in your way. I promise.

CISCO: Good.

KID: If those Arcadia guys come by here don't tell them where I am, OK?

CISCO: OK.

(The KID turns to go off left, then stops.)

KID: Oh, would you mind waking me up in the morning? I don't usually get up too easy.

BLUE: Don't worry, you'll hear the traffic.

KID: Thanks.

BLUE: Sweet dreams, boy.

(The KID goes off.)

CISCO: Boy, howdy, what'd I miss all them years?

BLUE: A whole lot, Cisco. A whole lot. Things change overnight now. One day there's a President, the next day he gets shot, the next day the guy what shot him gets shot.

CISCO: No foolin'.

BLUE: Next day they outlaw guns and replace 'em with nerve gas. Stuff can turn a full-grown man into a blithering fool. Then they change the government from capitalism to socialism because the government's afraid of a full-blown insurrection. Then they have a revolution anyhow and things stay just like they was.

(WILLIE rolls over and speaks on his back lying down.)

WILLIE: Cisco?

CISCO: That's me.

WILLIE: You made it. Good. Sycamore here yet?

CISCO: Not yet. Should be soon though.

(WILLIE sits up.)

BLUE: You feelin' better now, boy? That was some awful fit ya' had there.

WILLIE: Get prepared to see worse.

BLUE: Why? You plannin' on flippin' out some more?

WILLIE: In Nogoland there's men walking around with their brains eaten out, skinless, eyes turned inside out, frozen in pictures of terror. Men walking day and night like dogs on the end of a leash. You'd be happy if the worst you saw there was "flipping out," as you say.

CISCO: What's the scoop, Willie?

BLUE: How'd you know his name?

WILLIE: Long before we turned human, the magicians introduced us to the mysteries of telepathy, Blue. Your brother is able to know and understand things that he himself won't have the answers to.

BLUE: Well, how 'bout me? Why don't ya' clue me in on a few secrets?

WILLIE: It will take time. First of all you must undergo temporal re-arrangement.

BLUE: I don't get ya'.

CISCO: Yeah. Keep it simple, Willie.

WILLIE: Your brain has undergone cell breakdown with age and time, Blue. We have to regroup your temporal field to make you young enough to again become sensitive to telepathic and extrasensory reception.

BLUE: Yer gonna' make me young?

WILLIE: That's right.

CISCO: How 'bout that.

BLUE: I don't exactly know if I go fer that idea. I been on a long hard road fer so long now it feels kinda' good to know it's drawin' to a close. Now ya' want me to go through it all over again?

WILLIE: Whenever you want it, the scheme can be reversed back to your normal earth age. But for now we must transform you, for it's the only hope for the prisoners of Nogoland.

BLUE: Who are these dudes exactly? I don't even know if I like 'em yet.

WILLIE: People, like you and me, but with a strange history and stranger powers. These powers could work for the good of mankind if allowed to unfold into their natural creativity. But if they continue as they are they will surely work for evil, or, worse, they will turn it on themselves and commit a horrible mass suicide that may destroy the universe.

BLUE: Well, you seem like a decent enough Joe. What've I got to lose?

WILLIE: Fine.

CISCO: Good boy.

BLUE: How do I start?

CISCO: Sit down here in front of me.

(WILLIE sits with his feet out.)

BLUE: Right here? Like this?

(BLUE sits with his feet out facing WILLIE.)

WILLIE: That's right. Now push your feet against the soles of my feet. Real hard.

BLUE: Like this?

(BLUE presses his feet against WILLIE's.)

WILLIE: Press hard. Now grab my hands and squeeze.

(BLUE follows WILLIE's directions.)

BLUE: This ain't gonna hurt, is it?

WILLIE: Not a bit. You'll feel an interior shrinkage as your organs re-arrange themselves and grow stronger, but don't panic. Just push with your feet and grip my hands firmly.

BLUE: OK.

CISCO: Hang on, Blue. Yer halfway home.

(WILLIE *goes into another seizure but different this time. It's as though thousands of electric volts were being transmitted from* WILLIE *to* BLUE. *It should look like waves of shock being transformed. First* WILLIE *trembles and shakes violently, then* BLUE. BLUE *gradually becomes younger until at the end he is a young man of about thirty.*)

WILLIE: The truth of the spinning fire wheel! Steel brings you close! Strength in the steel! Strengthen! Electric smoking man power! The strength of a man! Power in the man! Tower of power! Texaco sucks! Texas man! Longhorn panhandle tough cowboy leather man! Send him home! Where the buffalo roam! It's daytime! It's bright day! Truth in the sun! Sun play! Mexican silver stud! Proud of his pride! Proud guy! Tall and lean and mean! Look out, Tuba City! Look out, down-and-out crumpled-up muffled old bad guy! Here's screaming new blood! A flood of new blood screaming straight to your raggedy heart! Churning new blood flooding your mind up! Sending you zigzag straight to your heart! Aaaaaaaah! Gyrode screen! The Hand! The Hand's got me, Blue! The Hand!

BLUE: Hang on, Willie. I'll see ya' through it.

(BLUE *grips* WILLIE's *hands tighter and pushes hard with his legs as* WILLIE *twists and grimaces trying to ward off the Hand.*)

WILLIE: No! No! Diminish laser count! Aaaaaah!

CISCO: Hang on, Blue! Don't let him go!

WILLIE: My brain! It's squeezing my brain!

BLUE: Hold his head, Cisco! Grab his head!

(CISCO *puts both hands on* WILLIE's *head and presses down.*)

WILLIE: Gamma build-up! System burn! Burning! Cell damage to block unit! Can't see! Can't see! They've smoked it good this time! Black wire smoke burn! There's a fire in code D! Disorient power pack! Aaaaaaaaaaah! Fading!

(*He shakes violently, then goes limp and unconscious as before.* CISCO *lowers his head to the ground as* BLUE *releases his grip.* BLUE *is now much younger than before. He stands.*)

CISCO: Poor devil.

BLUE: He'll be all right in a little while. The same thing happened to him before you came. Anyway, it worked.

CISCO: What?

BLUE: I'm young. Least I feel young. I still know it's me and everything but I feel much stronger. Tough, like I used to be.

CISCO: Hot damn! We're getting close now, Blue. It won't be long.

(BLUE *lets out a yell, takes a run across the stage and does a somersault.*)

How 'bout that.

(CISCO *takes a run and does a somersault right next to* BLUE. BLUE *stands and starts singing "Rock Around the Clock."* CISCO *stands and joins him, dancing around and doing the twist and all that jive.*)

CISCO & BLUE: One for the money. Two for the show. Three to get ready. Now go man go. We're gonna' rock around the clock tonight. We're gonna' rock, rock, rock until the broad daylight. We're gonna' rock, gonna' rock around the clock. . . .

(SYCAMORE MORPHAN *appears opposite them. They freeze.* SYCAMORE's *very tall and slick. Dressed like Bat Masterson with black tails, black hat, black vest, white shirt with ruffled cuffs and diamond cufflinks, black boots, black leather gloves and black cane with a diamond-studded handle and a pearl-handled revolver tied down to his hip in a black holster. He just stands staring at his two brothers.*)

BLUE: Sycamore.

CISCO: Hey, boy. Where you been? We been waitin' and waitin'.

(SYCAMORE *sidles over to* WILLIE *and pokes him with his cane.*)

BLUE: Thought you was probably lost or somethin'.

CISCO: Yeah. Don't know why we'd figure that though, since you know the trails better than any of us.

(Uneasy silence as SYCAMORE moves to the Chevy and pokes it with his cane, scanning the area with his eyes. He is cold and mean. He reaches in the car and turns the radio off with a sharp snap.)

BLUE: Sure is good to see us all back together again, though. Boy howdy, how long's it been, anyhow?

CISCO: Must be goin' on a hundred some-odd years, I'll bet.

BLUE: Sure. Must be that. At least a hundred.

CISCO: Yer lookin' mighty fit, Sycamore. Just like old times.

(SYCAMORE turns to them swinging his cane.)

SYCAMORE: Was there some specific reason behind choosing a rendezvous point right on the open highway?

BLUE: This here's Azusa, Sycamore. "Everything from A to Z in the USA." Nothing hardly but rock quarries and cement factories here. All the traffic dies down at night on account of most of the vehicles is trucks carrying gravel and they don't work at night.

SYCAMORE: The sun don't rise on Azusa, huh.

BLUE: Well, sure. But we'll be outa' here by then.

CISCO: Yeah, we should be long gone by mornin'.

SYCAMORE: I guess you boys know exactly where you're goin', then, and how you're gettin' there.

CISCO: Well, not exactly. But Willie's gotta set us straight soon as he comes to.

SYCAMORE: I reckon he's got you all set up with enough guns and provisions, then, huh.

BLUE: Hadn't thought a' that one.

CISCO: Well, we all got guns, ain't we? I got mine.

(SYCAMORE takes out a cheroot and lights it.)

SYCAMORE: We just meet 'em in the street, then, huh? Like old times. A showdown.

CISCO: Yeah, why not?

BLUE: I see what Sycamore's drivin' at, Cisco. There's only three of us with pistols against hundreds, maybe thousands.

CISCO: So what. We used to bring a whole town to a standstill just by ridin' in. They used to roll out the carpet for the Morphan brothers.

BLUE: This ain't a town Willie's talkin' about, it's a whole country, maybe even a whole planet. We ain't in the movies, ya' know.

CISCO: So what do you suggest we do?

BLUE: Round up some more men maybe.

CISCO: Why don't we wake Willie up and ask him.

SYCAMORE: I say we forget it.

(A pause as they both look at SYCAMORE.)

BLUE: The whole thing?

SYCAMORE: Why not? We don't stand a chance of freeing those baboons.

BLUE: But they ain't baboons anymore, Sycamore. They're human beings just like us.

CISCO: Yeah.

SYCAMORE: So what?

BLUE: They're bein' tortured and stuff. Brainwashed or somethin'. Experimented on.

SYCAMORE: What's that got to do with us? We're free now. We been brought back to life. What do you want to throw it away for a bunch of baboons? Look, I say we split up, go our different ways and lay low for a while. Then we meet up again in Tuba City or somewhere on the North Platte. That way it'll give us time to think things over.

CISCO: What things?

SYCAMORE: Reorganizing the gang, you pinhead. The Morphan brothers ride again, except this time in a whole different century. This time we don't make no mistakes. We stick to trains and forget about banks and post offices.

BLUE: There ain't no trains no more, Sycamore. Just planes and hover-crafts and such like.

SYCAMORE: What're you talkin' about?

BLUE: There ain't no trains to rob no more. Besides, we can't ditch Willie like that. He just give me back my youth. I can't go walkin' out on him.

SYCAMORE: No trains?

CISCO: Yeah, I feel kinda' bad about that too. I wouldn't even be here if it weren't for him. You neither, Sycamore.

SYCAMORE: No trains.

BLUE: I say we stay and see it through.

(WILLIE comes to.)

WILLIE: It's up to you. What Sycamore says is true. Why should you feel responsible for some species of hybrid in another galaxy? You could stay here and be free. Live like you want to.

CISCO: You mean you wouldn't mind if we took off on ya'?

WILLIE: I can't force you to help us. It must be left to your own conscience. All I can do is to try to persuade you to come.

SYCAMORE: No trains.

BLUE: Oh, this here's my brother Sycamore, Willie.

WILLIE: I know. I'm happy you came.

SYCAMORE: They got trains where you come from?

WILLIE: They used to have a system underground but it's long been made obsolete.

SYCAMORE: It's still there though?

WILLIE: Yes. As far as I know.

SYCAMORE: And it connects to all the parts of the city where these prisoners are?

WILLIE: Yes. I think it must. Throughout the whole planet, I think.

BLUE: What you gettin' at, Sycamore?

SYCAMORE: Sounds to me like it could be used as an escape route.

CISCO: Then we're goin' then! Waaaahoooo! Attaboy, Sycamore! I always knew ya' had a soft spot.

SYCAMORE: Well, if there's no trains here we might as well go there.

BLUE: Hot dog!

WILLIE: Good. Let me show you a plan of Nogoland.

(WILLIE stands and draws a huge map with his finger on the floor of the stage. As he indicates lines, different colored lines of light appear on the floor as though they emanated from the tip of his finger. The other three watch as WILLIE describes Nogoland and draws the map accordingly.)

In the northeastern sector is the Capitol, as you would say, contained in a transparent dome permitting temperature and atmosphere control. It is here that the Silent Ones conduct their affairs of state. Only members of the High Commission and Sorcerer Chiefs are allowed passage to and from the Capitol. Over here in the southwestern sector are the Diamond Fields where slaves work day and night under constant guard by the soldiers of the Raven Cult.

BLUE: Who're they?

WILLIE: Fierce morons cloaked in black capes. They ride on huge black ravens which continually fly over the area, patrolling and keeping a constant eye out for the possibility of an uprising amongst the slaves. Here in the west are the laboratories of the Sorcerers of the Nogo. Here is where my friends are kept. They are also watched by Raven guards but the control is not so heavy there since the power of the Unseen Hand is believed to be security enough.

SYCAMORE: What's in the middle?

WILLIE: Huge refineries and industrial compounds for the processing of the diamonds. It is here that the biggest and best diamonds are culled out of the crop.

BLUE: What do they do with them?

WILLIE: Each year a Great Game is played with the people of Zeron, a competition of some kind. The winner is allowed to extend the boundaries of his domain into the loser's territory and rule the people within that new area. The loser must also pay off the winner with certain secret information of magical knowledge.

SYCAMORE: What about the south?

WILLIE: A vast primitive region of swamps and lagoons. We must enter Nogoland by this route since we'll surely be spotted by Raven guards if we attempt to come in from the north.

BLUE: What's up there?

WILLIE: Desert. Nothing. The sky never changes. No day and no night. No atmosphere of any kind. Not even craters to break up the landscape. We would surely be seen.

SYCAMORE: How do they get back and forth from these different areas?

WILLIE: Only certain chosen ones are allowed to travel at all. These do so by means of teleportation. They beam themselves into a chosen area by displacing their bodies.

SYCAMORE: Does this underground railroad you're talkin' about go into the south there?

WILLIE: Just about. We'll have to be extra careful once we arrive there, though.

BLUE: Why's that?

WILLIE: This region is inhabited by the Lagoon Baboon, another experiment on our race. He watches over the Lower Regions and is also controlled by the Hand.

SYCAMORE: Uh, don't anybody let on to it but we're being watched.

BLUE: What do you mean?

SYCAMORE: Don't turn around. Act like we're still talkin' about the map. He's over behind the car. I'll try to circle around behind him.

CISCO: How ya' gonna' do that without him seein' ya'?

SYCAMORE: I'll go off like I'm goin' to take a leak, then come up behind him. You stay here and keep talkin'. Just act natural.

BLUE: OK.

CISCO: So ya' say this here Lagoon Baboon's an ornery critter, eh Willie?

WILLIE: Yes. Very ornery, as you say. He can eat three times his weight in human flesh in less time than it would take you to eat a doughnut.

SYCAMORE: Well listen, I gotta' go see a man about a horse so why don't you fellas carry on here.

BLUE: OK, Sycamore. Don't get it caught in the zipper now.

(SYCAMORE exits. The rest continue to act "natural.")

CISCO: Sounds to me like this Nogoland's a pretty depressing place. Don't they ever have no fun? No rodeos or nothin'?

BLUE: Yeah. What about that, Willie?

WILLIE: Twice a year they hold tournaments where my people are pitted against beasts from other galaxies. Also robots and androids are programmed to fight my people in the Gaming Arena.

BLUE: Where's that at?

WILLIE: Right here in the east.

(He draws another area of light with his finger.)

Many of my people are slaughtered each year in the tournaments.

CISCO: Don't they ever win?

WILLIE: It has only happened once and the Silent Ones were so impressed and stunned that they allowed the man his freedom but kept him still under the control of the Hand.

BLUE: Well, what happened to him? Where's he now?

WILLIE: Right here. It is me they set free.

CISCO: You? Hot dog! You must be a mean hombre, Willie.

BLUE: But how come they let you go?

WILLIE: The Silent Ones believed I could not survive the Southland and the Lagoon Baboon. Plus they still had control over me with the Hand. They thought if I was to return to my people I would cause trouble, so rather than kill me they played another game.

(Voice of the KID *yelling from behind the car. He comes out into the open with his hands raised and his pants still down and* SYCAMORE *right behind him with his gun out.)*

KID: Wait a minute! Wait a minute! Please. I didn't mean to bother you. I just couldn't sleep and I heard you talking so I came over. I just wanted to listen.

SYCAMORE: He's heard the whole shootin' match.

CISCO: I told you once, boy. How come you didn't listen?

KID: I know, but I can help you. I want to come with you.

SYCAMORE: I say we put a bullet through his head.

BLUE: Now wait a minute, Sycamore.

WILLIE: What makes you say you could help us?

KID: I know about that kind of fighting. I learned it in school.

SYCAMORE: Come on. He's seen our whole hand.

BLUE: Hear him out.

KID: Three things: Constant movement, absolute mistrust, and eternal vigilance. Movement: that is, never stay put; never spend two nights in the same place; never stop moving from one place to another. Mistrust: at the beginning mistrust even your own shadow, friendly peasants, informants, guides, contacts; mistrust everything until you hold a liberated zone. Vigilance: constant guard duty, constant reconnaissance; establishment of a camp in a safe place, and, above all, never sleep beneath a roof, never sleep in a house where you can be surrounded.

CISCO: I'll be damned.

WILLIE: And how does this apply to our mission? We go to free prisoners, not to start a revolution.

CISCO: Yeah.

KID: The two are inseparable. Freedom and revolution are inextricably bound up. To free the oppressed you must get rid of the oppressor.

This constitutes revolution. And the surest means to victory is guerrilla warfare. This has held true for hundreds of years.

WILLIE: Then you see no other way to liberate my people than to make war with the Silent Ones?

KID: Exactly.

SYCAMORE: Keep those hands up.

CISCO: And pull up yer pants, fer Christ's sake.

(The KID goes to pull up his pants.)

SYCAMORE: I told ya' to keep yer hands raised.

KID: Well, I can't do both.

BLUE: Let him pull up his pants, Sycamore.

SYCAMORE: This here is a spy in case you forgot. I say we plug him right here and now.

BLUE: And I say we let him pull up his doggone pants!

CISCO: What do you say, Willie?

WILLIE: I have come to find any means possible to free my people. If he has information we should listen.

SYCAMORE: OK. But keep yer hands high, mister.

(The KID talks with his hands raised and his pants down. The others listen.)

KID: First of all you need more men. A guerrilla unit should be small but four or five is not enough to be fully effective.

BLUE: Well, let's see, there's Red Diamond.

CISCO: And Slim and Shadow. We could get them easy.

SYCAMORE: What about Fatback?

CISCO: Yeah. And then there's Sloe Gin Martin, Cat Man Kelly, Booger Montgomery, the Mouse, Mojo Moses—

KID: That's enough. Ten to fifteen is all you'll need in the initial stages. It's important to remember that what you're organizing is more than a gang of bandits. Guerrilla warfare is a war of the masses, a war of the people. The guerrilla band is an armed nucleus, the fighting vanguard of the people. It draws its great force from the mass of the people themselves. Bandit gangs have all the characteristics of a guerrilla army, homogeneity, respect for the leader, valor, knowledge of the ground and often even good understanding of the tactics to be employed. The only thing missing is support of the people, and inevitably these gangs are captured and exterminated by the public force.

WILLIE: But the people you speak of, the masses, in this case are all held prisoner.

KID: Then you must liberate a few for reinforcements.

BLUE: How?

KID: Hit and run, wait, lie in ambush, again hit and run, and thus repeatedly, without giving any rest to the enemy. The blows should be continuous. The enemy ought not to be allowed to sleep. At every moment the impression ought to be created that he is surrounded by a complete circle.

SYCAMORE: Keep those hands high.

WILLIE: Go on.

KID: Acts of sabotage are very important. It is necessary to distinguish between sabotage and terrorism, a measure that is generally ineffective and indiscriminate in its results, since it often makes victims of innocent people and destroys a large number of lives that would be valuable to the revolution. Sabotage should be of two types: sabotage on a national scale against determined objectives, and local sabotage against lines of combat. Sabotage on a national scale should be aimed principally at destroying communications. The guerrilla is a night combatant. He thrives in the dark, while the enemy is afraid of the dark. He must be cunning and able to march unnoticed to the place of attack, across plains or mountains, and then fall upon the enemy, taking advantage of the factor of surprise. After causing panic by this surprise he should launch himself into the fight implacably without permitting a single weakness in his companions and taking advantage of every sign of weakness in the enemy. Striking like a tornado, destroying all, giving no quarter unless the tactical circumstances call for it, judging those who must be judged, sowing panic among the enemy, he nevertheless treats defenseless prisoners benevolently and shows respect for the dead.

BLUE: Now I say we let him pull his pants up.

CISCO: Yeah, let him, Sycamore. What the hell.

SYCAMORE: All right. Pull 'em up but nice and slow.

(The KID very slowly bends down and goes to pull up his pants. He gets them halfway up, then suddenly kicks SYCAMORE in the balls and grabs his gun.

SYCAMORE *falls on the round holding his crotch and groaning. The* KID *holds the gun on all of them.)*

CISCO: What the hell!

KID: All right! Now up, all of you! Get your hands up! Don't try anything or I'll shoot. Honest I will. All I'll have to tell the cops is I caught a bunch of subversives right in the act. They wouldn't think twice. In fact they'd probably call me a hero.

(They all raise their hands.)

SYCAMORE: I told you! I told ya' we shoulda' killed the bastard.

KID: He's right, you know.

BLUE: Well, you sure disappointed me, boy.

KID: Why? What do I owe you?

BLUE: Here I thought you was gonna' lead us on to victory and all.

CISCO: Yeah, me too. The way you was talkin' . . .

KID: Shut up! Don't say anything more or I'll kill all of you! I mean it.

CISCO: Ya' really ought to pull yer pants up though. It don't look right.

KID: Shut up!

CISCO: I mean we're your prisoners and you got yer pants pulled down like yer about to get whooped or something.

(The KID *struggles to pull up his pants with one hand while he holds the gun on them with the other. He gets them up around his waist and hangs on to them with one hand.)*

KID: You better shut up!

WILLIE: Don't tease him.

CISCO: That's right. He's had a rough night.

BLUE: What you gonna' do now, boy? How ya' gonna' go fer help?

KID: We'll wait until morning. There'll be plenty of trucks.

BLUE: Yer gonna' tell 'em you captured a bunch a' subversives single-handed, huh?

KID: That's right! And everything else too. How you were planning to take over Azusa.

*(*SYCAMORE *starts laughing hysterically then screams with pain, then back to laughter. The others join in laughing except for* WILLIE, *who watches.)*

SYCAMORE: Azusa!

CISCO: That's a good one! "Everything from A to Z in the USA." Yeah boy!

KID:

(In the background the old "C" "A" "F" "G" rock-and-roll chords are played to the KID's *speech.)*

Shut up! Shut up! I'll kill you all! I'll kill you! This is my home! Don't make fun of my home. I was born and raised here and I'll die here! I love it! That's something you can't understand! I love Azusa! I love the foothills and the drive-in movies and the bowling alleys and the football games and the drag races and the girls and the donut shop and the high school and the junior college and the outdoor track meets and the parades and the Junior Chamber of Commerce and the Key Club and the Letterman's Club and the Kiwanis and the Safeway Shopping Center and the freeway and the pool hall and the Bank of America and the post office and the Presbyterian

(They laugh louder and louder as the KID *keeps on.)*

church and the laundromat and the liquor store and the miniature golf course and Lookout Point and the YMCA and the Glee Club and the basketball games and the sock hop and graduation and the prom and the cafeteria and the principal's office and chemistry class and the county fair and peanut butter and jelly sandwiches and the high school band and going steady and KFWB and white bucks and pegger pants and argyle socks and madras shorts and butch wax and Hobie boards and going to the beach and getting drunk and swearing and reading dirty books and smoking in the men's room and setting off cherry bombs and fixing up my car and my mom, I love my mom most of all. And you creeps aren't going to take that away from me. You're not going to take that away from me because I'll kill you first! I'll kill every one of you if it's the last thing I do!

(They all stop laughing. WILLIE *goes into a trance, speaking a strange ancient language. The others watch.)*

WILLIE: Od i gniht tsal eht sti fi uoy fo eno yreve llik lli. Tsrif ouy llik lli esuaceb em morf yawa taht ekat ot gniog ton eruoy. Em morf yawa taht ekat ot gniog tnera speerc uoy dna. Lla fo tsom mom ym evol i mom ym dna rac ym pu gnixif dna sbmob yrrehc ffo gnittes dna moor . . .

KID: Shut up, you! Shut up!

WILLIE: . . . snem eht ni gnikoms dna skoob ytrid gnidaer dna gniraews dna knurd gnitteg dna hcaeb eht ot gniog dna sdraob eiboh dna xaw hctub dna strohs sardam dna skcos elygra dna stnap reggep dna skcub etihw dna bwfk dna . . .

(The KID fires the pistol into WILLIE but WILLIE keeps on speaking and getting very weird.)

. . . ydaets gniog dna dnab loohcs hgih eht dna sehciwdnas yllej dna rettub tunaep dna riaf ytnuoc eht dna ssalc yrtsimehc . . .

KID: Shut up!

(The KID fires again. WILLIE keeps on.)

WILLIE: . . . dna eciffo slapicnirp eht dna airetefac eht dna morp eht dna noitaudarg dna poh kcos eht dna semag . . .

(The KID empties the gun into WILLIE but WILLIE continues, accumulating incredible power from the language he speaks.)

. . . llabteksab eht dna bulc eelg eht dna acmy eht dna tniop tuokool dna esruoc flog erutainim eht dna erots rouqil eht dna tamordnual eht dna hcruhc nairetybserp eht dna eciffo tsop eht dna aciremA fo knab eht dna llah loop eht dna yaweerf eht dna retnec gnippohs yawefas eht dna bulc snamrettel eht dna bulc yek eht dna ecremmoc fo rebmahc roinuj . . .

(The KID screams and holds his hands to his ears. His whole body twitches and writhes as WILLIE did when the Hand grabbed him.)

KID: Stop it! Stop it! I can't— No! No more! Stop!

WILLIE: . . . eht dna sedarap eht dna steem kcart roodtuo eht dna egelloc roinuj eht dna loohcs hgih eht dna pohs tunod eht dna slrig eht dna

secar gard eht dna semag llabtoof eht dna syella gnilwob eht dna
seivom ni drive eht dna sllihtoof eht evol i . . .

KID: No! No! My head! My brain! Stop it!

(He falls to the ground holding his head and writhing, screaming for mercy.)

WILLIE: Asuza evol i. Dnatsrednu tnac uoy gnihtemos staht. Ti evol i.
Ereh desiar dna nrob saw i. Emoh ym fo nuf ekam tnod. Emoh ym si
siht. Uoy llik lli. Lla uoy llik lli. Pu tuhs! Pu tuhs! Free! Free! Free!
Free! Free! Free!

*(WILLIE goes into an elated dance as the KID screams on the floor. Very gradu-
ally Day-Glo painted Ping-Pong balls start to fall from the ceiling passing
through black light as they fall and bouncing on the stage as WILLIE screams
"Free" over and over again and dances.)*

BLUE: Willie! What's goin' on!

WILLIE: I have discovered their secret! The Hand is in my control! I have
the Hand! We are free! Free! Free!

KID: My brain! I can't stand it!

WILLIE: My people are free! Nogoland is exploding! The Silent Ones are
dying! Look! Look at the sky!

*(As they look up at the sky more and more Ping-Pong balls fall, Day-Glo strips
of paper flutter to the ground. CISCO joins WILLIE in his dance and yells "Free"
with him. SYCAMORE and BLUE look at the sky. SYCAMORE takes off his hat and
catches the balls and throws them up in the air. BLUE joins in.)*

CISCO: Free! Free! Yipeee! Wahoooo! Alaman left and swing her low!
Catch her on the backside and watch her glow!

BLUE: Then we don't have to go to no other galaxy after all. We can stay
right here!

SYCAMORE: We're free! Free!

KID: No! My brain!

WILLIE: It was all in my brain the whole time. In my mind. The ancient
language of the Nogo. Right in my brain. I've destroyed them by
breaking free of the Hand. They have no control. We can do what we
want! We're free to do what we want.

BLUE: Let's have us a party, Willie.

CISCO: Sure, we'll invite the old gang. You can call them all back, Willie. You've got the power.

WILLIE: So have you. Do it yourself. Do whatever you want. I've got to leave.

BLUE: How come?

SYCAMORE: You just got here, I thought.

WILLIE: My people need me now more than ever. Now we can start to build our own world.

BLUE: What's a' matter with this one?

WILLIE: I am a visitor here. I came for help. This is your world. Do what you want with it.

CISCO: But we're strangers too. We're lost, Willie.

WILLIE: Good luck.

BLUE: Wait!

(WILLIE exits. The KID is frozen in an attitude of terror.)

SYCAMORE: Well of all the damn nerve. He just used us.

CISCO: What're we gonna' do now?

BLUE: Anything.

CISCO: Stop talkin' like him, dammit. We're in some pickle, Blue. It's gonna' be mornin' and here we are stuck in some other century in some hick town called Azusa somewheres.

BLUE: "Everything from A to Z in the USA." That's us all right.

CISCO: Stop saying that over and over all the time!

SYCAMORE: What do you mean, "That's us all right"?

BLUE: Now they got us thrown in to boot.

CISCO: And I ain't sure they're gonna' go fer the idea. He sure didn't.

SYCAMORE: What're we gonna' do with him anyway?

CISCO: I say we plug him.

BLUE: He's free like us.

SYCAMORE: Free to kill us, ya' mean.

CISCO: Yeah, or turn us in to the law.

BLUE: If you waste him there's gonna' be a dozen more to take his place. Look at him. He's as good as dead anyway.

CISCO: He's right, Sycamore.

SYCAMORE: I don't know. Can't seem to think straight. Who runs this town anyhow? That's the dude to go to. Straight up to the top.

BLUE: The mayor?

SYCAMORE: The mayor.

BLUE: He runs the cops. The governor runs the mayor.

SYCAMORE: The governor. What's his name?

BLUE: Congress runs the governor. President runs the Congress.

SYCAMORE: What's his name? We gotta' get outa' this.

CISCO: We could hide in the drainage ditch.

SYCAMORE: Yeah, we could sit it out. We ain't done nothin' wrong.

CISCO: We could change our names. Get a haircut, some new threads. Blend right in.

SYCAMORE: That's it. That's the ticket. I could get me an office job easy enough.

CISCO: Sure. Western Union. Pacific Gas and Electric. Plenty of places.

SYCAMORE: Settle down with a nice little pension. Get me a car maybe.

CISCO: Yeah boy. And one a' them lawnmowers ya' sit on like a tractor.

SYCAMORE: Sure. We could fit right into the scheme a' things. Don't have to bust our balls for nobody. What do ya' say, Blue?

BLUE: Whatever you boys want. I'm gonna' be long gone by mornin'.

CISCO: What do you mean, Blue?

BLUE: I'm leavin'. I been hangin' around this dump for twenty years. Seems about time to get the lead out.

(He moves toward the car and pulls the suitcase out of the back seat.)

CISCO: But where you gonna' go? What you gonna' do?

BLUE: I'll answer them questions when they come up. Right now I just gotta' move. That's all I know.

CISCO: Well, let me come with ya' then. Please, Blue.

BLUE: All right.

CISCO: Sycamore? You comin'? We oughta' stick together since we're brothers and all.

SYCAMORE: Naw, thanks anyway. Think I'll stay awhile.

CISCO: All right. So long then.

BLUE: Sorry it didn't work out like you want, Syc. . . .

SYCAMORE: Don't matter. Seemed unreal from the start anyhow.

BLUE: Yeah. I know what you mean.

SYCAMORE: You boys go ahead on and take care, ya' hear. Don't worry about me.

CISCO: Good luck, Syc.

SYCAMORE: Yeah. You too.

BLUE: Peace.

(BLUE and CISCO exit. SYCAMORE looks down at the KID, still frozen grotesquely. He stares at the KID's face and slowly becomes older and older just with his body. He turns to the Chevy and talks to an imaginary driver as BLUE did in the beginning.)

SYCAMORE: *(In ancient voice)* Well now. Well. Sure is decent of ya' stoppin' so late of an evenin' fer an old wreck like me. Yes sir. Mighty decent. Cars get to rollin' by here, eighty, ninety, a hundred mile an hour. Don't even see the landscape. Just a blur. Just a blue blur. Can't figure it. Wouldn't hardly call it a vacation now, would ya'. Screamin' out to Desert Hot Springs, back to Napa Valley. Don't even see the country. Not to speak of. Most folks is too scared, I guess. That's what it mounts up to. A certain terrorism in the air. A night terror. That's what's got 'em all locked up goin' so fast they can't see. Me, I'm slow by nature. I got nothin' agin' speed now, mind ya'. I've done plenty a' speed in my time to know the taste good and well. Speed's a pleasure. Yes sir. Naw, that ain't it. Mind if I grab yer back seat here so's I can curl up? Feet are awful dogged. Good. Mighty kind. Mighty kind.

(He opens the door of the Chevy and slowly climbs in the back seat. The lights fade slowly as he gradually disappears in the back while he talks.)

It's just a hankerin' to take stock a' things. A man's gotta' be still long enough to figure out his next move. Know what I mean? Like in checkers, for example. Can't just plunge in. Gotta make plans. Figure out yer moves. Make sure they're yer own moves and not someone else's. That's the great thing about this country, ya' know. The fact that you can make yer own moves in yer own time without some guy behind the scenes pullin' the switches on ya'. May be a far cry from bein' free, but it sure come closer than most anything I've seen. Me, I don't yearn fer much anymore but to live out my life with a little peace and quiet. I done my bit, God knows. God knows that much. There comes a time to let things by. Just let 'em go by. Let the world alone. It'll take care of itself. Just let it be.

(As SYCAMORE disappears the lights fade out. Guitar music accompanies ending speech.)

The Rock Garden

The Rock Garden was first performed at Theatre Genesis, St. Mark's Church-in-the-Bowery, New York, on October 10, 1964, with the following cast:

BOY: Lee Kissman
WOMAN: Stephanie Gordon
MAN: Kevin O'Connor

It was directed by Ralph Cook.

SCENE ONE

As lights come up we see a dinner table center stage. Seated at the head of the table facing the audience is a MAN *reading a magazine. Seated to the left of the table is a teenage* GIRL. *A teenage* BOY *sits opposite her. The* GIRL *and* BOY *are drinking milk. They take turns sipping the milk and exchanging glances. The* MAN *is completely involved in his magazine. For a long period of time nothing is said. The only action is that of the* BOY *and* GIRL *drinking milk. The* GIRL *drops her glass and spills the milk. Blackout.*

SCENE TWO

A bedroom. There is a WOMAN *lying in a bed upstage with several blankets over her. To stage left is the teenage* BOY *seated in a rocking chair. The lighting is a very pale blue. There is a large bay window behind the bed. The silhouettes of trees can be seen through the windows. The* BOY *is dressed in underwear. As the lights come up there is no sound for a long while except the slow rocking of the* BOY.

WOMAN: Angels on horseback. That's what we called them. They're easy to make. Just salt crackers and marshmallows.

BOY: You have to toast them.

WOMAN: Yes. They're best when they're just barely toasted. Sort of a light brown so the marshmallow just barely starts to melt. (*A long pause.*) It seems like they're for summer. We always had them in the summer.

BOY: It's summer now.

WOMAN: Yes. That's what I mean. In the summer. Angels on horseback. (*A long pause.*) Pop liked them burned. You know? Burned to a crisp. Black and crispy. He'd sit there and chew all night on them. He'd sit in front of the fire and burn them all night. He loved them burned like that. It was funny.

BOY: Why?

WOMAN: I don't know. He just sat there a long time burning marshmallows and eating them. That's why his face was red. Everyone thought he just got out in the sun a lot but actually it was from sitting in front of the fire so long. He hardly ever went in the sun. It was funny. A whole beach and he stayed inside all the time. He'd look at the beach from the attic but he hardly ever went near it. The forest was what he liked. You know? He liked to go walking in the trees. He'd pick mushrooms. He could tell all the different kinds. He knew the poison ones from the edible ones. Once he made a mistake and got very sick. I remember. He picked up a lot of very small red ones that he'd never seen before. He made a big kind of stew out of them. He even mixed them with some of the other kind. He got very sick and threw up for a whole week. Poor Pop. He was a funny man.

BOY: Why?

WOMAN: He just was. I don't know. I mean he knew all about a lot of things but he still got sick. Like the mushrooms. And once he tried to make a tree house and fell down and broke his leg. Sometimes he just stayed in the attic. He'd stay up there for days and days and never come down. We thought he'd starved to death once because he'd been up there for ten days without food. But he was all right. He came out looking like he just had breakfast. He was never hungry.

BOY: Never?

WOMAN: Hardly ever. He would eat when we weren't around. He always ate alone.

BOY: Why?

WOMAN: He just liked to, I guess. He didn't like to eat around people. He ate with the cats in the attic. He had a lot of cats. He had one called Ty Cobb because it played ball so well. *(A long pause.)* He was a funny man. He knew a lot of people. They'd stop by to see him but he was always in the attic. I always wondered why they kept coming back. He was always in the attic. He loved animals. He had a whole bunch of cats. He kept them in the attic though so nobody could bother them. Mother went up there once and she said the place stank so bad she never went back. I guess he never cleaned up after the cats. They just went all over the place and he never cleaned it up. Ty

Cobb was his favorite one. I never saw Ty Cobb, but he told me that was his favorite.

BOY: He never let the cats out?

WOMAN: No, he kept them in the attic. He never let anyone up there. He'd stay up there for days.

BOY: What did he do?

WOMAN: I don't know. Mother told me he was a painter but I never saw him painting. He'd stay up there for days. I guess he was a painter. I don't know. Would you get me a glass of water?

(The BOY gets up and goes offstage. He comes back with a glass of water.)

Thank you.

(The BOY sits.)

I'm really thirsty. *(A long pause.)* Your legs are a lot like Pop's. Pop had the same kind of legs.

BOY: What do you mean?

WOMAN: Well I mean they were bony and—and kind of skinny.

BOY: They were?

WOMAN: Yes. And he had knobby knees.

BOY: He did?

WOMAN: And fuzzy brown hair all over them. He was a funny man. Would you get me another glass?

(The BOY goes off. He comes back with the water and wearing a pair of pants.)

Thank you.

(The BOY sits.)

I really don't know how I caught this cold. It was probably from being out in the rain too much. I used to play in the rain all the time but now I catch colds. I used to listen to the rain when I was sleeping. I mean not when I was sleeping but when I was in bed. Just before I fell asleep I'd listen to the rain. It made me fall asleep. It was like music sort of. It always made me fall asleep. Your feet are almost identical to Pop's. I mean the way the middle toe is. You see the way your middle toe sticks way out further than the other toes? That's the way Pop's toes was. His middle one. The way it sticks out.

BOY: Oh.

WOMAN: Isn't that funny? Pop would have liked you. I can tell. Would you get me another blanket, please?

(The BOY *goes off. He comes back on with a blanket and wearing shoes.)*

Oh, thank you. It's getting a little drafty. Can you feel it?

BOY: *(Sitting)* No.

WOMAN: It feels a little drafty. It's probably coming from the windows. It probably is. But you know Bill. He says he'll put new putty in and he never does. He never gets around to it. All they need is some new putty and there wouldn't be any more drafts. It's very simple, you know? Even I could do it. I'll probably have to if I want to get it done. I don't think he's ever done that kind of work. I know he does physical labor but I don't think he's ever done any work with putty. Putty is a hard thing to work with. It's very—very tricky and it takes a lot of know-how. You can't just expect to pick it up and start working it right off the bat. You have to know what you're working with. It's a tricky kind of material. You have to know all about how to prepare it with the right kind of pastes and think like that. You can't just take it and start puttying. You have to really learn all you can about it before you can start working with it. He'll never learn. I don't think he wants to. Can I have another glass of water?

(The BOY *gets off and comes back with a glass of water.)*

Thank you.

(The BOY *sits.)*

He can't learn about putty by working in the orchard and things like that. He needs to practice with it a few times in order to get the feel of it. He could practice on the windows in the shed but I don't think he wants to. Just a little practice is all he'd need. He doesn't have to do all that physical labor that he does. He really doesn't. It doesn't do anything for him. He gets all sweaty and everything. It would be so much easier just to practice a little and putty the windows. I don't think he wants to do it though. (*A long pause.*) It doesn't do anything for his physique. You know? He works and works all day and look at his physique. You've seen him without his shirt. You've seen his physique. He does all that labor for nothing. It's really too bad. You have the same kind of torso as he does. The same build. Only he works and you don't. That's the difference. He should just face up to it, that's all. It won't get any better. He's not going to develop any more by doing all that work. Could I have another glass?

(The BOY *goes off. He comes back with a glass of water and wearing a shirt.)*

Thank you.

(The BOY *sits.)*

It doesn't really matter to me except that the draft isn't good for me when I have these colds. Otherwise the drafts are fine. It's just when I catch these colds that they bother me. I guess I should gradually become used to the draft but I can't help it. You're not supposed to have drafts on you when you have a cold. Aren't you cold?

BOY: No.

WOMAN: I'm freezing. Would you bring me another blanket?

(The BOY *goes off. He comes back with a blanket and wearing an overcoat.)*

Thank you.

(The BOY *sits.)*

It's really cold. I shouldn't have walked in the rain. That's the problem. If I hadn't walked in the rain I wouldn't be cold like this. It's just that I love the rain and whenever I get the chance I walk in it. I like it after the rain stops, too. I mean the way everything smells and looks. Right after a good hard rain. Those are two of my favorite times. When it's raining and right after it rains. I like it just before it rains too but that's different. It's not the same. I get a different feeling just before it rains. I mean it's a different feeling from the one I get when it's raining. It's not the same. It's like—

(Footsteps are heard offstage. The footsteps get louder. A MAN walks by the window from stage right to stage left dressed in a hat and overcoat. The BOY stands suddenly. The MAN can be heard scraping his feet offstage. The BOY runs offstage right. The MAN enters stage left. He walks across the stage and exits stage right. After a while the MAN comes back on dressed in underwear. He crosses to the rocking chair and sits. For a long while the MAN just sits rocking. The WOMAN stares at the ceiling.)

MAN: Kind of drafty.
WOMAN: Yes.
MAN: Must be the windows.
WOMAN: I guess so.

(A long silence while the MAN rocks. The lights dim down slowly.)

SCENE THREE

The lights come up again on a bare stage except for a couch downstage left and a chair upstage right. The MAN sits on the couch. The BOY sits in the chair facing upstage with his back to the MAN. The BOY never turns to address the MAN but delivers all his lines into the air. They are both dressed in underwear. At different moments the BOY nods out from boredom and falls off his chair. He picks himself back up and sits again. The MAN goes on oblivious. There is a long pause as the two just sit in their places.

(Saturday afternoon—just after lunch, just before the ball game.)

MAN: It's uh—the lawn doesn't seem too bad this time of year. *(A long pause.)* Except around the sprinkler heads. It's always wet around the sprinkler heads so it grows all the time, I guess. *(A long pause.)* It's harder to mow around them too, I guess. It's hard to get the lawnmower in there close, I guess. It's pretty hard to get it in there close so it cuts, I guess. *(A long pause.)* The other house wasn't as bad as this one, was it? I mean the lawn wasn't. I mean the way the lawn was at the other place made it easier, I guess. I mean not the lawn itself but more the way it was. You know? The way it was just there. I mean it was just a square piece of lawn. You know? It wasn't the lawn so much as the way it was.

(A long pause. The BOY *falls off his chair, then sits back down.)*

The lawn here is different, you know. This one is different from the other one. It's the locality of it, I guess. You know? It's harder to get to. The other one didn't have as many sprinkler heads as this. The other one didn't have any, did it? No, the other one was easy. I remember the other one.

(A long pause.)

BOY: The other one was different from this.
MAN: Yes, the other was easier and didn't have so many sprinkler heads. *(A long pause.)* If we can get the fence painted by next week it would be nice. You know? It's not a good fence but if we could get it painted by next week it would be nice, I guess. *(A long pause.)* It needs to be saturated, you know? That way it will last. I remember the last one didn't last at all. You remember the last one, the way it fell down all the time? But if it had been saturated it wouldn't have fallen down at all. You know? *(A long pause.)* There's a new kind of preservative you can buy that will be good for it. It only takes a couple of coats.
BOY: Two coats?
MAN: Yes, just a couple will do it.
BOY: Two?
MAN: Yes, two or three.
BOY: Three or two?
MAN: Just a couple.
BOY: Two?
MAN: Yes.
BOY: Good.
MAN: Yes. *(A long pause.)* That ought to do it.
BOY: Good.

(A long pause.)

MAN: What color?
BOY: For the fence?

MAN: Yes.

BOY: What color is it now?

MAN: White.

BOY: White?

MAN: Yes.

BOY: How about white?

MAN: You mean paint it over white?

BOY: Yes.

MAN: Oh. Well, all right.

BOY: White would be good.

MAN: Sure. Maybe a kind of off-white. You know? What about a kind of off-white? You know what I mean? A kind of different white. You know? Just a little different. Not too much different from the way it is now. What do you think? A different kind of white. You know? So it won't be too much the same. It could be almost the same but still be a little different. You know?

(A long pause. The BOY *falls off his chair.)*

It would be fun, I think. Did you notice the rock garden? That's a new idea. It's by the driveway. You may have seen it when you pass by there in the mornings. It's not bad for my never having made one before. It's one of those new kind. You know? With rocks and stuff in it. It has a lot of rocks and stuff from the trip. We found afterwards that it was really worth carrying all those rocks around. You know? It's a nice rock garden. It gives me something to do. It keeps me pretty busy. You know? It feels good to get out in it and work and move the rocks around and stuff. You know? It's a good feeling. I change it every day. It keeps me busy.

(A long pause. The BOY *falls off his chair.)*

It's not the garden so much as the *work* it gives me. It's good to work in a garden. Remember when we found the rocks? I remember. That was a good trip, wasn't it? Maybe we can take another one and get some more.

BOY: Rocks?

MAN: Yes. We could start another garden. A bigger one.

BOY: Bigger than the one you have now?

MAN: Sure. We could start a whole lot of them. They're not hard to start, you know. All you need is some rocks. They have to be good rocks, though. I mean they can't be any kind of rocks. You know what I mean? I mean they have to be the right size and shape and color and everything. They can't just be ordinary rocks, otherwise there wouldn't be any point in making a garden at all. You know? That's why we'd have to go somewhere else to find them. Somewhere like Arizona or something. Like we did before. Do you remember? We went to Arizona before and we found a lot of rocks. We could really have some nice gardens like the one I have now. Only bigger and more fancy. I saw one with a fountain in it. We could put a fountain in ours. You know? And some of those Oriental statues and things like that. We could work on it together. You know? It wouldn't be hard. We could do it in our spare time.

BOY: Together?

MAN: Sure. And we could have bacon, lettuce, and tomato sandwiches afterwards.

BOY: After we work?

MAN: Sure.

BOY: With mayonnaise?

MAN: Yeah. And we both would have big appetites probably, from working so hard in the garden.

BOY: Hard?

MAN: I mean just working we would have appetites. Just from plain working.

BOY: We would?

MAN: Sure. *(A long pause.)* It wouldn't be hard work at all. Just plain good steady work in the outdoors. It would be good for us. Don't you think? *(A long pause.)* The orchard is the thing that really needs work. You know? It needs more work than the garden probably. It needs to be taken care of. It needs more water than it's been getting. You know what I mean. The new trees especially. They get brown pretty easily in this warm weather. I guess we should really take care of the orchard first. You know? Then maybe we can go to Arizona and pick up the rocks. We should disc the orchard first and then spray the new trees. It won't be hard once we get into it. It doesn't take a lot of work, really. You know? The irrigation needs to be worked on too. That will be the hardest. It's those damn pipes, you know? Whoever put them in when they were put in didn't put them in right. You know? They weren't put in right originally. That's the whole thing. They were put in wrong when they were first put in. You know what I mean? So I thought we'd take them all out and then put in some new ones. Some of those aluminum ones they have now. Have you seen the ones? They're lightweight. I thought we'd put some of those in.

BOY: We take all the ones that are in now out and then we put in some aluminum ones?

MAN: Yes.

BOY: And then we spray the new trees?

MAN: Yes, they need spraying. We could do all that and then go to Arizona. It wouldn't be bad at all once we got into it. This whole place will be looking like a new place. A new place. One of those new places with rocks gardens all over and fountains. You know? You come up the street and there'd be a nice green lawn with a lot of rock gardens and the irrigation running and the new trees all—all sort of green. You know? And the fence all painted with a different kind of white paint and the grass cut around the sprinkler heads and all that. You know?

(*A long pause.*)

BOY: When I come it's like a river. It's all over the bed and the sheets and everything. You know? I mean a short vagina gives me security. I can't help it. I like to feel like I'm really turning a girl on. It's a much better screw is what it amounts to. I mean if a girl has a really small vagina it's really better to go in from behind. You know? I mean she can sit with her legs together and you can sit facing her. You know? But that's different. It's a different kind of thing. You can do it standing, you know? Just by backing her up, you know? You just stand and she goes down and down until she's almost sitting on your dick. You know what I mean? She'll come a hundred times and you just stand there holding on to it. That way you don't even have to undress. You know? I mean she may not want to undress is all. I like to undress myself but some girls just don't want to. I like going down on girls, too. You know what I mean? She gives me some head and then I give her some. Just sort of a give-and-take thing. You know? The thing with a big vagina is that there isn't as much contact. There isn't as much friction. I mean you can move around inside her. There's different ways of ejaculation. I mean the leading up to it can be different. You can rotate motions. Actually girls really like fingers almost as well as a penis. You know? If you move your fingers fast enough they'd rather have it that way almost. I learned to use my thumb, you know? You can get your thumb in much farther, actually. I mean the thumb can go almost eight inches whereas a finger goes only five or six. You know? I don't know. I really like to come almost out and then go all the way into the womb. You know, very slowly. Just come down to the end and all the way back in and hold it. You know what I mean?

(The MAN *falls off the couch. The lights black out.)*

Chicago

Chicago was first performed on Good Friday, in 1965, at Theatre Genesis, St. Mark's Church-in-the-Bowery, with the following cast:

POLICEMAN:	Warren Finnerty
STU:	Kevin O'Connor
JOY:	Lyn Hutt
MYRA:	Lenette Reuben
JOE:	Paul Plummer
SALLY:	Susanne English
JIM:	Lee Kissman

It was directed by Ralph Cook on a double bill with *The Customs Collector in Baggy Pants* by Lawrence Ferlinghetti. *Chicago* was subsequently presented at Cafe La Mama on March 13, 1966, on a double bill with *This is the Rill Speaking* by Lanford Wilson and again on March 17, 1966, on a triple bill with *The Recluse* by Paul Foster and *Thank You, Miss Victoria* by William M. Hoffman.

Chicago was presented off-Broadway at the Martinique Theatre as part of *6 From La Mama* by Circle in the Square. It was directed by Tom O'Horgan. It opened April 12, 1966, with the following cast:

POLICEMAN:	Warren Finnerty
STU:	Kevin O'Connor
JOY:	Lyn Hutt
MYRA:	Jacque Lynn Colton
JOE:	Victor Lipari
SALLY:	Stephanie Gordon
JIM:	Michael Warren Powell

SCENE

The lights dim down in the house. A POLICEMAN *comes out in front of the curtain with a club. He beats the curtain several times with the club, then walks into the audience and up the center aisle. He goes to the back of the house and bangs his club three times on the back of a chair. Someone reciting the "Gettysburg Address" comes on very loudly through the sound system. The curtains open. The lights come up slowly on a bare stage. Upstage center* STU *is sitting in a bathtub splashing water and talking in a singsong manner. The "Gettysburg Address" fades out as* STU *continues.*

STU: And ya' walk through the town. With yer head on the ground. And ya' look all around through the town fer yer dog. Your dog Brown. He's yellow but ya' call him Brown anyhow. And sit in the hay. And ya' say. What a day. This is it. It's the day that ya' say is okay. Anyway. Anyhow. You know by now. That yer dog is dead and ya' don't care anyhow. 'Cause ya' didn't really like him in the first place. So ya' say. What a day. In the hay. Anyway. And ya' walk through the town and around. Then ya' see another tree. And ya' pee on the ground. 'Cause it's nice and ya' don't think twice. Ya' just do and it's done. And it's fun. Ho, ho.

JOY: *(Off right)* Biscuits!

STU: Biscuits in the sun. And ya' run. And it's fun. Ya' have a gun. It's yer own. Ya' don't care. You can even shoot a bear. If ya' have any hair. If ya' don't. Ya' don't. If ya' do. It's true. And yer through anywho.

JOY: *(Off right)* Biscuits are ready!

STU: Teddy and Freddy and all the stupid people having fun with a gun. And ya' run all around. Through the town. What a way. To spend a day. In the hay. By the way. It's okay. Stay away.

(JOY *comes on from right in a bathrobe; she yells at* STU.)

JOY: Biscuits! Biscuits! Come on!

(*She goes off right.* STU *stands suddenly in the bathtub; he is wearing long pants and tennis shoes without a shirt.*)

STU: Just a second! Just a second!

(JOY *comes back on from right.*)

JOY: What?
STU: A towel.
JOY: Just a second.

(*She goes off right.*)

STU: If it was warm I could go without a towel. Seeing as how it's cold, I'll need one.

(JOY *comes back on with a towel; she throws it at* STU, *then goes back off right.* STU *stays standing up in the tub drying himself.*)

Thanks.
JOY: (*Off right*) Okay.
STU: I meant if the sun were out. That kind of warmth. Not just warm but a sun kind of warmth. You know? Like the beach.
JOY: (*Off right*) The beach has sun.
STU: I know. You just lie there and the sun dries you and the sand gets all stuck to you. It sticks all over. In your toes. In your ears. Up your crotch. Aaah! Sand between your legs! Aaah! Sticking in your pores. Goddamn!

(*He sits back down in the tub and puts the towel over his head; he talks like an old lady, using the towel as a bandanna.*)

All you young little girlies out there paradin' around in yer flimsies. Makes me all ashamed and pink in the face to think a' that.
JOY: (*Off right*) What?

STU: Two-pieces and one-pieces and bare-chested things going on. No upbringin'. That's it. That's where it comes from. A lack a' concern on the part a' the parents and all. Flimsy morality. Dirty shame.

(JOY comes on fast from right.)

JOY: Cold biscuits! Do you dig cold biscuits? The butter's cold, too. The jam's cold. I hope you're glad.

(She goes off right. STU stands again with the towel still draped over his head; he talks like an old lady.)

STU: Looky here, missy. Don't be so high and mighty and flashy, all of a sudden. Just 'cause ya' got big boobies. Thank the Lord fer that. But that happens to be a gift. Ya' were bestowed with that chest a' yours. And don't forget it. Praise the Lord!

JOY: *(Off right)* Fuck off!

(STU takes the towel off his head and starts drying himself again; he talks in a normal voice.)

STU: Biscuits. Who needs biscuits at this hour? Who ever needs biscuits? Joy?

JOY: *(Off right)* What?

STU: Who needs biscuits?

JOY: Peasants in Mexico.

STU: Peasants make their own. Biscuits were invented to trick people into believing they're really eating food! They aren't any good at all. They're just dough. A hunk of dough that goes down and makes a gooey ball in your stomach. It makes you feel full. Biscuits are shit!

(JOY throws a bunch of biscuits from off right; they hit STU in the head, STU picks one up and takes a bite out of it, he sits back down in the tub and continues eating the biscuit; a phone rings off left, JOY crosses the stage and exits left still wearing the nightgown, she answers the phone, she talks off left.)

JOY: Hello. Hi. Oh, you're kidding. Is that right? Oh Myra. Well when's he leaving? He left? He's gone? You do? Oh fine. Yes. I got the job. Yes, it's final. Well they called last night. Last night. Uh-huh. Two weeks. A week maybe. The sooner the better. I'll see. Well I have a few things to do. Yes. Okay. 'Bye.

(She hangs up; she comes on from left dressed in a bra and slip, she crosses the stage.)

How's your biscuit?
STU: Good. How's yours?

(She exits right.)

JOY: *(Off right)* Myra's coming.
STU: Did you say you got the job? Did I hear you say that?
JOY: I said Myra's coming.
STU: On the phone. Did you say you got the job?
JOY: Yes.

(STU stand suddenly in the tub and starts yelling.)

STU: You did not!
JOY: *(Off right)* Yes!
STU: They hired you!
JOY: Yes!
STU: Good! I'm really glad!
JOY: Good!
STU: I'm really, really glad. When are you going?

(JOY comes on from right brushing her hair and still wearing the bra and slip.)

JOY: Oh, I don't know.
STU: You don't?
JOY: Soon.
STU: Good.

(JOY climbs into the tub with STU.)

Don't! You can't get in here!
JOY: How come?
STU: Because there's not enough water.

JOY: Don't be stupid. We can fill it up.

STU: It'll overflow.

JOY: Myra's coming.

STU: You told me.

(JOY *kisses* STU; *they embrace for a while, then sit in the tub facing each other;* JOY *brushes her hair.*)

JOY: It's really nice out here.

STU: Out where?

JOY: On the water.

STU: (*Putting the towel on his head and talking like an old lady*) All you young things are the same. Corny. Corny young girls. That's what.

JOY: I love the water.

STU: Ya' all love the water. Water in the nighttime. With the moon hangin' over yer filthy little head.

JOY: It's so quiet.

STU: Yeah. Ya' like the quiet 'cause ya' don't take the time to listen when it's not quiet.

JOY: Listen to the waves.

STU: Listen yerself, missy. I heard water slappin' on the pier before. I got ears.

JOY: I could stay here forever. Feel the breeze.

STU: A corny young virgin. That's what.

JOY: It's so nice.

(*She leans over the side of the tub as though it were a boat.*)

STU: Nice, nice. No nicer than most things.

JOY: Look at the fish.

(STU *leans over and looks.*)

STU: Them's barracuda, lady. They eat people when they feel like it.

JOY: They wouldn't eat me.

STU: They'd eat you like nobody's business.

JOY: They're really big.

STU: Big as they come.

(MYRA *comes on from left dressed in a fur coat and dark glasses and carrying a* *suitcase. She stands looking on.*)

JOY: That's awful.
STU: See the way they flash around. That's 'cause they're hungry.
JOY: Really?
STU: Starvin' to death.
JOY: Damn.
STU: Just lookin' fer a nice young virgin.
JOY: They don't eat people.
STU: Just lookin' fer somethin' to bite.

(*He grabs her and tries to push her out of the tub.*)

JOY: Stop it!
STU: All them fishies gettin' ready fer a feast.
JOY: Cut it out!

(*They stand struggling with each other.*)

STU: Big striped fishes with long teeth and pink tongues.
JOY: Stop!
STU: (*Normal voice*) They like you. They want you for their very own. They want to eat you up!
JOY: No!

(*They kiss for a while.*)

STU: Myra's here.
MYRA: Hello, Joy. Are you ready?
JOY: No.
STU: She's ready.
JOY: I am not.
STU: She got hired.

(JOY *climbs out of the tub and starts brushing her hair.*)

MYRA: It's a good job.
JOY: It's all right.

(JOY *exits right brushing her hair,* MYRA *follows behind her, they go off.* STU *stands looking down at the floor.*)

STU: Tough luck, fish. You're really ugly anyway. Eat some little fish. Minnows or something. Seaweed. Try some seaweed for a change. You're going to be in bad shape if you keep going around like that. In schools. In all that crappy black water. Bumping your dumb heads into rocks and boulders and making your tongues bleed. Stupid. Swim. Go ahead. Let me see you. Don't just hang there treading water.

(*He kneels down in the tub looking over the edge.*)

What's wrong? I see you, stupid. Go down. Dive or something. Beat it! All right! Stay there. See if I care.

(*He lies back in the tub and puts his feet up on the edge.*)

You can't wait forever. You'll have to go when it gets dark. People will start looking for you when it gets dark. They'll be out in boats. They'll have long hip boots and pipes and mosquito juice on their faces. They'll have bottles of worms and poles for you. They'll get in all their little boats and push them out in the water. Then they'll whisper to each other about what a nice night it is and how still it is and look at all the fireflies. Then they'll row very softly out to the middle. Out in the deep part. And they'll break out their thermos bottles full of coffee and split-pea soup. And they'll drink and whisper about you. About how big you are and how striped you are and how nice it would be to have your head cut off and mounted over the fireplace. They'll get out their poles and the worms and the hooks and drop them over the side. The worm will just float for a while, then he'll have a little spasm and wriggle on the hook. Then he'll drown and sink all the way to the bottom and die in front of your long noses. You'll watch him for a while, see. Then you'll move a little bit. You're pretty hungry but you're not sure. So you take your time. You're down there moving slowly around this worm, taking your time. And they're up there drinking split-pea soup and grinning and pointing at the moon and the pier and all the trees. You're both hung up.

(The phone rings off left, JOY *crosses the stage and exits left.* STU *remains standing and looking off left.)*

JOY: *(Off left)* Hello. How are you, Joe? Sure. Okay. Yes, I got the job. Of course. How about you? Well, pretty soon I guess. Yes, I bought my ticket. Uh-huh. Well, as soon as I can. Yes. Sure. Come on over. Okay. Good. 'Bye.

(She hangs up and comes on from left carrying a fishing pole; she crosses to STU *and kisses him on the stomach, then exits right.)*

STU: That was Joe, huh?

(He sits.)

JOY: *(Off right)* Yes. He's coming over.
STU: Good.
MYRA: *(Off right)* Good biscuits, Joy.
JOY: They're all right.
STU: Are you packing, Joy?
JOY: What?
STU: Are you getting your stuff ready?
JOY: Yes.
STU: That's going to be a good trip.
JOY: I guess so.
STU: All that way on a train. The seats fold back so you can sleep if you want to. You can look out the window too. You can see all kinds of different houses and people walking around.

*(*JOE *comes on from left wearing a suit and dark glasses and carrying a fishing pole and a suitcase; he looks at* STU *for a while, then crosses the stage and exits right.)*

They have one whole car where you eat. And another car just for drinking. The tables are nailed to the floor so they don't jiggle. You can buy a whole dinner for about five bucks. They even give you a full pitcher of ice water. They just leave it on the table so you don't have to keep asking for water. And a silver cup full of toothpicks. You sit there and pick your teeth and look out the window. Then you have to leave. They force you to leave because there's a whole line of people waiting to eat. They're all hungry.

JOY: *(Off right)* Hi, Joe.

JOE: *(Off right)* Hi.

MYRA: *(Off right)* Have a biscuit.

JOE: Thanks.

STU: They stop once in a while but you can only get off at the big stations. You can only get off at places like Saint Louis or Cincinnati. None of the small towns. And your butt aches after a while. Your butt really starts to ache. You can hardly stand it. So you have to get up and walk around. Up and down the aisles. Back and forth.

JOE: *(Off right)* Hm. Real butter.

JOY: *(Off right)* Yes. It's starting to melt though.

STU: Your butt aches so bad that your legs even start to ache. Your legs can fall asleep on a train. Then your feet. You have to walk fast. It's better to sit in the restroom because you can stretch. You can stretch your legs out in there. And there's old men in there taking nips on little wine bottles. They get drunk in there and throw up on the floor. Their wives don't even know it because they're asleep in the folding chairs.

MYRA: *(Off right)* Delicious.

JOE: *(Off right)* Good jam, too.

STU: Then everyone falls asleep. Almost everyone at once. It's dark so they figure they have to, I guess. The porter turns the lights out and right away everyone's asleep. There's a little girl running up and down the aisle. She doesn't make any noise because everyone's sleeping. There's a Marine making it with somebody's wife because her husband's drunk in the restroom. There's a cowboy picking his teeth and spitting little gobs of food into the aisle. Some fat guy is farting and he doesn't even know it. The smell drifts down the aisle and stinks up the whole car. One fart after another. Big windy farts that sort of make a whizzing sound. Nobody can hear him but it stinks the whole car up.

(SALLY *enters from left wearing dark glasses, fur coat, and carrying a suitcase and a fishing pole; she watches* STU *for a while, then crosses to the tub and stands there.)*

He moves a little in the seat because he can feel it, I guess. His wife moves a little and rubs her nose. Then they keep on sleeping. The car stinks more and more. The smell gets into the seats and the pillows and the rug. Everyone's smelling it at the same time. They sleep more and more. Then it's morning.

SALLY: Hi.

STU: (Sitting up and yawning) Whew! What time is it?

SALLY: Seven.

STU: Are you going, too?

SALLY: Yep.

STU: Do you have all your stuff?

SALLY: Yep.

STU: It's a good day to leave.

SALLY: Why?

STU: I mean's it's sunny. The sun's out.

SALLY: It's cold though.

STU: But when the sun's out you don't notice it.

SALLY: I guess. I'm going to eat.

STU: Okay.

(She exits right.)

The water's up. The sun's on the water already.

(He stands and yells off right.)

Hey, everybody! The sun's on the water!

MYRA: (Off right) Really?

STU: Yeah. And the tide's up. We should take a swim.

JOY: (Off right) It's too early.

(STU puts the towel over his head.)

STU: (Talking like an old lady) Dainty little things. Too early. Too early to swim. Water's too cold. There's a little bitty wind skippin' over the sand. The shells are too sharp for them dainty feet. Tsk, tsk. Got to wear your tennies on account of the shells.

(JIM comes on from left wearing a suit and dark glasses and carrying a suitcase and fishing pole; he watches STU.)

Got to wear a shirty on account of the sun. Can't lay around in the sand on account of your crotch. Smear a lot a' chicken fat on yer tiny fragile legs. Get back in the cabin, girlie! Don't go faintin' on the beach!

JIM: Are you going, Stu?

STU: *(Still old lady)* None a' yer business, sonny! Get away from this beach! Go on! Get off my sand! Get away from the shells! Git! Git!

JIM: Hey Stu.

(He gives STU *the finger and goes off right.)*

STU: That don't shock me, sonny! I been around. That kind a' smut don't bother no one nowadays. This is the twentieth century, buddy!

MYRA: *(Off right)* Hi, Jim.

JIM: *(Off right)* Hi.

JOY: Are you ready?

JIM: Sure.

STU: You ain't gonna' bother nobody nowadays. You're a bunch a' sissies! A bunch a' pantywaists! Nobody cares about the likes a' you! No moxy! No spunk! Can't even swim on account a' the smoke ya' put in your lungs. A bunch a' fatsoes. A bunch a' fag-prancin' around. Dancin' in the streets with yer make-up on. Swishin' into yer gay restaurants! No balls! That's what! No hair on yer chest!

JOE: *(Off right)* Do you have everything?

MYRA: *(Off right)* I think so.

JIM: Toothpaste?

JOY: Yep.

STU: *(Still old lady)* Anyway the water's up. There won't be a boat for days. They don't come in when it's high like this. The tide and all. Boats are chicken, too. Chickens run boats. A bunch a' cowards. They'll wait for it to calm. It'll warm up and they'll come in with their sails down and their nets hangin' over the edge. They'll all be drinkin' gin and singin' sea songs. They'll all be horny for the young virgins that walk the beaches in their two-piece flimsy things. Then they'll come onto the land and start screwing everything in sight. The boats'll be hung up for days because everybody's screwing on the beach. They'll like it more and more. Once they get the taste for it they won't stop. The boats will be there for months because everybody's screwing. Nobody wants to go nowhere because screwing is all they need.

Screwing and screwing. And all those boats just sitting out there with their sails down and their nets hanging and rotting in the sun. Years go by and they're still screwing. Old sailors with bald heads and old virgins with gray hair. The whole beach littered with bodies on top of each other. The boats are sinking! All those rotten boats falling into the ocean. One at a time. They sink. Pieces of wood float and wash up onto the beach but nobody cares. Nobody needs boats or wood or sails or nets. There's a whole new crop of corny virgins walking around. Up and down the beach in their two-pieces. Nobody stops. More babies from the virgins. Males and females up and down the beach. No clothes anymore. A mound of greasy bodies rolling in sperm and sand sticking to their backs and sand in their hair. Hair growing all over. Down to their feet. Pubic hair without bows or ribbons.

(He talks in normal voice and takes the towel off his head.)

Hair on their toes. Fires! Fires at night. All over the island there's huge fires flaring and they all lie around. They lie there fucking by the fire and picking each other's nose. They lick each other's arms and growl and purr and fart all they want to. They roll around farting and spitting and licking up and down. Long tongues and wet legs. Then they build a house. A big house way up on the side of a hill. It takes a year to build. It's one house with one room and fire pit in the middle. They all go in and sit on the floor and make rugs. They make rugs because the floor is cold and they don't like the cold. They start weaving and sewing. Big huge heavy rugs with fringe around the edge and diamond shapes in the middle. Orange and red rugs with yellow diamonds. They stop screwing, see, and they just make rugs. All day. Years of making rugs until the whole house is covered. The walls are covered and the ceiling and the floor. The windows are blocked up and they sit. The fire's out because of the rugs. It's warm. They're very warm inside. Sitting. It's dark, see. Pitch black and no sound. Because of the rugs. Then they start to giggle. One of them starts and they all start. One after another until they can't stop. The whole house is giggling. Then they scream, see. They start screaming all together because they can't breathe. On account of the rugs. The rugs are all sewn together and it's very warm. It's boiling hot inside. They start to sweat and run around. They bump into each other because it's dark. They can't see so they hit and claw each other with their nails. They have long nails. They kick and scream and the sweat is rolling off them. They can't breathe and it's hot. They're screaming, see.

(Off stage right the actors giggle, STU *sits slowly in the bathtub, the giggling stops.)*

And they come out. One at a time. They walk in a line out of the house. One behind the other. Down the side of the hill. Through the woods. They don't say anything. They don't even breathe. They just walk in a line. Down to the beach. They walk across the beach and right into the water. One behind the other. They just keep walking until you can't see them anymore.

(He lies back in the tub so that his head is out of view and his feet hang over the edge. JOY *comes on from right dressed in a bright red hat and a red dress; she is pulling a wagon loaded with all the suitcases. The rest of the actors come on whistling and cheering, they all hold their fishing poles, they stand in a group stage right waving and throwing kisses at* JOY *as* JOY *backs up slowly with the wagon waving back to them.)*

MYRA: Have a good time!
SALLY: So long, Joy!
JOE: So long!
JIM: Good luck out there!
JOE: See you, babe!
JIM: 'Bye!
JOE: 'Bye, 'bye!
JOY: 'Bye!
MYRA: Say hello for me!
JOE: Don't forget!
JIM: Have fun!
JOE: Good luck!
JOY: Thanks!
JOE: See you later!

*(*JOY *keeps backing up with the wagon and exits left. The four actors throw kisses, then walk slowly downstage; they stand in a line across the stage facing*

the audience, then they all cast their lines into the audience. They sit simultaneously and look at the audience while holding their poles.)

STU: *(With his head still unseen)* Then the water goes out again because it's nighttime. I guess it goes out. Yes. At night the water always goes out. And the sand gets all dry in the place where the water used to be. You can hear it making little slapping sounds and getting farther away from the pier. There's a breeze sort of. One of those high breezes that just hits the top of your head and blows paper cups down the beach. Your back shivers a little and you get goose bumps on your legs. Your toes start to sweat. The sweat runs down between your toes and your feet swell up and stick to your socks. You can't move because your feet are stuck. You can't move your head. Your head stays straight and your eyes are wide open. You can't blink your eyes. Your hands sweat just like your feet. Your fingers swell up like your toes.

(The lights start to dim slowly.)

The sweat runs down your arms and down your legs. You're looking out and you can see the water. You can see it in the dark because it's white. Like milk. The whole top is covered with milk. It smells. Your nose is burning from the smell but you can't move. You keep looking to the other side. The smell gets worse and your ears start to hum. You can see these little clots on the other side. These lights. Your eyes stay open. Then you move. You start to move slowly up the beach. Your feet hurt and your nose is bleeding from the smell. Then you see the light again. And they blink. One after the other. Between the trees. You can see them blinking. On and off. A whole town.

(JOY backs on stage from left again pulling the wagon; she exits right.)

Your eyes start blinking with the lights. Your feet start moving. You can feel them move inside your socks. Then your arms. You're running. You can feel the breathing. Panting sort of. The wind comes in through your nose and dries the blood. You can taste it. Your mouth opens and the wind comes in. Your body's moving. The sweat dries on your legs. You're going now. Much faster and the breathing gets harder. You can see the lights better now. Yellow lights between the trees. The smell stops. The humming stops. The lights go out.

(The lights come up to their full brightness, STU jumps out of the bathtub and crosses very fast downstage center facing the audience, the other actors remain sitting and staring at the audience.)

STU: Good! *(He breathes in and out very fast.)* That's great! See my stomach. In and out. It's breathing. I'm taking it in. The air. What a fine bunch of air I'm taking in. Now I'm taking it in through my nose. See. *(He breathes through his nose.)* Aaah! Great! Now my mouth. *(He breathes through his mouth.)* Good! In and out! Ladies and gentlemen, the air is fine! All this neat air gathered before us! It's too much!

(The other actors start to breathe slowly, gradually, making sounds as they inhale and exhale.)

The place is teeming with air. All you do is breathe. Easy. One, two. One, two. In. Out. Out, in. I learned this in fourth grade. Breathing, ladies and gentlemen! Before your very eyes. Outstanding air. All you need to last a day. Two days. A week. Month after month of breathing until you can't stop. Once you get the taste of it. The hang of it. What a gas. In your mouth and out your nose. Ladies and gentlemen, it's fantastic!

(They all breathe in unison as JOY backs on stage from right pulling the wagon; she exits slowly left as the lights dim and go out. There are three loud knocks from the back of the house.)

Icarus's Mother

Icarus's Mother was first produced at the Caffe Cino on November 16, 1965, with the following cast:

BILL: John Kramer
JILL: Lee Worley
PAT: Cynthia Harris
HOWARD: James Barbosa
FRANK: John A. Coe

It was directed by Michael Smith. It was subsequently produced by David Wheeler at the Theatre Company of Boston.

SCENE

The stage is covered with grass. A low hedge upstage runs the width of the stage. Behind the hedge is a pale blue scrim. Center stage is a portable barbecue with smoke rising out of it. The lighting is bright yellow. On the grass down left is a tablecloth with the remnants of a huge meal scattered around it. BILL *lies on his back down left staring at the sky.* HOWARD *lies up left,* JILL *up right,* PAT *down right and* FRANK *center stage—all in the same position as* BILL *and staring at the sky. Before the lights come up the sound of birds chirping is heard. The sound lasts for a while. The lights come up very slowly as the sound fades out. The lights come up full. A long pause, then all the people start belching at random. They stop.*

BILL: *(Still staring at the sky)* Does he know there's people down here watching him do that?

JILL: Sure.

PAT: It's skywriting.

HOWARD: No, it's not skywriting. It's just a trail. A gas trail.

PAT: I thought it was.

FRANK: It's gas.

BILL: I don't like it. I don't like the looks of it from here. It's distracting.

FRANK: It's a vapor trail. All jets do it.

BILL: I don't like the way he's making it. I mean a semicircle thing like that. In a moon shape.

JILL: I like it.

BILL: If he knows what he's doing, that means he could be signaling or something.

FRANK: Jets don't signal.

PAT: It's gas, Bill.

BILL: You mean that whole long stream of cloud is just excess gas?

HOWARD: Right.

BILL: He has no other way of getting rid of it?
HOWARD: Nope.

(BILL *stands, looking up at the sky.*)

BILL: And he's spreading it all over the sky like that?
HOWARD: That's right.
BILL: He's staying in the same general area, though. How come he's not moving to some other areas? He's been right above us for the past hour.
FRANK: He's probably a test pilot or something.
BILL: I think he sees us. I don't like the looks of it.
HOWARD: He's a million miles up. How could he see us?
BILL: He sees our smoke and he's trying to signal. *(Yelling at the sky)* Get away from here! Get out of our area!

(HOWARD *stands, looking up at the sky.*)

HOWARD: He can't hear you, Bill. You'll have to be louder than that.
BILL: Hey! Get your gas away from here!
FRANK: Sit down.
BILL: We don't know what you want but we don't want you around here!
JILL: He can't hear you. What's the matter with you?
HOWARD: He can see us, though. He knows we're looking at him.
BILL: If you need help you'll have to come down!
HOWARD: *(Yelling at the sky)* We ate all the food so we can't give you any!
FRANK: Sit down, you guys.
BILL: Get away from the picnic area! Go somewhere else! Go on! Get away from the park!
JILL: Will you guys cut it out. Leave the poor guy alone. He's just flying. Let him fly.
HOWARD: He's not just flying. If he were just doing that it would be all right. But he's not. He's signaling.
JILL: Who would he be signaling to?
HOWARD: His mother, maybe. Or his wife.
BILL: He could be signaling to anybody.
FRANK: Not likely.
PAT: What if he is? So what?
BILL: So, someone should be told about it. The community should know.

PAT: Let him signal his wife if he wants to. He's probably been away for a while and he just got back. Let him show off a little.

HOWARD: But he's right above us. His wife isn't down here.

JILL: I'm his wife.

BILL: Are you his wife, Jill?

JILL: That's right.

BILL: Then we should tell him, so he doesn't have to waste any more time.

HOWARD: Come on down! Your wife's down here!

BILL: Come on down here!

(JILL stands and yells at the sky.)

JILL: Come here, honey! Here I am! *(She waves.)*

BILL: Come and get her!

(FRANK stands and yells at the sky.)

FRANK: Come and get your wife, stupid!

(The following lines should happen on top of each other, with whistling and ad-lib shouts from all the actors.)

HOWARD: Come on! Land that thing!

JILL: Here I am, sweetheart! *(Throwing kisses)*

FRANK: You'd better hurry!

(PAT stands and yells at the sky.)

PAT: Come on down! Here we are! Yoo hoo!

BILL: Your other wife's here, too!

FRANK: Two wives!

PAT: Come on, sweetie! Where have you been!

JILL: We've been waiting and waiting!

FRANK: Two ripe juicy wives waiting for you!

HOWARD: Come on!

BILL: You've been up there too long, mister!

FRANK: We can see you! Come on down!

BILL: Land that thing!

PAT: Come to me, booby! Boobsy, boobsy, boobsy.

(JILL and PAT start shimmying around the stage.)

HOWARD: We've got your wives, mister pilot! You'd better come down or we'll take them away.
BILL: We'll use them ourselves! There's three of us here!
FRANK: He's leaving! Look! Hey!
HOWARD: Hey don't! Come back here!
JILL: He's leaving us! Stop!
PAT: Darling! The children!
BILL: You're running out on your kids!

(They all yell and shake their fists at the sky.)

JILL: Don't leave us! Come back here!
HOWARD: You're no good, mister pilot!
PAT: Come back! The children!
JILL: Don't leave us, darling!

(They all boo loudly.)

BILL: What a rotten guy!

(They stop booing and just stare at the sky.)

FRANK: He's gone.
HOWARD: That makes me sick.

(A pause as they all stare at the sky.)

PAT: Well, when do they start this thing?
FRANK: Are you in a hurry?
PAT: No. I just want to know so I could take a walk or something in the meantime.
BILL: They don't start till it gets dark.
FRANK: Where are you going to walk to?
PAT: Just down the beach or something. To rest my stomach. That was a big meal, you know.

FRANK: Walking doesn't rest your stomach. When you're full and you walk, that just irritates it.

JILL: He's right.

PAT: All right! I'll walk just to loosen my legs up or something. I'm not going to lie around here waiting for it to get dark, though.

HOWARD: What happens if they start while you're on your walk?

JILL: That'd be terrible, Pat.

PAT: They shoot them in the sky. I can watch fireworks while I'm walking just as easy. It isn't hard. All I have to do is tilt my head up and watch and continue walking.

BILL: You may trip, though, and there you'd be unconscious on the beach somewhere and we'd have to go looking for you.

JILL: Yeah.

HOWARD: Then we'd miss the fireworks just on account of you, Pat.

FRANK: We'd be looking all over. Through the bushes and up and down the beach for hours. Everyone would miss everything.

JILL: Then maybe someone else would trip while they were looking for you and we'd have two missing people on the beach unconscious instead of just one.

BILL: We might all trip and be there on the beach for weeks unconscious.

PAT: All right!

(She sits; the rest remain standing and close in on her, slowly forming a circle.)

HOWARD: You can walk if you want to, Pat. While it's still light. We don't mind.

JILL: We don't want to wreck your fun, Patsy.

BILL: But you have to get back before it gets dark. Because that's when the fireworks start. And you don't want to miss them.

FRANK: You don't want to be lost on the beach by yourself and suddenly hear loud booming sounds and suddenly see the sky all lit up with orange and yellow and blue and green and purple and gold and silver lights.

(They gather around PAT *in a circle, looking down at her as she remains seated.)*

JILL: That'd be scary.

HOWARD: You might run and fall and scream. You might run right into the ocean and drown or run right into the forest.

BILL: They'd have to send helicopters out looking for you.

JILL: Or jets.

BILL: Your husband in the jet would find you.

(PAT stands suddenly.)

PAT: Shut up! I don't have a husband in a jet and neither does Jill! So stop kidding around! If I want to walk, I will! Just to walk! Just to walk down the beach and not come back till after dark. To loosen my legs up after a big dinner like that.

FRANK: We were just kidding, Pat.

(They all sit slowly around PAT.)

PAT: Boy! That's something. Trying to scare me into not walking. What a group.

FRANK: We were kidding.

PAT: Shut up, Frank! Jesus. All of a sudden picnics are localized events. We all have to hang around the same area where we eat. We can't even walk. We eat a big steak and we can't walk it off.

(HOWARD stands and grabs PAT's hand; he starts pulling her stage left.)

HOWARD: Let's walk! Come on, Pat. Here we go walking. Where do you want to walk to? *(The rest remain seated.)*

PAT: Cut it out! Let go! Let go of my hand!

(He holds her hand tightly, staring at her.)

HOWARD: I would like very much to take a walk. You're absolutely right about the steak. We need to walk it off.

PAT: Let go, Howard, or I'll kick you.

BILL: Let her go, Howard.

HOWARD: But she's right. We should all walk after steak dinners. The stomach works best when the whole body's in motion. All the acid gets sloshed around.

(PAT struggles violently to get away, HOWARD grabs her other arm and holds her tightly, they face each other.)

PAT: Let me go! Let go of my arm, Howard! I'll kick you. I really will.

FRANK: Come on. Let her go.

HOWARD: But she's right, Frank.

FRANK: Her husband may come back in his jet plane and see what you're doing. Then you'll be in trouble.

PAT: Very funny.

BILL: He might.

JILL: Then he'll land and do you in with a ray gun or a laser beam.

HOWARD: But we'll be way up the beach. Jets can't land on a little strip of beach. We'll be under some bushes even. He won't even see us. Will he, Pat?

(He shakes her.)

Will he, Pat?

PAT: He might.

JILL: See?

HOWARD: Pat's lying, though. Jets fly at an altitude of approximately five thousand feet and move at a minimum of approximately five hundred miles an hour with an air velocity of approximately—and a wind velocity and the pilot can't even hear or see or anything. He's just hung in space and he can't hear or see. Can he, Pat?

(He shakes PAT *more violently.* PAT *gives no resistance.)*

Can he or can't he? No he can't! Oh yes he can! He can see fireworks because fireworks explode at an altitude of approximately five hundred feet and give off powerful light rays and make swell patterns in the sky right under his keen old plane! Right? Beautiful Just think how beautiful, Pat. We'll be down here on the grass and he'll be way, way, way up in the air. And somewhere in between the two of us there'll be a beautiful display of flashing fireworks. I can hardly wait for nighttime

(He lets go of PAT. *She moves downstage slowly, then turns and walks slowly upstage; she stands upstage staring at the scrim.* HOWARD *and the others watch her.)*

HOWARD: Of course you have to let yourself go into aeronautics gradually, Pat. You can't expect to grasp the sensation immediately. Especially if you've never been up before. I mean in anything bigger than a Piper Cub or a Beachcraft Bonanza. Single- or double-propeller jobs of that variety usually don't get you beyond say a sore ear or two sore ears from the buzzing they make. The booming of a jet is something quite different.

JILL: She knows that.

HOWARD: Of course the sound isn't all of the problem. Not at all. It's something about being in the cockpit surrounded by glass and knowing that glass is solid, yet it's something you can see through at the same time. That's the feeling. You know what I mean, Pat? Looking through this glass enclosure at miles and miles of geometric cow pastures and lakes and rivers. Looking through and seeing miles and miles of sky that changes color from gray to blue, then back to gray again as you move through it. There's something to look at all around you. Everywhere you turn in the cockpit you have something to see. You have so much to see that you want to be able to stop the plane and just stay in the same position for about half an hour looking all around you. Just turning your seat from one position to the other until you take it all in. Even then you get the feeling that you'd like to spend more than just half an hour. Maybe a whole hour or two hours or maybe a whole day in that very same position. Just gazing from one side to the other.

(He crosses up to PAT slowly and stands behind her.)

Then up, then down. Then all the way around until you realize you don't have enough eyes for that. That maybe if you had a few more eyes you could do that but not with just two. Then you get kind of dizzy and sick to the tum tum and your heads starts to spin so you clutch the seat with both hands and close your eyes. But even inside your closed eyes you can see the same thing as before. Miles and miles of cow pasture and city and town. Like a movie. Lake after lake with river after river running away from the lake and going to the ocean. House after house turning into city after city and town after town. So you quick open your eyes and try to fix them on the control panel. You concentrate on the controls and the dials and the numbers. You run your hands over the buttons and the circles and the squares. You can't look up now or around or from side to side or down. You're straight in front straining not to see with peripheral vision. Out of the sides of your eyes like a bird does but straight ahead. But the sky creeps in out of the corner of each eye and you can't help but see. You can't help but want to look. You can't resist watching it for a second or two or a minute. For just a little bitty while.

(JILL *stands.*)

JILL: All right! Leave her alone!
HOWARD: Sorry.

(*He crosses back down left and sits;* JILL *crosses up to* PAT *and stands beside her, patting her on the back.*)

JILL: We're all going to see the fireworks together. So there's no point in getting everyone all excited. Pat's going to see them with us and nobody's going to walk anywhere.
FRANK: Oh, thanks a lot.

(*He stands;* BILL *and* HOWARD *remain sitting.*)

Thanks for the consideration, Jill. My stomach happens to be killing me. I could use a walk. And besides I'd like to see the beach.
BILL: We can walk later. After the fireworks.
FRANK: I can't wait and besides I have to pee too. I really do.
JILL: Well go ahead.
HOWARD: Pee here.
FRANK: No!
HOWARD: Pee in your pants.
FRANK: Look, Howard—
BILL: You can pee in front of us, Frank. It's all right. Pee your heart out.
HOWARD: We don't mind. Really. We're all friends.
JILL: We'll close our eyes, Frank.
FRANK: I would like very much to take a nice little walk and pee by myself, alone. Just for the enjoyment of peeing alone.
BILL: Well go ahead.
FRANK: Thank you. (FRANK *goes off right.*)
HOWARD: How's the girl?

JILL: She's all right. All she needs is some rest.

BILL: Listen, Pat, why don't you and Jill go up the beach with Frank and pee together under the bushes?

HOWARD: And we'll stay and wait for it to get dark.

(At this point the lights start to fade, almost imperceptibly, to the end of the play.)

BILL: Pat?

HOWARD: We'll wait here, Pat, and save you a place. We'll save all of you a place to sit.

BILL: How does that sound, Patricia?

HOWARD: It would give you time to rest and settle your stomach and empty your bladder and loosen your legs. What do you think?

BILL: You could take as much time as you wanted.

HOWARD: You could even miss the display altogether if you want to do that. I mean it's not mandatory that you watch it. It's sort of a hoax, if you really want to know the truth. I mean if it's anything at all like the one they had last year.

BILL: Last year's was a joke.

HOWARD: That's right, Pat. Most of them didn't even work. The city spent thirty thousand dollars for twenty-five hundred fireworks last year and fifteen hundred of them exploded before they even got off the launching pad. They just made a little pop, and a stream of smoke came out, and that was it. A joke.

JILL: Some of them were beautiful.

BILL: Some of them *were* beautiful. The big gold and silver ones with sparklers on the ends. Then they had rocket ones that went way up and disappeared and then exploded way out over the ocean. They'd change into different colors. First orange, then blue, then bright yellow. Then this little parachute came floating down very softly with a tiny silver light on it. We just watched it slowly falling through the air hanging from the parachute. It went way out and finally sank into the water and the light went out. Then they'd shoot another one.

PAT: *(Still facing upstage)* I'm not going to miss the display. I've seen every one of them for the past ten years and I'm not going to miss this one.

JILL: Of course not, Pat.

(She strokes her hair.)

PAT: They get better and better as the years go by. It's true that some of them didn't work last year and that the city got gypped by the firecracker company. But that doesn't mean it will happen again this year. Besides, as Bill said, some of them were beautiful. It's worth it just to see one beautiful one out of all the duds. If none of them work except just one, it will be worth it to see just that one beautiful flashing thing across the whole sky. I'll wait all night on my back, even if they have to go through the whole stack without one of them working. Even if it's the very, very last one in the whole pile and everybody who came to see them left and went home. Even if I'm the only one left in the whole park and even if all the men who launch the firecrackers go home in despair and anguish and humiliation. I'll go down there myself and hook up the thing by myself and fire the thing without any help and run back up here and lie on my back and wait and listen and watch the goddamn thing explode all over the sky and watch it change colors and make all its sounds and do all the things that a firecracker's supposed to do. Then I'll watch it fizzle out and I'll get up slowly and brush the grass off my legs and walk back home and all the people will say what a lucky girl. What a lucky, lucky girl.

JILL: We'll see them, Patty. Don't worry.

BILL: Jill, why don't you take Pat up the beach for a little walk? We'll wait for you. It would do you both good.

JILL: Do you want to walk, Patty?

PAT: Will we be back in time?

JILL: Sure. We'll just take a short walk and come right back.

(PAT *turns downstage.*)

PAT: All right. But just a short one.

BILL: That's a girl.

(JILL *leads* PAT *by the arm; they go off right.*)

HOWARD: Take your time and we'll save your places.

(BILL *and* HOWARD *look at each other for a second, then they both get up and cross to the barbecue.* HOWARD *picks up the tablecloth and drapes it over the barbecue,* BILL *holds one side of the tablecloth while* HOWARD *holds the other, they look up at the sky, then they lift the tablecloth off the barbecue and allow some smoke to rise; they replace the tablecloth over the barbecue and follow the same procedure, glancing up at the sky; they do this three or four times, then* FRANK *enters from left in bare feet and carrying his shoes.)*

FRANK: What a beach!

*(*HOWARD *and* BILL *turn suddenly to* FRANK *and drop the tablecloth on the ground.)*

It's fantastic! The beach is fantastic, you guys.

(They just stare at FRANK.*)*

You ought to go down there. No beer cans, no seaweed, no nothing. Just beach and water and a few rocks. It's out of the question. We ought to go down there and sit. That'd be the place to watch fireworks from. Right on the sand. We could move our stuff down there. What about it?

HOWARD: There's flak and little particles that fly off in those explosions. It gets in your eyes.

FRANK: Well it would get in our eyes up here just as easy.

HOWARD: Not likely. We're above sea level here.

FRANK: So what?

HOWARD: So the air is denser above sea level and the flak and shrapnel and—well, it's just safer up here. Besides there's waves to contend with at sea level. And there's sand and we're away from the smell up here. There's a nice little breeze up here.

FRANK: I'd like to be down there myself.

(He crosses upstage and stares over the hedge as though looking down at a beach.)

BILL: Why don't you go.

FRANK: I'd like to. It'd be nice lying there with the waves right next to me and explosions in the air.

HOWARD: Go ahead, Frank. We'll stay here.

FRANK: Well we could all go. Like an expedition or an exploration. We could all find out what there is to know about the beach before it gets dark.

BILL: There's nothing to know. The beach is composed of sand which is a product of the decomposition of rock through the process of erosion. Sand is the residue of this decomposition which, through the action and movement of tides controlled by the location of the moon in relation to the position of the other planets in the hemisphere, finds itself accumulating in areas which are known to us as beaches.

FRANK: But it stretches so far out. It'd be nice to walk to the end of it and then walk back.

HOWARD: Go, then! Nobody's stopping you! Have fun! Go roll around in it.

(FRANK *turns downstage.*)

FRANK: Boy! You guys are really something. It interests me to know that I've been living in this community for ten years and never knew about this beach. I mean I never knew it was so clean. I expected trash all over and a huge stench from dead fish. But instead I find a long old beach that seems to go out to some kind of a peninsula or something. That's nice to see. I'd like to try hiking out there some day. That's an interesting thing to know. That you could spend a day hiking with a nice group of friendly neighborly neighbors and pack a lunch and make a weekend of it even. Or maybe two weekends' worth, depending on the weather and the friendliness of the neighbors and the cost of the baby-sitters involved.

BILL: That sounds very nice, Frank.

FRANK: I think so.

BILL: We'll have to try that.

FRANK: Where are the girls?

HOWARD: They left. They said they were going to look for you.

BILL: They wanted to tell you something.

FRANK: What?

BILL: They wouldn't say. Something important.

FRANK: They're just kidding.

(*He crosses down left.*)

HOWARD: No. It was something big, though, because they wouldn't tell us even. We asked them what it was and they said they could only tell you.

FRANK: Something big?

HOWARD: Some kind of secret.

FRANK: Did they giggle about it?

BILL: Yeah but they wouldn't tell. We even threatened them. We told them we'd take them home before the fireworks started if they didn't tell.

(FRANK *crosses down right.*)

FRANK: And they still didn't tell?

BILL: Nope. Something exciting, they said.

FRANK: But they giggled a lot?

BILL: Yep.

FRANK: I bet I know what it is.

HOWARD: You do?

FRANK: If it's what I think it is I'll kill both of them. Do you want to know what I think it is?

HOWARD: No. They said it was top secret. We don't want to know until you find out first.

FRANK: Well I already know.

HOWARD: Not for sure. Go find out for sure, then come back and tell us.

FRANK: Okay, but it's really a joke if it's what I think it is. And if it is what I think it is they're going to be in real trouble.

HOWARD: Go find out.

FRANK: Which way did they go?

(HOWARD *and* BILL *both point off right.*)

FRANK: Thanks a lot. I'll see you later. (*He goes off right.*)

BILL: Good luck.

(BILL *and* HOWARD *pick up the tablecloth and drape it over the barbecue again; they look up at the sky, then lift the tablecloth. They do this a couple of times, then* JILL *and* PAT *enter from left, laughing hysterically and slapping each other on the back; they are in bare feet and carry their shoes.* BILL *and* HOWARD *drop the tablecloth and turn to the girls.*)

JILL: Too much! What a nut!

(They both double over with laughter as BILL *and* HOWARD *watch them.* PAT *falls on the ground and rolls around, laughing and holding her sides;* JILL *stands over her.)*

PAT: Oh my side!

JILL: Do you know—do you know what this idiot did? Do you know what she did! She—we're walking up the beach, see—we're walking along like this.

(She walks very slowly with her head down.)

Very slowly and dejected and sad. So suddenly she stops. We both stop and she says, Guess what? And I said what? She says I really do— I really do have to pee after all.

(They both break up.)

So I said all right. I'm very serious with her, see. I say all right, Patsy dear, if you have to you have to. So then she said I have to pee so bad I can't even wait. I have to go right now. Right this very minute. So we're in the middle of the beach with nothing around but sand. No bushes or nothing. So she whips down her pants and crouches right there in the middle of the beach very seriously. And I'm standing there looking around. Sort of standing guard. And do you know what happens?

(They crack up.)

All of a sudden I have to pee too. I mean really bad like she has to. So I whip my pants down and crouch down right beside her. There we are sitting side by side on the beach together.

(She crouches down in the position.) Like a couple of desert nomads or something. So. You know how it is when you have to pee so bad that you can't pee at all?

(BILL and HOWARD nod their heads.)

Well that's what happened. Neither one of us could get anything out and we were straining and groaning and along comes our friend in the jet plane. Except this time he's very low. Right above our heads. Zoom! So there we were. We couldn't stand up because then he'd really see us. And we couldn't run because there was nowhere to run to. So we just sat there and pretended we were playing with shells or something. But he kept it up. He kept flying back and forth right above our heads. So do you know what this nut does?

(HOWARD and BILL shake their heads.)

She starts waving to him and throwing kisses. Then he really went nuts. He started doing flips and slides with that jet like you've never seen before.

(She stands with her arms outstretched like a plane.)

He went way up and then dropped like a seagull or something. We thought he was going to crash even. Then I started waving and the guy went insane. He flew that thing upside down and backwards and every way you could imagine. And we were cracking up all over the place. We started rolling in the sand and showing him our legs. Then we did some of those nasty dances like they do in the bars. Then we both went nuts or something and we took off our pants and ran right into the water yelling and screaming and waving at his plane.

PAT: *(Lying on her back and staring at the sky)* Then he did a beautiful thing. He started to climb. And he went way, way up about twenty thousand feet or forty thousand feet. And he wrote this big sentence across the sky with his vapor trail. He wrote "E equals MC squared" in huge letters. It was really nice.

BILL: Are you sure he saw you?

JILL: Well he wasn't doing all those tricks for nothing.

BILL: But are you sure it was the same guy?

JILL: Of course.

HOWARD: It couldn't have been anyone else?

JILL: Not a chance.

HOWARD: Because Frank told us that guy crashed.

(PAT stands suddenly.)

PAT: What?

HOWARD: He said that he saw that very same jet go down in the middle of
the ocean.

PAT: When?

HOWARD: Just before you came back.

JILL: So where did Frank go?

BILL: To get some help. They're trying to fish him out right now.

PAT: You mean he crashed into the water?

BILL: That's what he told us. It could be a different guy, though.

JILL: I doubt it.

HOWARD: The plane exploded just before it hit the water.

PAT: No!

BILL: That's what Frank said.

JILL: Well let's try to find him, Pat.

BILL: He went that way. (*He points off right.*)

PAT: Aren't you guys coming?

HOWARD: We'll wait here.

JILL: Come on, Pat.

(*She pulls* PAT *by the arm, they go off right.* HOWARD *and* BILL *pause to look at
the sky, then grab the tablecloth quickly; they are about to drape it over the barbecue when* FRANK *enters slowly from left. He seems to wander around the stage
undeliberately and staring blankly in front of him.* HOWARD *and* BILL *drop the
tablecloth and watch* FRANK.)

HOWARD: Frank?

(FRANK *continues to walk as he speaks; he moves all over the stage in a daze as*
HOWARD *and* BILL *watch.*)

FRANK: Boy, oh boy, oh boy, oh boy. You guys. You guys have missed the
fireworks altogether. You should have seen—this is something to behold, this is. This is the nineteenth wonder of the Western, international world brought to you by Nabisco Cracker Corporation for the
preservation of historians to come and for historians to go by. This is.
If only the weather and the atmospheric conditions had been better
than they were it would have beaten the Hindenburg by far more
than it did.

(The lights by this time have become very dim, so that the scrim takes on a translucent quality.)

By that I mean to say a recognized world tragedy of the greatest proportion and exhilaration to make the backs of the very bravest shudder with cold sensations and the hands moisten with the thickest sweat ever before known, ever. And the eyes to blink in disbelief and the temples swell with pounds and the nose run with thick sticky pus. Oh you guys should have come, you guys should have. What a light!

(There is a tremendous boom offstage, followed in a few seconds by flashes of light onstage changing from orange to blue to yellow and then returning to the dim lighting of before; the flashes should come from directly above them. This all occurs while FRANK continues, oblivious to everything but what he's saying; HOWARD and BILL remain in their positions.)

And to happen while walking head down looking at your toes and counting your steps. To happen under private conditions on sand. To be thinking about killing your baby boy or your baby girl or your wife or your wife's sister or your pet dog. And to come to a standstill.

(Another boom followed by the same lighting and returning to the dim; the sound of a vast crowd of people starts faintly and builds in volume to the end of the play.)

To stop still in your tracks, thinking about the night to come and how long it takes to build a beach given the right amount of sand and the right amount of time and the right amount of water to push everything up. Bigger bodies of water with more rain and less sun. More water than land ever. In volume, in density, in the stratospheric conditions. And to hear a sound so shrieking that it ain't even a sound at all but goes beyond that into the inside of the center of each ear and rattles you up so you don't know exactly or for sure if you'll ever hear again or if it actually exactly matters. And it pulls your head straight up off your shoulders in a straight line with the parallel lines of each leg and so each tendon leading to your jawbone strains to its utmost.

(Another boom followed by the lighting; the crowd increases.)

So your eyes bob back and roll around in their sockets and you see the silver-sleek jet, streamlined for speed, turn itself upside down and lie on its back and swoop up, then give itself in so it looks like it's floating. Then another boom and it falls head down just gliding under its own weight. Passing cloud after cloud and picking up its own speed under its own momentum, out of control. Under its own force, falling straight down and passing through flocks of geese on their way back from where they came from. Going beyond itself with the pilot screaming and the clouds breaking up.

(Another boom and light.)

And the windows cracking and the wings tearing off. Going through seagulls now, it's so close. Heading straight for the top of the flat blue water. Almost touching in slow motion and blowing itself up six inches above sea level to the dismay of ducks bobbing along. And lighting up the air with a gold tint and a yellow tint and smacking the water so that waves go up to five hundred feet in silver white and blue. Exploding the water for a hundred miles in diameter around itself. Sending a wake to Japan. An eruption of froth and smoke and flame blowing itself up over and over again. Going on and on till the community comes out to see for itself.

(Another boom and light.)

Till the houses open because of the light, they can't sleep. And the booming goes on. And the porches are filled with kids in pajamas on top of their fathers shielding their eyes. And their mothers hold their fathers with their mouths open and the light pouring in and their cats running for cover.

(The booming sounds come closer together now and the lighting keeps up a perpetual change from color to color in bright flashes; the crowd noise gets very loud. FRANK moves faster around the stage, almost shouting the lines; HOWARD and BILL hold hands and stand very close together.)

And the sound keeps up and the doors open farther and farther back into the city. And the whole sky is lit. The sirens come and the screaming starts. The kids climb down and run to the beach with their mothers chasing and their fathers chasing them. Oh what a sight to see with your very own eyes. How lucky to be the first one there! And the tide breaks open and the waves go up!

BILL: Stop it, Frank!

FRANK: The water goes up to fifteen hundred feet and smashes the trees, and the firemen come. The beach sinks below the surface. The seagulls drown in flocks of ten thousand. There's a line of people two hundred deep. Standing in line to watch the display. And the pilot bobbing in the very center of a ring of fire that's closing in. His white helmet bobbing up and bobbing down. His hand reaching for his other hand and the fire moves in and covers him up and the line of two hundred bow their heads and moan together with the light in their faces. Oh you guys should have come! You guys should have been there! You guys—

(He staggers off left. HOWARD and BILL stand very still, facing out to the audience and holding hands. JILL rushes on from right.)

JILL: Come on, you guys! The plane went down. Come and look! Come on!

HOWARD: Get away from here!

JILL: Everybody's down there! It's fantastic. The plane crashed, Bill! It really did!

BILL: Get away from the picnic area!

JILL: All right. But you guys are missing out.

(She runs off right, HOWARD and BILL stand very still, the crowd noise becomes deafening, the lights dim slowly out, the sound stops.)

4-H Club

4-H Club was first presented by the Playwrights Unit at the Cherry Lane Theatre in September 1965, with the following cast: Paul B. Price, John Fink and Kevin O'Connor. It was directed by Charles Gyns.

SCENE

An empty stage except for a small kitchen extreme upstage left. Three flats compose the walls of the kitchen with a swinging door in the upstage wall. On the floor downstage left of the kitchen is a hot plate with a coffee pot on it. The floor of the kitchen is littered with paper, cans and various trash. There is a garbage can in the upstage right corner. The walls are very dirty. The lighting should be equal for the whole stage with no attempt to focus light on the kitchen. The lights come up slowly. JOHN is downstage facing the audience kneeling beside the hot plate. He is stirring something in the pot with a spoon. BOB stands in the middle of the kitchen jumping up and down and laughing wildly. JOE stands upstage beside the door with a broom. He is hitting the door with the broom and laughing with BOB. They are all dressed in torn, grimy clothes. BOB and JOE laugh hysterically and fall to their knees. They fall on the floor and roll around stomping their feet. They stop laughing. A pause. JOHN hits the spoon on the pot several times.

JOHN: You can't call it coffee anymore. Brown powder for coffee, white powder for cream, saccharin for sugar. Water's the only thing that stays the same. Put it all together and it comes out coffee.

BOB: Put it all together.

JOHN: I am.

JOE: Three.

JOHN: Three colored waters.

(He pours water out of the pot into three coffee cups; he hands a cup to BOB, and a cup to JOE, then sits on the floor with the last cup. BOB and JOE sit; a pause as they all sit and drink from the cups. BOB slurps, a pause, JOE slurps loudly, JOHN slurps even louder. They all stand suddenly and smash the cups on the floor. BOB and JOHN start kicking the pieces back and forth across the kitchen.)

JOE: Hey! Hey! Cut it out! Stop!

(He grabs the broom and tries to sweep up the pieces as JOHN *and* BOB *continue kicking them.)*

Cut it out! Stop it! We got to keep this place neat! Cut it out! Stop!

*(*BOB *and* JOHN *stop and watch* JOE *as he sweeps the pieces into a pile.)*

JOHN: That's very nice, Joe.
JOE: Thanks.
JOHN: It's neat the way you're sweeping that all up nice and neat.
JOE: Thanks.
JOHN: Could I do it, Joe?
JOE: Nope.
JOHN: Come on.
JOE: Nope.

(A pause as JOE *continues sweeping. He gets the pieces into a pile, then looks at* JOHN *and* BOB. BOB *and* JOHN *kick the pieces all over the floor, then run out the door laughing.* JOE *looks after them, then starts sweeping again.)*

I don't care myself. I mean it doesn't matter to me about the neatness part of it. I was thinking in terms of someday having bare feet and walking in here and getting cut.

(He continues sweeping.)

That's all. I'm leaving the country anyway, so it doesn't matter.

(He stops and yells at the door.)

It don't make no difference! Hear me?

(He starts sweeping again.)

Not just glass, either. There's bottle caps and tin can edges and razor blades too. All the stuff that cuts is bad for bare feet. That's all I was thinking of as far as sweeping goes. As far as clean goes, if I was thinking of clean we could get a fire hose in here and blast the walls and the floors and the stove. Just a great huge blast of hot water. That would do it.

(*He goes to the garbage can and drags it over to the pile of glass. He puts the pile into the can as he continues talking.*)

You'd need permission, I guess. How much would it cost to hire a fireman for one day to blast this place? I don't think he'd do it. It would knock down the walls, anyway. It would probably wash the stove out into the audience. It'd take a week to dry anyway. There'd be puddles of water all over the floor.

(*He drags the garbage can back into the corner, then crosses down to the hot plate.*)

No good. Leave it as it is for the time being. I'm going anyway.

(*He looks into the coffee pot.*)

Coffee.

(JOHN *enters through the door eating an apple. He stands upstage of the kitchen watching* JOE *and eating the apple with loud crunches.*)

Water and powder. That's kind of bad when you think about it. If a fire starts, all they do is knock down the walls with blasts of water. They have to build all over again anyway.

JOHN: (*Still upstage*) It puts the fire out, though.

JOE: (*Without turning around*) Yeah, but the walls are all broken down. Hunks of wet wood and pieces of cement all broken to pieces. Do they put floods out with fire? Nope. It works the other way around.

JOHN: It's chemical. Oxygen. Water cuts off oxygen. Simple.

JOE: Then all the firemen stand around in puddles of water and grin. The fire's been stopped and all the people stand there in puddles of water looking at this mound of rubbish with smoke rising off it. Then the firemen grin some more and coil up the hoses and put them back on the trucks and ride off into the night grinning and waving. And all the people stand there looking at this mound of rubbish.

(He turns around suddenly and looks at JOHN.*)*

JOHN: What?

JOE: An apple!

JOHN: Yeah.

JOE: Where'd you get it?

JOHN: It's mine.

JOE: Where'd you get it?

JOHN: None of your business.

*(*JOE *approaches* JOHN *slowly;* JOHN *backs up.)*

JOE: Come on, John. That's a brand-new red apple.

JOHN: So what?

JOE: So it crunches.

JOHN: Crunches?

JOE: Crunches. It sounds good.

*(*JOE *approaches* JOHN *slowly.* JOHN *backs up in a circle around the kitchen.)*

JOHN: It is good. It's a "Washington Delicious."

JOE: It looks delicious, John.

JOHN: Get back.

JOE: I've eaten green apples before, but never a bright red one.

JOHN: Green ones are for cooking.

JOE: Red and crunchy.

JOHN: Yeah. Get back!

JOE: A "Washington Delicious."

JOHN: Look, stay away from my apple, Joe.

JOE: Apple juice! We could make a lot of apple juice.

JOHN: I'm eating it!

(He takes big bites out of the apple as JOE *continues backing him up.)*

JOE: Take it easy! You're eating it all up.

JOHN: It's mine, stupid! Of course I'm eating it.

JOE: What about the juice?

JOHN: That was your idea. Get back.

JOE: We could salt it.

JOHN: No salt!

JOE: We could cut it into little slices and put salt on it. Come on, John. Diced apple is what they call it.

(They go faster in a circle, JOHN backing up and eating the apple as JOE follows.)

We'd leave the skin on it for more protein. We could eat the seeds and boil the core. Apple-core soup we could have. We'd put salt in that too. Salt and pepper. Maybe some sugar and salt and pepper. It'd last for days, John. A whole week of diced-apple soup and sugar. Stewing. That's a whole stewing apple you have in your hand. A bright red "Washington Delicious" stewing apple for us to eat!

(JOHN runs out the door laughing. JOE yells at the door, standing in the middle of the kitchen.)

Fuck your apple, John! Apples grow on trees! Green and red ones, John! As many as you can carry in your pockets and stuffed inside your shirt! One apple is nothing compared to what I've seen! And I've seen plenty, John! Don't forget that! I'll bring some when I get back! I'll bring all the apples I can get my hands on! A ton! There's apples all over, you know. Not just in Washington!

(He starts talking to himself. He walks aimlessly around the kitchen kicking pieces of trash on the floor.)

"Washington Delicious" is a brand name. It doesn't fool anybody. They grow all over the place. It's a stupid thing to name apples anyway. "Florida Oranges." There's another one. "Maine Cherries!" "Wisconsin Cheese!" "Minnesota Watercress!" "Arizona Spinach!"

(He starts kicking the trash violently and yelling.)

"New Jersey Cottage Cheese!" "Nebraska Mayonnaise!" "Oklahoma Malted Milk!" "California Scrambled Eggs!" "Viet Nam Corn on the Cob!" "Mexico Peanut Butter!" "Alaska Turnips!"

(He stops, crosses downstage and looks into the coffee pot. A pause.)

Hey, John! Hey, John and Bob! Do you want some coffee? That water's boiling. It's all hot and ready. Hot boiling coffee for you people if you want it!

(He turns to the door.)

Hey! The coffee's ready! You guys bring the apples in here and I'll give you some coffee. There's enough for three! I know you guys have apples! I know you have all the apples you need and I have the coffee!

(BOB enters through the door eating an apple. He stands upstage facing JOE.)

Hi, Bob.

BOB: Hi.

(He stares at JOE and takes large bites out of the apple.)

JOE: Do you want some coffee?
BOB: We broke the cups.
JOE: Yeah, I know.
BOB: We couldn't drink coffee out of the pot.
JOE: I guess not.
BOB: How would we drink it?
JOE: Well, I don't know.
BOB: We don't have any more cups around.
JOE: I guess not.
BOB: The water's ready, huh?
JOE: Yeah, it's all ready.
BOB: Gee, I could really go for some coffee.
JOE: Me too.

(They start walking in a circle slowly as they talk to each other, JOE following BOB.)

BOB: It's too bad we broke all the cups.
JOE: Yeah.
BOB: We could be having coffee right now if it wasn't for that.
JOE: With cream and sugar.
BOB: However you take it.

JOE: We could be sitting around on the floor talking and drinking.

BOB: Yeah. It would have been nice.

JOE: It's too bad.

BOB: Maybe we'll do it sometime.

JOE: Sure.

BOB: We'll get some more cups and sit around drinking.

(They both start laughing as they circle the kitchen.)

JOE: We'll even clean the floor so we can sit down.

BOB: We'll get all this junk out of here.

JOE: We'll clear it all away. We'll put it in the can and throw it in the street.

BOB: Throw it out the window.

JOE: We'll hit somebody in the head.

BOB: It'll smash somebody in the head.

JOE: That's a heavy can.

BOB: It'd really smash, wouldn't it?

(They laugh harder.)

JOE: It'd break to pieces.

BOB: We'd kill a lot of people with that can.

JOE: Little kids and old ladies. Some old lady buying potatoes for her invalid husband.

BOB: Right!

JOE: She's down there limping along with a bag full of potatoes, and this garbage can smashes her in the head.

BOB: Potatoes all over the street!

JOE: She wouldn't even know what hit her!

BOB: Then after that there's a whole crowd of people. They come running from all over. The whole street is running toward this old lady with her head smashed in.

JOE: They're yelling and screaming and trying to get a look.

BOB: There's more and more people!

JOE: All over!

BOB: Then do you know what we do?

JOE: What?

BOB: We're looking out the window, see.

JOE: Yeah?

BOB: And we start throwing apples!

JOE: Right! Right!

(BOB *tosses the apple to* JOE. *They throw it back and forth, laughing harder and still going in a circle.*)

BOB: We could hide behind the window so they wouldn't know where they were coming from.

JOE: Apples out of the sky!

BOB: Right! All these apples sailing through the air and crashing their skulls!

JOE: More and more people come. They think it's a riot or something.

BOB: They call the cops!

JOE: There's sirens all over!

BOB: Everybody's head is bloody from the apples!

JOE: They're lying in the street moaning and groaning.

BOB: The cops can't figure it out!

JOE: The cops get hit. There's dead cops lying on the sidewalk with bloody heads.

BOB: Apples!

JOE: They call the National Guard!

BOB: They bring tanks! A whole string of armored cars and tanks charging up the street.

JOE: Apples from the sky!

BOB: They shoot at the sky!

JOE: *Get back in your houses, ladies and gentlemen! There's apples falling out here!*

BOB: *This is an emergency, people!*

JOE: *We're going to shoot the sky and we don't want anyone to get hurt!*

BOB: *Stay inside your houses! We shall open fire in exactly ten seconds!*

(BOB *catches the apple and holds it. They both start making gun sounds and firing at the sky. They stop going in a circle.*)

JOE: *Pow! Blam!*

BOB: We're getting them, ladies and gentlemen! Just stay inside! There's a lot of apples left!

JOE: Blam! Blam! Blam! I think we're winning!

BOB: Pow! Blam! I think we've done it! (*To the audience*) Ladies and gentlemen, this is the end of the apples.

(JOHN *enters through the door eating an apple.* BOB *and* JOE *sit on the floor.* JOHN *stares at them.*)

JOHN: Is there any coffee?
BOB: Nope.
JOE: There's coffee but no cups.
JOHN: That's too bad.

(*He goes out the door.*)

BOB: (*Still sitting*) We should clean up, you know.
JOE: Yeah.
BOB: Just a little sweeping and some elbow grease.
JOE: I don't mind sweeping.
BOB: Me either.
JOE: I used to sweep driveways a lot.
BOB: Really?
JOE: Yeah. Leaves. The driveways would get covered with leaves and dirt so I'd sweep them for a quarter.
BOB: A quarter each?
JOE: Yeah. They were long driveways though, so it wasn't as easy as it sounds.
BOB: I guess not.
JOE: Six in the morning I'd start.
BOB: How come so early?
JOE: I don't know. I just wanted to get up. I'd do the whole block before eight o'clock.
BOB: That's pretty fast.
JOE: Sometimes I'd use a hose. Just spray the leaves down the driveway and into the street.
BOB: That was probably faster.
JOE: Yeah. They paid by the job, not by the hour, so it didn't matter.

(JOHN *enters through the door again and stands watching* JOE *and* BOB *as they continue to talk.* JOHN *and* BOB *eat their apples slowly.*)

BOB: I just cut lawns.

JOE: I did some of that too. Trouble was there was this older guy who sort of had a monopoly on all the lawns.

BOB: Oh yeah?

JOE: Yeah. He was old enough to drive, see, and he had a car, a station wagon. He had all kinds of power tools that he used. Power mowers and edgers and hedge clippers. Things like that. And he was a kissy. I mean he'd smile at all the old ladies that owned all the lawns and he'd bring their milk in for them in the mornings and their newspapers. He was like a trained dog, sort of. He even went on errands because some of them couldn't walk. He'd buy them orange juice and cod liver oil and calcium tablets, all that junk. Then he moved in on them. He started vacuuming their rugs and polishing their silver and washing their dishes. They really loved this guy. He was like their son or something.

JOHN: Sounds like a fairy.

JOE: After a while he bought a new car—a truck, rather. A bright red pickup truck, and he painted white letters on the side of it that said "Mike's Gardening Service." He wasn't even out of high school and he owned a whole business. He cut every old lady's lawn in the whole town. He even had a telephone number in case of emergency.

BOB: Like a doctor.

JOE: Right. They'd call him in the middle of the night sometimes.

BOB: How come?

JOE: I don't know. But he was making more and more money. Then more old ladies started moving into the town. One after the other. They heard about this guy, see, and they came from all over. They all bought a little white house with a green lawn and a driveway. He was so busy he had to hire some help. He had a whole crew of special gardeners after a while. I was his special driveway sweeper. He had one man for each job and he just came around to check on us. He started wearing a suit and he'd drive up in his truck just to see how we were doing.

(JOHN *crosses downstage and looks into the coffee pot as* JOE *continues.*)

He quit school after a while because the business got so big. And the town was growing. A whole town of old ladies with green lawns and white houses. He'd visit them and have tea and cake and talk about their lawns and their driveways. The mayor even gave him a prize for improving the community. Then he started giving speeches at luncheons and benefits. They paid him lots of money to talk in front of all these groups. He'd talk about horticulture and fertilizer and ground-improvement plans. Then he started giving talks on zoning and housing facilities. He drew up a whole plan for a children's recreation area. All these old ladies were going to let him build a children's recreation area and pay him to boot. He got bigger and bigger and richer and richer until one day he left the town. He just drove off in a Rolls-Royce or something and all those old ladies died. One at a time.

BOB: What do you mean?

JOE: They just died. Nobody new came to the town after that. The houses got all dirty and the lawns grew out into the driveways and the leaves covered all the sidewalks.

BOB: They died?

JOE: That's what they said.

(JOHN *kneels facing the audience and stares at the audience as* JOE *continues.*)

BOB: Who?

JOE: All the guys. We'd go into the town sometimes on weekends. We had to get a bunch of guys together because we were all scared. We hiked into the town and then waited till it got dark. Those were the rules. It had to be dark. Then one of us would go at a time. Each one of us walked from one end of the town to the other. The thing was, we had to keep our eyes closed. We couldn't look. We could just feel the sidewalk with our feet. That's all we had to go on. If we touched the grass we knew we were getting lost. This one guy, Ernie, he got lost once and wandered right into one of the houses. He told us later that he was in this tiny living room with a fireplace. There were all these books lying around on the floor and big tall lamps and yellow lampshades and pictures of swallows and dogs hung on the walls. There was a little round table with a checkerboard and a chess set. Then he told us that he went through this doorway with beaded curtains hanging in it. He walked down this hallway and he could smell all the wallpaper. Then he walked into the huge bathroom that was painted blue and there was this old lady lying on her stomach with a spoon in her hand.

(JOHN slams the coffee pot down on the hot plate. BOB and JOE stand suddenly.)

JOHN: The water's cold!

(He stands still facing the audience.)

JOE: It was just boiling.

JOHN: Now it's cold.

BOB: It was boiling before, John. We were going to have some coffee.

JOHN: Yeah. Well, cold coffee doesn't exactly turn me on. I thought you
    were leaving, Joe.

JOE: I am.

JOHN: When?

JOE: When I can.

JOHN: When can you, Joe?

JOE: I'm not sure.

JOHN: Well, before you were yelling about it, and now you're not sure.
    You were yelling, "It doesn't matter because I'm leaving the country!"

JOE: I know.

JOHN: Then you started yelling about apples or something.

BOB: We both were.

JOHN: I remember.

BOB: We were both doing that.

JOHN: I remember! I remember! Now the water's cold and there aren't
    any cups!

JOE: We broke them.

BOB: You broke one of them, John. Remember?

JOHN: I remember that! Seems like we could make some soup or some-
    thing.

JOE: Sure.

JOHN: Sure! And sweep! Clean up the kitchen, goddammit! We can't eat
    apples in a dirty kitchen!

BOB: It's all right, John.

JOHN:

(He turns upstage and paces back and forth kicking the debris on the floor.)

It's all right, John! It's all right! Rats don't eat much. They don't eat
apples. Rats eat cheese. Rats and mice and everything nice.

JOE: There's no mice, John.

JOHN: There's no mice, John! The mice ran away. They went away for food. They left the country! A whole troop of mice marched out the door and said, "Fuck it! We're going to go out! We're going to hunt some food on our own! We're going to get fat and lie around burping all day!"

BOB: We'll clean it up.

JOHN: Clean it up! Clean it up! Forget it! The apples are running out and the mice don't care anyway so just forget it!

(He goes out through the door.)

BOB: *(Yelling at the door)* John! There aren't any mice around here! John!

JOE: *(Yelling at the door)* John! The mice are all gone! There's none left!

JOHN: *(Offstage)* There's some around. I've seen them.

BOB: Where?

JOHN: Inside the walls. In the garbage can. All over!

BOB: They're all gone, John!

JOHN: You just haven't looked!

BOB: I'll look.

(He looks in the garbage can and then under the hot plate.)

JOHN: They're hard to see. They're grayish and small so they blend right into the floor. You probably can't find them.

JOE: There's none here, John!

JOHN: They're there if you look.

BOB: I don't see them, John.

JOHN: They're there!

(JOE looks in the garbage can, then searches around the floor. BOB does the same.)

BOB: They couldn't just hide, John. It's impossible.

JOE: We'd hear them wriggling around.

JOHN: *(Still off)* They're very quiet.

BOB: They're just small little animals. They wouldn't have a chance.

JOE: We'd kill them!

JOHN: They bite. They have sharp little razor teeth and they cut.

(BOB and JOE start kicking the trash and looking for the mice.)

JOE: They're all skinny and weak, John. They don't stand a chance.
BOB: One smash of the foot and it'd be all over.
JOHN: They're tough.
JOE: They're too weak, John.
BOB: They're flimsy little animals. They run.
JOHN: They don't scare easy.
BOB: They're all gone, John.
JOE: You just stomp them on the head, John.

(They kick the trash and look on the floor.)

BOB: You break their necks.
JOE: We'd hear them if they were in here. We'd hear them moving around.
BOB: There's none left, John.
JOHN: They're there.
JOE: All you do is squash them!
BOB: *(Stomping his foot on the floor)* Smash!
JOE: *Squash!*
BOB: *Smash!*

(BOB and JOE stomp their feet loudly on the floor, yelling the lines.)

JOE: Come out, mice! *Smash!*
BOB: Crush the mice! *Crunch! Crunch!*
JOE: Little tiny mouse bones! *Smash!*
JOHN: You'll never find them! They hide!
BOB: *Crunch! Smash!*
JOE: Little gray-headed mice!
JOHN: They're in the walls!
BOB: We'll smash your heads!
JOE: Come out, mice! *Smash!*
BOB: Break your backs!
JOE: *Smash! Crunch!*
BOB: Come out! Come out!
JOE: Little gray mothers! We'll squash your heads to pieces!

(He goes to the garbage can and dumps it out on the floor. BOB *and* JOE *kick the garbage all over, yelling and screaming. They jump up and down wildly.)*

JOE: You don't stand a chance!

JOE: We're big! *Squash! Crunch!*

BOB: Come out, mice! You're dead!

JOE: We'll make some soup!

BOB: You're dead, mice!

*(*BOB *picks up the broom and hits it against the door.)*

JOE: It's all over, mice! Your time is up!

BOB: *Smash!* It's all over! Come out!

JOE: We have big feet, mice! Big strong feet with shoes!

BOB: We'll bust your heads!

JOE: Kill the mice!

BOB: *Come out! Come out!*

(The lights black out in the kitchen; the rest of the stage remains in light. JOHN *walks slowly into the bare stage area from behind the kitchen. He is eating an apple and carries several apples inside his shirt. He crosses downstage right and stands looking at the kitchen while he eats the apple.* BOB *and* JOE *continue yelling inside the kitchen.)*

JOE: You don't have a chance!

BOB: You'll die if you show your face!

JOE: Come on, chickens! We see you!

BOB: Come out of there!

JOE: We can see your eyes! We know you're there!

BOB: Show yourself!

JOE: Smashed to death by a foot!

BOB: *Crash! Crunch! Die!*

JOE: *Kill! Smash!* Come out of there!

BOB: Give it up, mouse!

JOE: Give it up! Come on out!

BOB: You're dead!

JOE: We see you! We know you guys!

BOB: We can see you!

JOE: We know you're there! Come out!

BOB: You guys have had it!

JOE: Come on out!

(They stop banging their feet.)

BOB: All right, you guys, come on. We know you're in there!

JOE: You can come out now.

BOB: It's all over, you guys.

JOE: You can come out now.

BOB: You're not fooling anyone.

JOE: Mouse! Come out. We can see you in there!

BOB: Come out of there before we get you.

JOE: We could tear this place apart with our bare hands. You know that, don't you?

BOB: We're bigger than you—let's face it.

JOE: Mice?

BOB: We have all the strength. You're too little.

JOE: We'll wait for you. We'll wait here all night until you decide.

BOB: You'll have to come out sooner or later.

JOE: You're going to be sorry.

(BOB and JOE sit on either side of the kitchen and light cigarettes. JOHN continues to crunch loudly on the apple.)

BOB: John? We're going to wait for them.

JOHN: Good.

(He leans against the proscenium down right.)

BOB: It won't take long. If we're quiet they'll think we left.

JOHN: OK.

BOB: We could tear the place apart, but it's easier to wait.

JOHN: Sure.

BOB: So don't come in for a while.

JOHN: I won't.

BOB: Good.

JOE: There's probably just a couple of them anyway, John. It won't take long to do.

JOHN: Good.

JOE: They might have a family, though, so it may take longer. I mean a whole bunch of babies. We'll just step on them and sweep them up later.

BOB: There'll be a little blood, though. We may have to boil some water and scrub the place down. The walls and the floor.

JOE: Yeah. There'll be some blood on the walls, John. They spurt when you step on them. Especially the babies.

BOB: The babies haven't grown any fur yet, so they're more fragile. Their skin is very thin and they just pop open.

JOE: They look like little embryos. They can't see because their eyes haven't opened yet. They're blind, so it'll be easier to get them.

JOHN: Don't you think you should be quieter?

JOE: *(Whispering)* You're right, John. We have to be quiet, Bob.

BOB: *(Whispering)* Sit very still.

JOHN: It may take a while, you know.

JOE: *(Whispering)* It's all right. We'll wait.

JOHN: They can hear you breathing. It's very hard to trick a mouse. I've tried everything from baseball bats to machetes. I even tried throwing hatchets, but it was no good.

JOE: *(Whispering)* He's right. My uncle even used a shotgun and that didn't work.

JOHN: I used pistols and swords and everything, and they kept coming back. I sat very still until they showed their heads. Then I'd fire. I emptied a whole chamber into this one mouse and he just limped away.

BOB: *(Whispering)* Did he die?

JOHN: Nope. He just kept coming back. I kept shooting him and he kept coming back. Then he had lots of babies that followed him around. There was blood all over the house, but none of them died.

JOE: *(Whispering)* Did they bite?

JOHN: I never let them get that close. I never gave them a chance.

(A pause as JOHN *crunches loudly on the apple.)*

BOB: *(Whispering)* Sure wish we had some coffee.

JOE: Yeah.

BOB: *(Whispering)* I saw a man hit a mouse with a wrench one time and the mouse just ran away.

JOE: *(Whispering)* Maybe it was a rat. Rats are bigger.

BOB: It might have been a rat. It had a long tail. It didn't hurt him at all, though. It just made a big cracking sound. He hit him right in the head too.

JOHN: Rats are different. More ferocious. They can actually charge you if they get into a corner.

BOB: *(Whispering)* It had big huge fangs on each side of its mouth. There was all this green pussy stuff hanging off them.

JOHN: They carry tetanus and different bacteria. Some Indian tribe uses rat pus for poison arrows. It kills the victim instantly.

JOE: *(Whispering)* They carry that junk on their tails too. And their feet. All you have to do is brush up against them and you die.

JOHN: Rats usually go around in large groups. Ten at a time. They're like coyotes in that respect. Constantly ravenous. They can never get enough to eat.

(He takes another apple out of his shirt and tosses it up in the air and then catches it. He continues to do this as he talks.)

Baboons too. There's one kind of baboon called a mandrill that is known as the fiercest animal in the world. I think it's a toss-up really between the mandrill and the wolverine. Wolverines run in packs too. Twenty or thirty at once.

BOB: *(Whispering)* They close their eyes in the dark when they know they're being watched. That way you can't see them. You can't see their eyes.

JOHN: I'll send you some postcards when I get there. They have big color postcards of the mandrills. They're hard to find because photographers are afraid to go into that area. Only a few have survived.

JOE: *(Whispering)* We couldn't tell if they were here or not, Bob. They may be walking around in here right now. I mean if they close their eyes like you said.

BOB: They do.

JOE: Maybe we should make some noise to scare them off.

BOB: No.

JOHN: The country around there is really beautiful. Completely wild. There's little patches of green woods and tiny lakes where the mandrills go to drink water. There's a few small villages inhabited by fishermen and hunters.

JOE: We should make some noise, Bob.

BOB: No. Sit still.

JOHN: The plane goes right over the area and you can look out the window and see these long beaches and fishing boats all lined up.

BOB: *(Whispering)* Sit very still.

JOHN: There's a guide on the plane who tells you all you need to know about mandrills.

BOB: Very quiet. They'll never see us.

JOHN: He says they have red and blue faces and no hair on their rumps. They're about twice as big as a chimpanzee and have brownish red hair.

JOE: Can you see them?

BOB: Shhh!

JOHN: They're mainly carnivorous but will occasionally eat succulent plants that grow near the lake. Their incisors are surprisingly doglike and they are known to pick their teeth with bones.

JOE: *(Whispering)* We should make some noise.

BOB: *(Whispering)* Sit still.

JOHN: The guide shows the specific areas where the mandrills live and warns the passengers to keep clear of them. He says they are extremely temperamental and will charge a human without any provocation. He says they scream in high staccato voices and run on all fours. They charge in groups of four and tear mercilessly at the victim's throat. They cut the jugular vein and then rip the head off. They eat the brain first, then devour the body. They tear off the arms and legs and carry them back to their mates.

JOE: *(Yelling)* We have to make some noise!

BOB: *(Yelling)* No!

(JOE goes to the coffee pot and starts banging it on the hot plate. BOB wrestles with him in the dark.)

JOE: We'll scare them away, Bob!

BOB: No noise! Stop!

(They continue wrestling as JOHN keeps talking.)

JOHN: It's always good weather for some reason. I mean every time I've gone there the sun has always been out and the air has been clear.

The water is so blue you can see all the way to the bottom. Clear as a bell.

BOB: Cut it out, Joe!

(JOE *keeps banging the pot on the hot plate in a steady rhythm.*)

JOE: Noise! We have to make some noise!
BOB: Stop it! No noise!
JOE: Loud! Loud! Loud!
JOHN: Then you land and go to the hotel. The air smells so good you can taste it. They have breakfast all ready for you. It's sitting there on this glass table in front of a huge picture window. You just sit there and eat and look out over the ocean.

(JOE *continues banging the coffee pot in a steady rhythm as the lights dim down slowly.*)

BOB: No noise, Joe! Stop! No noise!
JOE: Louder! Get away! Loud! Loud!
JOHN: I'll send you some postcards. I'll buy a dozen or so and send one a week. It's a great place. I'm going to do some swimming too. Floating on my back. You just float and stare at the sky. You just float and stare at the sky. You just float and stare at the sky. You just float and stare at the sky.

(*The lights dim out as* JOE *continues banging the coffee pot in a steady beat.*)

Fourteen Hundred Thousand

Fourteen Hundred Thousand was first produced in the Firehouse Theatre, Minneapolis, under the auspices of the Office of Aid to Drama Research at the University of Minnesota. It was directed by Sydney Schubert Walter and played by Steve Friedman, Antoinette Maher, Raymond Henry Stadum, Greta Giving, and David Burns. It was subsequently produced on National Educational Television.

SCENE

A white wall upstage running the width of the stage. A door in the wall stage left. A large bookcase stands from floor to ceiling stage right up against the wall. There are no books in it and it looks as though it's in the process of being built. Sawdust, nails, pieces of wood, saws, etc., are scattered around the floor. TOM stands on a stool in front of the bookcase with a hammer in his hand and nails in his mouth. He wears no shirt and is sweating a great deal. ED stands in the doorway with the door half open, talking to TOM, whose back is to the audience. The lights come up fast to bright blue.

ED: The leaves change color now so it looks even more protected than it really is. Vacant is better. No, protected. Something like that. Come up anyway if you get a chance.

(ED shuts the door behind him and exits, the lights change very fast to white, one of the shelves falls off the bookcase onto the floor, TOM looks at the shelf for a while, then climbs down off the stool, picks up the shelf, and climbs back up; he replaces the shelf in its former position, the lights change back to blue, the door opens, and ED reenters carrying some lumber, sets the lumber on the floor downstage center.)

TOM: *(With his back to ED)* This is a rented cabin or something?
ED: No.
TOM: You bought it?
ED: No. It was given to me, donated to me. It's mine to use. One full room. I have to fix it, though. It needs patching, plumbing, electricity, et cetera.
TOM: That's nice of them.

(He hammers a nail into one of the shelves.)

ED: *(Yelling to be heard over the hammering)* Nice of who?

(TOM stops hammering.)

TOM: What? Oh—nice of whoever gave it to you.

(TOM starts hammering again.)

ED: *(Yelling)* Not so nice! I mean they didn't even give it that much thought one way or the other! They weren't really trying to be nice at all. Like I said, it was more in the spirit of a donation!

(ED sits on the lumber with his back to the audience.)

TOM: *(Looking at the bookcase; he stops hammering)* That's even nice, though. They don't have to be necessarily aware of the niceness of what they were doing. In fact if they had been it would have made it anything *but* nice. It would have gone into the realm of charity. I mean the spirit of charity. But they gave it out of no particular spirit at all. It was devoid of any spirit whatsoever, which makes it beautiful and free from emotional claptrap.

(TOM hammers loudly for a while as ED looks up at him.)

ED: *(Yelling)* Anyway it's a full room if you want to come up! Bring a sleeping bag or something! Take the train and come when you can!

(TOM stops hammering.)

TOM: *(Still staring at the bookcase)* You're going to walk out on me. Is that it? Right in the middle of a job.
ED: Look, I got the structure built for you. You can put in the shelves yourself.
TOM: Thanks, friend.
ED: I have to finish the cabin before it snows.

(ED stands as though to leave.)

TOM: *(Without turning)* And it does snow up there! Boy, oh boy, the way it can snow when it wants to. A little tiny, eety, beety, teeny, weeny cabin like yours in the midst of a raging blizzard. In the midst of hail and snow and sleet. Calling out for some insulation. Calling for someone to warm its little hearth and seal up its cracking paint. Run to its side before it's too late! Run to its aid and attention!

(A shelf falls off the bookcase onto the floor, the lights change to white, they both stare at the shelf; DONNA enters carrying two cans of white paint and two brushes, she kicks the door shut and smiles at TOM and ED.)

DONNA: Hello there and I got some paint. Isn't that fine? So we'll paint it all up between the three of us.

(She sets the cans downstage left on top of each other and sits on them with her back to the audience, TOM climbs down off the stool, picks up the shelf, climbs back up, and replaces the shelf.)

TOM: Ed was just thinking about us going to his cabin in the woods.

(ED sits back down on the lumber.)

DONNA: Seems to me as though that's a bad idea offhand. Bad for several reasons. Bad because we're meeting people, bad because we're building shelves, and bad because we have to paint them. Of course it's good for Ed, however. It could be good for us too if we didn't have so many strikes against us already.

TOM: It's an idea that we had tossed haphazardly into the air without considering all the strikes against us or pondering it for long periods of time.

DONNA: Well.

(She stands and slaps her thigh, she crosses to the bookcase.)

How's it coming?

ED: Tom thinks it could be finished in short order. Seeing as how the frame is all finished, the rest should be easy.

DONNA: Good boy!

(She slaps TOM *on the butt.)*

ED: The thing is I can't wait around for the grand finale. I have to leave.

DONNA: Oh, it won't be anything to see, Ed. It's just a functional piece of basic furniture for around the house. For everyday use, so to speak.

TOM: Everyday. Everyday nothing. Once! It will be put to use once in its lifetime and that'll be the end. You never read the books to begin with. The ones you did read you read halfway. The rest you bought for their color or thickness or just to fill up some space. Fourteen hundred thousand books to put in a bookcase once and never touch them again till the day you die.

DONNA: I read like a fool, Tom. You know that and yet you'd like Ed to believe otherwise. In fact you'd like him to believe the exact opposite which is a lie. I could even prove it if it came to a matter of my having to defend my knowledge of books. Would you like me to prove it?

ED: No.

TOM: I don't really care actually. It just seems that books read once are better off in the trash can than they are sitting around on dusty shelves. That's a personal point of view.

ED: Not really. At times I've found myself very briefly getting very attached to books. Very emotionally attached. Like you would with a pet dog. It becomes something that's very hard to give up. You can't just throw it in the garbage with any kind of ease.

TOM: You throw away the book, not the effect. The response of the book stays with you wherever you go, whatever you do. In sickness and in health and through the long sad wintertime.

(He starts hammering; DONNA *yells.)*

DONNA: We're not going on no vacation until this gets done! Until it's nailed, sanded and painted, and stacked with books on every shelf! Then it's waxed, polished, and smells like the great outdoors! After that then we go! Not before or in the middle!

*(*TOM *stops hammering, the lights change to blue.)*

TOM: It's an impossibility. We'll be here forever. The winter will pass without a vacation, without a change of scenery. There'll be no free moments to wander around through yellow fields or climb purple trees. The task will last forever.

(The door opens very slowly and MOM *enters with her arms full of books, the other three watch her as she slowly crosses downstage right and stacks the books in a pile on the floor, she sits on the books with her back to the audience;* DONNA *sits on the cans of paint, all three of them look up at* TOM, *who turns around now on the stool to see them.)*

MOM: Whew! It's such a long ways up. It's like climbing three or four mountains in succession. It's also very much like rowing a rowboat in a rowboat race or running many miles over rough terrain in the freezing coldness. My goodness. Dearie.

TOM: I'm not on display, you know.

DONNA: *(Still sitting)* Hi, Mom. I see you brought up some of the books for me. Thanks.

MOM: Yes. A few. They made it very much tougher on me. They must weigh a great deal nowadays. They've changed since I was a schoolgirl in my schooling days.

TOM: I'm not up here for my health, you know. I have a job to do.

DONNA: It's worth it though, Mom. When they're all stacked in and divided into topical categories, it's really a sight to see.

MOM: Oh indeed. Libraries fascinate me to death. Like ancient tapestry or Chinese urns or butterfly collections that I've seen in the past. Many times. Goodness yes.

TOM: This is not a show! I happen not to be a professional carpenter or an expert nailing person. There's no reason to watch me work.

ED: It's not you in particular. It's what you're making.

TOM: But *I'm* making it! You're watching *me* make *it!*

MOM: Should we leave here?

DONNA: No, no, no.

TOM: It's turned into some kind of funny picnic or something which I don't like. I prefer to do it alone if I have to.

ED: We won't pay attention. We'll talk to each other.

DONNA: Right.

(DONNA crosses over to ED *and* MOM *and sits on the floor; they gather around in a circle and talk, ignoring* TOM.*)*

Ed suggested we go up to his cabin, Mom, for the weekend.

ED: That's right.

MOM: Oh that'd be very fine. I'd like it. I certainly would.

(TOM *turns back to the bookcase and starts hammering loudly again; the other three yell at each other.*)

DONNA: Such peace in the mountains!

MOM: Yes! And birds!

ED: Singing all the time!

DONNA: Such fun!

MOM: Lovely! Lovely!

(TOM *throws down the hammer and goes out the door, slamming it behind him; the three stare at the door, then* DONNA *stands and picks up the hammer, she climbs slowly up on the stool with her back to the audience;* ED *and* MOM *watch her.*)

DONNA: The time I spent deciding which books to choose and how and why. All that time perusing tiny bookstore shelves and never a thought as to where they'd wind up. Never one little thought about how to store books, how to keep them.

ED: I know.

DONNA: And it could be so lovely, too. So very pleasing to the eyeball. With various sizes and shapes and groups together. Without concern for what they're about or what they mean to me and who wrote them when. Just in terms of size and shape and color.

MOM: Yes, dear.

DONNA: But I'm at a loss. I'm really not ready to hammer and nail just yet. I can't bring myself around to it. I'd like it all done. I'd like to see it all finished and done and through with.

(ED *stands.*)

ED: I was going to—

(DONNA *turns abruptly on the stool toward* ED.)

DONNA: Sit down!

ED: I started—

DONNA: Sit back down!

(ED *sits on the lumber again.*)

Do you have to feel guilty about something you have nothing to do with!

MOM: That's true.

DONNA: Do you! I didn't ask you to apologize to me for not having finished my bookcase. Did I? No I didn't. As a matter of fact I was talking to myself rather than to anyone in particular. I wasn't even conversing actually. Of course there was no way of your knowing that.

ED: I was just saying—

DONNA: You were just going to say that you felt bad inside your heart because you didn't finish my bookcase when you were supposed to. That instead of finishing you pawned the job off on my husband and went off on a nifty little vacation in the woods somewhere. And finally that you allowed my poor old mother to haul books up eight flights of stairs in the midst of her old age.

ED: I—

(*The lights change to white; the door opens slowly and* POP *enters with his arms full of books, he crosses slowly down left and stacks the books in a pile, then sits on them with his back to the audience as the others watch.*)

MOM: There he is. I love him.

DONNA: But you don't need to.

(*She turns slowly upstage again, facing the bookcase.*)

It's quite all right with me. In fact it's perfect. It gives you something to project into the future as a future reference. Next time we'll know what to do. We'll have gathered together our joint experience and be able to use it as a kind of guidepost or maybe even a kind of guiding light.

POP: Boy, oh boy. Lots of stairs. I'll say that.

DONNA: (*Without turning around*) Lots of books, Pop. I'm glad to see you helping, even though it must be painful.

POP: There's many more. Never seen so many. Tons and tons down there. All piled up.

MOM: *(Still sitting stage right)* Poor baby.

(ED stands again.)

ED: I should go down maybe.

(DONNA turns on the stool.)

DONNA: No! Sit down there and stay sitting!

(ED sits back down.)

The books will make their way up gradually. Ever so slowly. They'll come up an armload at a time. Carried by friends or relatives or people who might pass them accidentally and offer a helping hand.

ED: I'd like to help.

MOM: Yes, dear.

DONNA: That's fine. That's really all right but I've just decided against it, Ed. I've decided you might just gum up the works. And we can't have that. Not at this stage of the game.

POP: It's like climbing hills.

DONNA: Not that we have to be overly careful. But selectivity has its good points now and then.

POP: There's nothing like a climb now and then.

DONNA: After a while, in fact, you forget the whole business. The preparation, the blueprint, the ideas, the measurements. We just pass through the room and take the whole shmear for granted.

MOM: Yes.

ED: I know, but I made it to order. It's precisely done. Just nail up the shelves and it could be considered a finished piece of work. Not even painted it would serve its purpose.

POP: What I was thinking was about a pulley. A dolly arrangement with heavy cables to pull up so many books as that.

MOM: Yes, dear.

DONNA: You mean out the window? Very good, Pop! Hang some pulleys out the window.

(ED *stands.*)

Where are you going now?

ED: My cabin.

MOM: Oh.

DONNA: That's right. A one-room place, right? In the woods somewhere?

ED: Yes.

DONNA: How did you come by such a nice little place as that?

ED: It was given — donated, rather.

MOM: Oh yes.

DONNA: It could be fixed into a year-round house, I imagine.

ED: That's what I'm working on.

DONNA: With heat and gas and electric lights all around. Like a Christmas house.

ED: Christmas?

POP: In the snow.

DONNA: Comfortable and homey, I imagine. Somehow I see it lost in the woods and nobody even living there.

ED: Really?

DONNA: Yes. And somehow it maintains itself all year round. Somehow it adapts itself to every change in the weather and turns on its own lights at night and then turns them off again in the morning. It even flushes its own toilet and builds its own fires and makes its little bed. There's no footprints around at all. Just buried one-quarter of the way in snow, and smoke coming out its chimney. Just sitting there in a small clearing about half a mile from a frozen lake. A Christmas house.

ED: There's no lake at all and I haven't even built the chimney yet.

POP: Oh too bad.

DONNA: But you're going to?

ED: I might.

DONNA: Well how will you stay there all year round if you don't have a chimney?

ED: Who says I'm staying?

DONNA: You did. You told me that.

ED: I might.

DONNA: You will. I can tell you will. You won't ever come back once you get all moved in.

ED: You make it sound very definite. Like I have no choice.

DONNA: I'm sorry.

ED: It's a place for retirement, if you really want to know. A place for rest-
ing and walking and not doing much else.
DONNA: Well that's fine then. You should have no trouble. This then is
your very last job on earth, I take it. And to think you're leaving it unfinished. That gets to me a little when I think of it. An unfinished
piece of work.
ED: For Christ's sake, I finished the frame.

*(The lights change to blue; the door opens and TOM enters, his arms full of
books, he kicks the door shut, he stands holding the books and looking around
at all the people.)*

TOM: You still here?
ED: I guess.
POP: Tommy boy.
TOM: Are you finishing up, my dear?
DONNA: Yes, I thought I would.

*(She turns toward the bookcase and starts hammering loudly on the shelves; the
rest yell their lines.)*

ED: I really have to leave! I'm sorry!
TOM: Well go then! Go! It's under control! It's not going to be hard at all,
once we get it organized!
MOM: A Christmas house!
ED: But I'd like to help some more!
TOM: No need! We have enough hands as it is! You're only in the way!

(DONNA stops hammering but does not turn around, TOM still holds the books.)

ED: I'm really sorry. Well all right. So long then.

(ED slowly crosses to the door and exits as the others watch him.)

'Bye.

(He waves to them, then closes the door behind him.)

DONNA: *(Still facing the bookcase)* Pop used to talk about a house like that when I was a girl and he was a father. How come you stopped thinking of that house, Pop?

(TOM crosses slowly to extreme stage right and sets the books in a pile, then sits on them with his back to the audience.)

POP: Whereabouts?

MOM: Oh dear.

DONNA: How could it happen like that? I mean so easily. Without any regrets. To start hauling books for your very own daughter.

MOM: Yes, dear.

POP: They're all heavy.

DONNA: Not minding at all one way or the other. Letting things slip away from you as though it didn't matter. As though it were all a joke and talking about a Christmas house doesn't really mean there will ever be one. I can see that!

TOM: Donna!

(She turns slowly around on the stool and faces TOM.)

DONNA: Yes, dear?

TOM: Shall we paint or not?

DONNA: Not just yet, I don't think. I don't care that much one way or the other.

TOM: We can't leave them plain.

(He crosses to the cans of paint and opens them.)

DONNA: We could. Of course we could. If worse came to worse we could sit on the books all year round and forget about the shelves. Like a bunch of hens. How about it? They might even hatch.

MOM: Yes, dear.

(TOM kneels facing the audience and stirs the paint with one of the paintbrushes.)

TOM: We can't leave it plain no matter how you look at it. We bought the paint already.

DONNA: That doesn't matter now. The color's unimportant.

(She gets down off the stool and crosses to the pile of books that TOM brought in, she picks a few of the books up; she turns as though to go back to the book-case, TOM stands with the paintbrush in his hand.)

TOM: Just leave the books where they are.

(DONNA stops and faces TOM, her arms full of books.)

DONNA: Look. I don't give a damn anymore about how it looks.
TOM: That's just too bad. We started it and now we'll finish.
DONNA: We started nothing. You never even wanted a bookcase at all. In the beginning.
TOM: But now it's there and it has to be finished.
DONNA: Has to be nothing. We leave it as it is.

(She approaches the bookcase.)

TOM: Stay where you are!

(DONNA stops, MOM and POP remain indifferent throughout all this.)

DONNA: Is it that important to you really? I mean in your heart of hearts?
TOM: Most important. It's become essential. It's become overpowering to me. Coloring every moment of my waking hours. I wake up thinking of this bookcase and I sleep dreaming of it. I walk around with the smell of it in my nose and I can see it in the future. I have a picture in my head of what it might become and I plan to fulfill that picture if it's the last thing I do.
DONNA: Swell!

(She drops the books abruptly on the floor, TOM swings the paintbrush through the air so that paint streaks down the front of DONNA.)

Shithead!

(They stare at each other but do not move, MOM and POP simultaneously pull a book out from each of their respective piles and start reading them with their backs still to the audience.)

TOM: I could have compromised a day or two ago while it was still in the planning stage. But now it's too late. Now it's definitely too late.

DONNA: You've become very definite very fast.

(She moves slowly toward the second paintbrush as TOM *stalks her, holding the brush in front of him like a weapon.)*

TOM: I find it helps. I'm not so wishy-washy and I can make fast decisions on a moment's notice.

DONNA: Right on top, as they say.

TOM: Exactly.

DONNA: Must be nice.

TOM: It is. I feel at home in any situation. I baffle everyone around me and I'm known for my wit.

DONNA: A joy to be with.

TOM: Of course.

*(*DONNA *grabs the other brush and dips it in the paint,* TOM *makes a lunge toward her but backs away, they hold the brushes in front of them and crouch for attack.)*

DONNA: People must flock to your side. You must have what they call "magnetism," a pulling sensation. That's the opposite of repulsion. Something like yin and yang.

TOM: Very close to it.

(They rush at each other and slap the brushes across each other's face—this should happen almost as though they were making a mockery of the fight, like two old gentlemen slapping each other with gloves—they back away and resume the crouch more typical of a street fight with knives. MOM *and* POP *gradually turn toward the audience while sitting on their stacks of books, they become very engrossed in their reading,* POP *turns toward stage left and* MOM *toward stage right.)*

DONNA: How could it lie dormant for so many years? Just under the surface and itching to pop out.

TOM: I had no chance. No field to practice in. I'd throw rocks now and then but there was always something left over. Some extra zest.

DONNA: All the windows you broke in preparation. All the dirt clods you threw. And the people chasing you across acres of vacant lots, firing shotguns and swearing your name.

TOM: My name was death in the neighborhood. I hung around with enemies of the town. Even enemies of myself.

DONNA: But now!

(They charge and slap each other again with the brushes, then back away.)

TOM: Yes! And my health has changed for the better. Even my eyes sparkle and my ears are clear. My whole body pulses with new life.

DONNA: The trouble is the longevity. Its lasting power. It seems like a stage to me. Just a frame of mind. Temporarily manic is the way I'd put it.

TOM: But that's so wrong. So easily overlooking what's right in front of you. You can't see it the way my veins stand out? The way my temples throb?

(They charge and slap each other, this time more deliberately and enjoying it less, they back away.)

DONNA: You'll fall back into it again. Wait and see. You'll sleep for days, afraid to get up. You'll wet your bed.

TOM: I'll jump out of bed! You don't even know. You haven't seen me when I'm at my best.

DONNA: You'll tremble under stacks of blankets, afraid to show your face. How will you account for the lies you've told?

TOM: Nothing false about it. I've gone through that stage. That pubic stage.

(By this time MOM and POP are directly facing the audience and remain that way to the end of the play, deeply absorbed in reading.)

DONNA: Prone on your back forever and ever. You'll cry to be read to. You'll want a bedtime story twenty-four hours a day. And no lights. I'll have to read to you with a flashlight tucked under my arm. The room will be dark and you'll whimper until you fall asleep.

TOM: It could never happen now!

(They charge and viciously paint each other with the brushes, then back away; they are both covered with white paint by now.)

DONNA: All you'll have is a tiny little glimmer of your present excitement. The rest will have gone and you'll lie there forever, trying to get it back. The bed will be your house and home and your head will be glued to the pillow. Your arms will be stuck to the sheet and your legs will be paralyzed from the hip down. You can't turn your head because you drool from the mouth and pus will run out your nose. Your eyes fill up with water and pour over onto your cheeks and each ear hums from hearing nothing. You lie in pools of urine and feces for days on end until the bed and you become one thing. One whole thing and there's no way of telling where the bed stops and you begin. You smell the same, you look the same, you act the same, you are the same.

(The lights change to white; the door opens and ED enters with his arms full of books, he kicks the door shut, DONNA and TOM drop the brushes on the floor and look at ED, MOM and POP keep reading.)

ED: Hi.

DONNA AND TOM: Hi.

ED: Decided to bring up a load.

DONNA AND TOM: Good.

ED: Where should I set them?

DONNA AND TOM: Oh, anywhere is all right.

(ED crosses and piles the books down center, then turns and looks at the book-case.)

ED: How's it coming?

DONNA AND TOM: Not bad.

ED: There's not as many down there as you had me believe. I mean by the way you were talking anybody would think you were flooded with books. But there's just a few. A couple more trips and you'll have it done.

DONNA AND TOM: We decided to stay.

ED: What? No, I mean a couple more trips up the stairs and you'd have it all finished. The books.

DONNA AND TOM: We're staying up here.

ED: Well, I can't bring them all. One trip is all I have time for. It won't take very long and you forget the climb after a while. You were probably counting the flights as you came up. That's always bad. If you stop counting, it'll go much faster. I can assure you of that. I personally find work to be easier if I distract myself rather than pour my full concentration into it. That way you forget about your body and therefore you're not conscious of being fatigued or exhausted. In fact I usually finish up a day's work fully refreshed. I know that seems odd to most people but it's true. Work tends to boost my energy rather than diminish it.

DONNA AND TOM: That does seem strange.

ED: The trouble is I don't have enough time. I wouldn't mind bringing the rest up for you but I really have to go.

DONNA AND TOM: That's quite all right.

(They both turn upstage and stare at the bookcase with their backs to ED.)

ED: It's just too bad all the way around. We should all take some time off. You know? Why don't we do that? We could all go up there this very minute and take a little rest. We'd be just in time for the first snow. And we could make some kind of special dinner. You know, a turkey dinner with cranberry sauce. Then we could build a fire and sit around drinking hot chocolate. Then we could—

MOM AND POP: *(Reading from the books)* And the snow started early and came so soft that nobody even noticed. The only way we could really tell was the way the trees slowly changed from green to white.

ED: We could do that. It would just be a visit. I'm all moved in so I don't need any help.

MOM AND POP: It fell for hours and hours, then days and days, and it looked like it wouldn't stop. In fact everyone decided that it wouldn't stop and it kept going on. Falling down and down.

ED: There's really enough room even though it's small.

MOM AND POP: But the funny thing was that there wasn't any wind and there wasn't any cold. It just fell and changed everything from the color it was to white. But it got thicker and thicker so the people went outside but it didn't get any better. It got thicker and thicker and covered all their trees.

ED: I really can't hang around. I have to get back to my house now.

MOM AND POP: It got so bad that they had to climb a hill and watch from the top while their houses disappeared. It happened very slow but they never sat down and their legs got very strong.

ED: I'll even buy the food and cook it all myself.

MOM AND POP: It happened very slow and they stood very still until the smoke went away from their little chimney tops. Then the trees disappeared while they all just looked and didn't say a word but stood in a line looking straight ahead. The blanket moved up and the valley disappeared but the people didn't cry and it kept coming down and it kept piling up and they all just stared and didn't say a word.

ED: If I *could* stay I would!

(*Everyone but* ED *says the next lines simultaneously in perfect synchronization.* MOM *and* POP *still reading and facing front,* DONNA *and* TOM *still facing the bookcase, and* ED *somewhere in the middle.*)

ALL BUT ED: The place was in white as far as they could see and not a sound or a wind or a hint of cold or hot. Not a taste in their mouth or a sting in their nose. And they moved very slow away from the place. And they moved and they moved and they didn't say a thing. Didn't laugh, didn't cry, didn't moan, didn't sigh, didn't even cough as the snow came down.

ED: *It's just too bad!*

ALL BUT ED: And once they turned they didn't turn around and once they walked they didn't even stop and they met more people as they went along, all new people as they went along, and the ground was white for as far as they could see and the sky was white, as white as it could be, and the crowd was thick and the air was thin but there wasn't any cold and there wasn't any hot and they couldn't even stop.

(ED *joins in at this point as they all say the lines in perfect unison; they don't wait for* ED, *he simply joins them.*)

ALL: So they just moved on and on and on and as the story goes they never did stop, they never did drop, they never lagged behind or even speeded up. They never got tired and they never got strong and they didn't feel a thing. And nobody knows how they ever got lost, how they ever got away. To this very same day nobody knows how they ever got away.

(The lights change to blue, all the shelves fall off the bookcase onto the floor, none of the actors move; the blue light dims out very slowly to the end of the play, MOM and POP stand slowly as the other actors start to hum "White Christmas" very softly, begin picking up all the debris from the floor and carrying it offstage through the door. MOM and POP read alternately from the book, staying on either side of the stage; the other three clean the entire stage, starting with the debris, then the books, then dismounting the entire set and taking it off so that the stage is completely bare by the end of the play; they hum the tune more loudly as they continue, likewise MOM and POP read more loudly.)

POP: The original plan unfortunately hasn't changed, despite publicity to the contrary. The radial city exists much the same as it always has in the past. In fact it never really occurred out of a preconception on the part of individual architects or city planners.

MOM: It occurred more out of a state of frenzy and a complete lack of consideration for the future function of a place to live and/or work. The present condition is only the outcome of that lack of consideration.

POP: Consequently the city as it exists today affords certain people who live in certain areas many more benefits and varied ways of living than it does certain other people. This situation occurs in terms of center points similar to the hub of a wheel. The center of a city always offers people more diversions, more necessities, and more of everything they need to stay alive.

MOM: Therefore the center is densely populated and has a greater coagulation of excitement in the air. The farther one gets from this center point the less one is aware of the excitement. As one moves toward the country and more rural areas the excitement has all but disappeared.

POP: The problem seems to be one of accommodating people with the pleasures and necessities of the city and at the same time offering them plenty of open green space—since city parks are nothing more than tiny breathing places or overly synthetic versions of the real thing and they also make it tremendously difficult to forget the city (if that be their function) for the simple fact that they were conceived in the midst of horrendous skyscrapers.

MOM: Skyscrapers, too, have never solved any congestive problems since they were built more out of the need for space than with any consideration for the human being. Hence when the day's work is done, there is a terrible conglomerate of people pushing their way out of the base of each building and rushing to more rural developments.

POP: The obvious alternative to this radial concept seems to be what might be called the "linear city" or the "universal city." As an example the city would stretch in a line from the tip of Maine to the tip of Florida and be no wider than a mile. The city would stop immediately at its mile width, at which point the country would commence. This would allow any citizen with the ability to use his or her legs to walk from the midst of the city into the midst of the country.

MOM: Unexcelled transportation systems would be put into use for the traversing of the city's length. An underground system traveling at the speed of two hundred miles an hour. An overhead system traveling at the rate of four hundred miles per hour. Two very wide belts, much like conveyor belts, would stretch from Florida to Maine and be in perpetual motion twenty-four hours a day, seven days a week. One belt moving at the rate of four miles per hour, the other at eight miles per hour.

POP: These would be primarily used for any person walking from someplace to someplace and if they couldn't afford the higher-speed systems. A person walking on the four-mile-an-hour belt would obviously be walking four miles an hour faster than his normal pace. If he or she became tired he could then sit down on the eight-mile-an-hour belt and maintain the same speed.

MOM: Skyscrapers would be eliminated in preference to elongated parallel structures with many outlets along their sides. Thus eliminating heavy congestion at one exit.

POP: Cultural centers would be evenly distributed along the entire length of the city. Museums, concerts, movies, theater, et cetera, would be readily available to everyone rather than the chosen few.

MOM: State borders would disintegrate and all police cars would be the same color as well as all license plates.

POP: Schools would be functional rather than regional and the children could walk to the country on their lunch hour.

MOM: Employment opportunities would vastly increase.

POP: Water shortage would be extinct.

MOM: Cross-country linear cities would develop.

POP: Stretching from coast to coast and crisscrossing the vertical cities.

MOM: The vertical cities stretching north through Canada and south through Mexico.

POP: All the way into South America.

MOM: Each city no less than ten miles from the next city.

POP: Forming ten-mile squares of country in between.

MOM: Desert cities and jungle cities where cities have never been.

POP: Ocean cities and sky cities and cities underground.

MOM: Joining country to country and hemisphere to hemisphere.

POP: Forming five-mile squares in between.

(The stage is bare by this time, the other three actors are offstage but still humming the tune, MOM and POP still face front.)

MOM: Elevated cities suspended under vacuum air.

POP: Forming two-mile squares in between.

MOM: Cities enclosed in glass to see the sky.

POP: Forming one-mile squares.

MOM: Cities in the sky to see the glass.

POP: Forming squares in between.

(MOM and POP close their books, the lights dim out, the other three actors stop humming offstage.)

Red Cross

Red Cross was first produced on January 20, 1966, at the Judson Poets' Theatre with the following cast:

CAROL: Joyce Aaron
JIM: Lee Kissman
MAID: Florence Tarlow

It was directed by Jacques Levy.

SCENE

The bedroom of a cabin. There is a screen door up center leading out to a small porch. A window stage left and stage right. There are twin beds, one under each window with the heads facing upstage. The tops of trees can be seen through the screen door and each of the windows to give the effect of a second story. As the lights come up JIM *is sitting on the bed to stage left facing* CAROL, *who is sitting on the other bed. Everything in the set plus costumes should be white.*

CAROL: Look at it closely.

JIM: I am.

CAROL: You can't see it, then?

JIM: Yes.

CAROL: Then it *is* bad. I can't believe it. The tingling. It's like a tingling thing under each eye. It goes into the nose, too.

JIM: Maybe it's just sinus or something.

CAROL: No. I can see the results. If you can see something happening, then it couldn't just be sinus. The whole face and ears and nose and eyes. And my hands. Feel my hands.

(She holds her hands out, JIM *holds them.)*

JIM: Hm.

(She pulls her hands back.)

CAROL: Feel them? What's that, Jim. Something's happening. My hands never sweat like that. And my feet. Hold my foot.

(She raises her foot, JIM *holds it.)*

Just feel it. The other one, too. Feel them both. What's that? Under the eyes is what bothers me. It's from wearing those glasses. I can tell. It's from the glasses. My head aches so bad. I can't believe my head.

JIM: Why?

CAROL: It hurts. It's breaking open all the time. It crashes around inside.

(She gets up and starts pacing around the stage as JIM remains sitting on the stage-left bed.)

JIM: What's the matter?

CAROL: It's anything. Beer or water or too many cigarettes and it starts to break. One day it'll break clear open and I'll die, I'll be dead then.

JIM: Take it easy.

CAROL: It'll just burst and there I'll be lying in the middle of the street or in a car or on a train. With a bursted head.

JIM: Somebody will take care of you.

CAROL: It might happen when I'm skiing or swimming.

JIM: There's always lots of people around those places. They'll see you and help.

CAROL: They'll see my head.

(She crosses to the stage-right bed and stands on it facing JIM and begins to act out the rest as though she were skiing on a mountain slope.)

It'll be in the snow somewhere. Somewhere skiing on a big white hill. In the Rockies. I'll be at the top of this hill and everything will be all right. I'll be breathing deep. In and out. Big gusts of cold freezing air. My whole body will be warm and I won't even feel the cold at all. I'll be looking down and then I'll start to coast. Very slowly. I'm a good skier. I started when I was five. I'll be halfway down and then I'll put on some steam. A little steam at first and then all the way into the egg position. The Europeans use it for speed. I picked it up when I was ten. I'll start to accumulate more and more velocity. The snow will start to spray up around my ankles and across my face and hands. My fingers will get tighter around the grips and I'll start to feel a little pull in each of my calves. Right along the tendon and in front, too. Everything will be working at once. All my balance and strength and breath. The whole works in one bunch. There'll be pine trees going past me and other skiers going up the hill. They'll stop and watch me go past. I'll be going so fast everyone will stop and look. They'll wonder if I'll make it. I'll do some jumps and twist my body with the speed. They'll see my body twist, and my hair, and my eyes will water from the wind hitting them. My cheeks will start to sting and get all red. I'll get further and further into the egg position with my arms tucked up. I'll look down and see the valley and the cars and houses and people walking up and down. I'll see all the cabins with smoke coming out the chimneys. Then it'll come. It'll start like a twitch in my left ear. Then I'll start to feel a throb in the bridge of my nose. Then a thump in the base of my neck. Then a crash right through my skull. Then I'll be down. Rolling! Yelling! All those people will see it. I'll be rolling with my skis locked and my knees buckled under me and my arms thrashing through the snow. The skis will cut into both my legs and I'll bleed all over. Big gushes of red all over the snow. My arms will be broken and dragging through the blood. I'll smell cocoa and toast and marmalade coming out of the cabins. I'll hear dogs barking and see people pointing at me. I'll see the road and college kids wearing sweat shirts and ski boots. Then my head will blow up. The top will come right off. My hair will blow down the hill full of guts and blood. Some bluejay will try to eat it probably. My nose will come off and my whole face will peel away. Then it will snap. My whole head will snap off and roll down the hill and become a huge snowball and roll into the city and kill a million people. My body will stop at the bottom of the hill with just a bloody stump for a neck and both arms broken and both legs. Then there'll be a long cold wind. A whistle, sort of. It'll start to snow a little bit. A very soft easy snow. The squirrels might come down to see what happened. It'll keep snowing very lightly like that for a long time until my whole body is covered over. All you'll see is that little red splotch of blood and a whole blanket of white snow.

VOICE OFFSTAGE: Miss Littles! Miss Littles, are you ready!

CAROL: What?

JIM: You have to go.

CAROL: Oh. Yes.

(She crosses to the door, she opens the door and yells down.)

I'll be right there!

(She crosses to JIM *and kisses him on the forehead.)*

You'll meet me, right? Please?

JIM: Yes.

CAROL: I'll see you then at six. *(She kisses him again.)* Six o'clock.

JIM: Right.

(She exits. JIM *gets up and crosses to the door, he hums some kind of tune, he looks out, then goes back to the bed and sits, he scratches his legs, then he stands up and takes his pants off, he sits back down and starts scratching his legs, he starts picking little bugs out of his skin and then stepping on them, he gets up and starts doing pushups downstage center. A* MAID *appears on the porch through the screen door, holding two pillows, sheets, and bedspreads in her arms, she is rather fat and older than* JIM, *she watches* JIM *as he does his pushups, then she knocks on the door;* JIM *continues, she knocks again, then a third time very loudly.)*

JIM: *(Still doing pushups)* Come in, come in, come in. Have a seat or something.

MAID: It's the maid, dear.

JIM: *(Without turning to look)* Come in, come in and have a bed or a seat. Whatever you want.

MAID: *(Still on the porch)* I want to change the beds is all.

JIM: *(He stops and turns to her, sitting on the floor.)* Well come in. The beds are in here.

MAID: Thank you.

(She enters and sets the linen down on the stage-right bed, JIM *sits on the floor looking at her.)*

I always seem to catch you, don't I?

JIM: Yep. You catch me every time. I think you plan it.

MAID: No.

JIM: I think you do. You like catching me.

MAID: It's just the time of day. You're the only one left this time of day.

JIM: Come on. Where do they go?

MAID: It's true.

JIM: Where do they go? I've seen them around during the day. They hang around. They play tennis or something.

MAID: I just make the beds.
JIM: You know where they go. They go into town. Right?

(She starts to change the stage-left bed.)

Hey leave my bed alone!

(He stands.)

MAID: Well I have to change it, dear.
JIM: It's got stains. I don't want you to see the stains. I get embarrassed.

(He jumps on the stage-left bed facing the MAID.)

I do. It embarrasses me. I get pink and everything.
MAID: All right.

(She turns and starts making the other bed.)

I've seen yellow spots before, you know. It don't bother me.
JIM: Well it bothers me. I get pink.
MAID: I'm sorry about that.
JIM: Do you know anything about crabs?
MAID: About what?
JIM: Crabs. Bugs that get in your pubic hair and eat your skin and suck your blood and make you itch.
MAID: Like nits or something?
JIM: What's a nit?
MAID: Like lice.
JIM: Yeah. Except on a smaller scale. Almost microscopic. With legs and red heads. They twitch when you grab hold of them. I can show you one if you want to see it. Do you want to see one?
MAID: Not really.
JIM: Oh, come on.
MAID: All right.

(JIM sits on the edge of the bed and picks at his legs, the MAID sits on the other bed facing him, he gets hold of a small bug and hands it carefully to the MAID, who looks at it in the palm of her hand.)

They must be part of the lice family to get in your skin.

JIM: There. See it? They crawl around.

MAID: Mm. You got these all over?

JIM: No. They're localized.

MAID: Can't you get some medicine?

(She hands the bug back to JIM.*)*

JIM: I don't want it back.

MAID: Well I don't want it.

JIM: Throw it on the floor.

(She throws it down, JIM *steps on it.)*

What kind of medicine?

MAID: Sheep dip or something.

JIM: Sheep dip!

(He stands on the bed again.)

Why sheep dip?

MAID: I'm sorry.

(She starts changing the bed again.)

JIM: Sheep dip is for woolly animals or dogs or something. Human lice are different from animal lice. The whole treatment is different.

MAID: Well that's the only thing I can tell you.

JIM: Who uses sheep dip for crabs? That's ridiculous. I mean that's really stupid.

MAID: Well I don't know, then. You'll have to find something pretty soon, though.

JIM: Why?

MAID: Well if I had parasites eating off me and draining me of all my blood and reducing my physical strength twenty-four hours a day, making me weaker and weaker while they got stronger and stronger, I can tell you that I'd do something. I'd get it taken care of. That's all I know. And I'm not smart.

JIM: You'd put sheep dip on them and kill your skin along with the crabs. Is that it?

MAID: I'd have enough sense to have my bed changed, knowing that crabs lay eggs inside the sheets and the blankets and that eggs hatch and that when eggs hatch new crabs are born. Baby crabs are born and baby crabs grow up like all crabs have to. And when they're grown they lay new crabs and it goes on and on like that indefinitely for years.

JIM: I'm talking about the immediate possibilities of killing the live crabs that are already there. Not the ones that haven't been born, maidy, maidy.

MAID: How 'bout a doctor?

JIM: Terrific.

(He jumps off the bed and crosses down center, doing arm exercises.)

I'm in the middle of the forest and you're talking about a doctor. Thank you. A country doctor, I suppose.

MAID: Isn't there someone to take you?

JIM: Not till six.

MAID: Can you wait?

JIM: I don't know. They really get to me every once in a while. You know what I mean? They pinch so hard I think they're going all the way through. They grab and squeeze. I think they must have teeth too. Along with the pincers I think they have teeth.

MAID: Can you wait till six?

JIM: *(He crosses right.)* It's a long time to go on itching like this. To have any itchy skin, I mean. And they're moving up, too. They've gotten to my navel and yesterday I found one in my armpit. Six is a long way off when this is happening to me.

(He crosses left.)

I can ignore them for periods of time. An hour at the longest if I'm preoccupied with something else. If I concentrate. They go away and then come back. It depends on the concentration.

(He stops doing the arm exercise.)

MAID: I could take you. I have a car.

JIM: I climbed a tree yesterday and it went away for a couple hours. I climbed all over the tree. Through the branches and clear up to the top. I sat up there for a couple hours smoking cigarettes. That did it for a while. Then I went swimming and that helped. Swimming always helps. Then I ran around the lake at a medium fast trot. I jogged all the way around. I got up a good sweat and I was breathing very hard and my heart was pounding. All the blood was going through me at once.

MAID: Have you had them for a long time?

JIM: I've had crabs for about ten years now and it gets worse every year. They breed very fast. It's nice, though. It's like having two bodies to feed.

MAID: Well I could take you. I have a car.

(JIM turns to her.)

Do you want to go now?

JIM: You drive in every day?

MAID: Well I don't walk.

JIM: You drive from town all the way into the middle of the forest to change somebody else's beds?

MAID: That's right.

JIM: Aren't there any beds in town?

MAID: I like the drive.

JIM: Me too. It's nice. Calm. Smooth. Relaxing. Comfortable. Leisurely. Pleasurable. Enchanting. Delightful.

MAID: Yes.

JIM: Is there a doctor in town, did you say?

MAID: Well sure. I suppose. We could probably find one if you want to go.

JIM: There isn't one out here, huh? I mean they don't by any chance have a country doctor out in this neck of the woods. One a' them country guys in a Model T Ford and beat-up leather bag full of sheep dip. Maybe even a veterinarian. I hear veterinarians can take as good care of you as a physician or a real doctor. Have you heard that?

MAID: Do you want to go into town or not?

JIM: Gee! I'd like the ride. I'd like that a lot. To ride in the car into town and get this taken care of. And then ride back. That'd be a lot of trips for you to take, though. A lot of extra hauls. Out and back and out and back. Coming and going.

MAID: I don't mind.

JIM: I could give you some gas money.

MAID: Forget it.

JIM: I insist. I absolutely insist.

MAID: Look—

JIM: Hey! Hold it! Hold it! I have an idea.

MAID: What?

JIM: You'll have to help me. Are you willing to help me?

MAID: I guess.

JIM: Okay. Come on.

(He starts pulling the stage-right bed down center.)

Push. Push it.

(The MAID starts pushing the head of the bed as JIM pulls.)

Come on, push. Push. Hup, hup.

MAID: What's this for?

JIM: You'll see. Come on. Get it down here. Hup, hup. Heave ho!

MAID: I have to go pretty soon, you know.

JIM: It won't take long.

(They pull the bed downstage, then JIM crosses to the stage-left bed.)

Very good. Beautiful. Come on now. Help me with this. Come on. Hup, hup.

MAID: All right.

(They push the stage-left bed across stage into the former position of the other bed.)

What are you doing?

JIM: Rearranging. It'll be much nicer. Much, much nicer. More better for everyone concerned. Hup, two. Hup, two.

MAID: I don't know.

JIM: Heave ho!

(They get the bed into position, then JIM crosses down to the other bed.)

All right, maidy baby. The last lap. Come on. It's almost done. Have faith.

(The MAID crosses down to the bed and helps him push it stage left.)

Heave, heave. Push, push. Put your back into it! A little more sweat there. Hup, two. 'At's it! Beautiful! Muy bien! Qué bonita!

(He jumps on top of the stage-left bed, the MAID sits on the stage-right bed facing him.)

Este es demasiado!

(He jumps up and down on the bed.)

Que bella! Que bella! Muy bien!

MAID: Why did you do that?

JIM: *(He stops jumping.)* Now I have a clean bed, right? A changed bed. New, fresh, white, clean sheets imported from town. A downy, soft, airy pillow and a freshly washed bedspread. Guaranteed to be free of crabs and crab eggs and lice and ticks and nits. Guaranteed to smell sweet and pure. I have all this and you didn't even have to change my old bed. Isn't that nice? Now we don't have to go to town at all. We can stay here and jump around.

MAID: Yes.

(She gets up and starts changing the stage-right bed.)

And I'm all worn out.

JIM: Now what are you doing! Leave that bed alone! Stop that!

MAID: It's no longer yours, remember? We just switched. The one you're standing on is yours. You can't have both, you know. Make up your mind.

JIM: It doesn't matter. Leave it alone! You'll catch something!

MAID: You're getting very selfish, aren't you? You forget somebody else sleeps in this bed. Somebody else who might not like to catch crabs.

JIM: She doesn't care!

(He flops down on the bed and lies on his stomach with his head toward the audience as the MAID *continues to change the stage-right bed.)*

MAID: I know she doesn't.

JIM: Is this the last room you have?

MAID: Yep.

JIM: You save it for last?

MAID: No. I just make a point to come here last. I keep hoping one day I'll come and you won't be here. All I'll have to do is come into this room and make the beds and go right back out. One day I'll be able to do this room in no time at all and just go straight home. What a day that will be.

JIM: You go straight home from here?

MAID: That's right.

JIM: You don't hang around at all?

MAID: Nope.

JIM: You don't hang around to climb a tree or run around the lake or nothing? You should come at night, maidy. You'd like it better at night. We could go swimming.

MAID: No thanks.

JIM: It's really better at night. You'd be surprised the way it changes. All the different sounds and the air gets wetter. Sometimes it rains. That's the best time for swimming. When it rains. That way you get completely wet. A constant wetness.

MAID: Don't you catch cold?

JIM: No. Not a chance. Your body stays warm inside. It's just the outside that gets wet. It's really neat. I mean you can dive under water and hold your breath. You stay under for about five minutes. You stay down there and there's nothing but water all around you. Nothing but marine life. You stay down as long as you can until your lungs start to ache. They feel like they're going to burst open. Then just at the point where you can't stand it anymore you force yourself to the top. You explode out of the water, gasping for air, and all this rain hits you in the face. You ought to try it.

MAID: I'm too fat for swimming.

JIM: What do you mean? You won't sink. You just do the strokes, you know.

(He starts kicking his feet and stroking with his arms.)

You learn how to breathe and you kick and you stroke and there's nothing to it.

(The MAID turns and looks at him.)

You know how, don't you?

MAID: Not really. I can never put it all together. I mean I either stroke faster than I kick or vica-versa.

JIM: Watch me. It's easy once you get started.

(He starts going through the motions as the MAID watches.)

The kicking is important. You have to keep your legs straight and kick from the waist. No bending the knees. And the arms too. Once the arm hits the water on the downsweep, you have to keep it straight. No bending the elbow.

MAID: *(She tries to copy him, moving her arms in an arc.)* Do you keep your elbow straight?

JIM: Well no. Just as it goes through the water. That's the only time you have to worry. You can bend it as you take it back. Lie down over there and watch me.

(She lies down on the stage-right bed with her head toward the audience, she watches JIM as he demonstrates the Australian crawl.)

Now the coordination has to come from knowing how to synchronize the speed. The rate of speed that your feet are taking has to match that of your stroking speed. The reason you can't put the two together is because you're not concentrating on the whole mechanism. That is, you're becoming more concerned with one end or the other rather than the collaboration of the two as a total unit.

MAID: I see.

JIM: Now start out slowly, keeping that in mind.

(She starts doing the crawl, JIM watches her for a while, then starts doing it himself.)

Keep it slow, trying to work on the points where you derive the most power. Think of the way an oar or a paddle is constructed. Regard your arms and legs as being paddles. A paddle has a broad surface and reaches its highest point of thrust when it is perpendicular to the surface line of the water. This is the way you should use your arms. Keep your fingers close together to make a broader surface. Be careful not to let any water pass between them. That's it. Now the breathing is important. This requires added concentration and coordination. You will be able to breathe instinctively in the right manner if you keep in mind that the human being cannot inhale water.

MAID: (*Still doing the stroke*) Really?

JIM: Your head should pivot on your shoulders, always to the left. Inhale as your head comes out of the water and exhale as it goes into the water. Breathe in. Breathe out. In, out. In, out.

(*They both breathe and continue the stroking.*)

MAID: In, out. In, out.

JIM: One, two. One, two. That's right. Remember the whole thing is working at once.

MAID: I'm getting tired.

JIM: It's no sweat. Keep it up. You can't poop out in the middle of a lake. Stroke! Stroke! Keep it moving. One, two. One, two. 'Atta girl.

MAID: It's my back. There's a pain in my back.

(*She continues to swim,* JIM *goes faster.*)

JIM: That's good. It's good when it hurts. It's working then. Keep it up! We've almost got it. Hup, two! Hup, two!

MAID: It really aches, Jim.

JIM: That's all right. We're halfway already.

MAID: I'll never make it! My back.

JIM: Use it all. Everything at once. Make it work. One, two. One, two.

(*He is going very fast with perfect coordination.*)

In, out. In, out. Breathe! Breathe!

MAID: My leg! I've got a cramp, Jim!

(*She continues very slowly.*)

JIM: Hup, two! Hup, two! Shake it off. Use it! Keep using it so it doesn't tighten. Keep it loose! Hup, two! Hup, two!

MAID: My side now! It's in my side!

JIM: Move it! Work it out! Keep it up!

MAID: Oh my leg! I can't. I can't do it!

(She continues slowly.)

It's killing me!

JIM: We're almost there!

(The MAID screams in agony, she lies very still on the bed with her face in the blanket, JIM stops and looks at her, he sits on the edge of the bed.)

Did you drown, maidy?

(She remains very still.)

Did maidy drown in the middle of the lake? Tsk, tsk, tsk, tsk.

MAID: I got a cramp.

JIM: A leg cramp and a side cramp. What a shame.

MAID: It's not very funny.

JIM: I guess we can't go then, right?

MAID: Go where?

JIM: Swimming. At night. Night swimming. Swimming in the dark in the middle of the forest. Like we wanted to do. Remember?

MAID: We could if you'd take it slower. If you wouldn't rush. How can I learn all that in one sitting? In, out. In, out. Breathe! Breathe! You can make it! I'm not an advanced swimmer, you know. I'm not even an intermediate swimmer. I'm a beginner. I know nothing about swimming and suddenly I'm supposed to have everything under my belt. Just intuitively I'm supposed to. It's pretty unfair, Jim.

JIM: I know.

MAID: If I get a cramp, I get a cramp. I can't go plodding on like an Olympic champion or something. Jesus Christ.

JIM: I'm sorry.

MAID: It takes time to be a swimmer.

(She sits up on the bed, JIM remains where he is.)

I can't just become a swimmer in one lesson like that. I mean what is that? There's no water or anything and you expect me to swim! How can I swim on a bed! How can I do it!

JIM: I don't know.

MAID: I don't know either. I really don't. I can see me in a lake. Can you imagine me in a lake in the middle of the night with nobody around? Me and you in the middle of the forest, in the middle of a lake. And there you are, fifty yards ahead of me yelling: "In, out! In, out! You can make it! You can make it! Keep it up!"

(She stands and crosses down center, limping and holding her side.)

And I'm sinking fifty yards behind you. That's what I'd be doing, you know. Do you know that! I'd be sinking!

JIM: Yes.

MAID: Yes. The maid is slowly sinking. Gurgling, yelling, floundering for help. Sinking to the bottom of the lake on her first swimming lesson. Her first time out.

JIM: Well take it easy. It's not my fault.

(The MAID limps more deliberately and holds her side in mock agony.)

MAID: The maid bobbing up and down, up and down with her hands slapping the water, her mouth gasping for air, her side screaming with pain.

JIM: I thought you'd swam before.

MAID: Wading is what I did before! Tiptoeing in shallow water with my sneakers on! Not in seventy-five feet of lake water with no one around. Stranded there at night with my family in town and me in the forest and you wandering around smoking cigarettes in a tree and not giving a damn at all!

(JIM stands and crosses to the MAID.)

JIM: Try to keep it moving. Work it out.

MAID: I can't now. It's cramped for good. I'll never swim again.

JIM: I know but keep it going. Keep the blood moving.

MAID: It'll never work. The pain is unbelievable.

JIM: Come on. Hup, two! Hup, two! You can make it.

MAID: Nobody able to eat at home because I'm drowning out here! Nobody knowing where I am. Everybody forgetting my name! And I'm getting worse all the time! I'm sinking more and more! With seaweed up my nose and tangled all around me and I can't see a thing in the night!

(She sinks to her knees and starts crawling around the stage on all fours as JIM follows her.)

JIM: Will you please cut it out?

MAID: So you don't like me screaming out here, is that it? You don't like me getting carried away with my cramps and my pain in the middle of the night, in the middle of the forest. Well let me tell you it hurts me to do it. I don't like screaming myself. I try to keep a calm house, an easy home with everyone quiet and happy. It's not an easy thing, Jim. At my age, in my condition.

JIM: Get up off the floor.

MAID: I make the beds and cook the meals. Everyone gets fed on time at my house.

JIM: I don't care. It's six o'clock now!

MAID: So the screaming shouldn't hurt you at all, knowing I don't do it all the time. Knowing that I save it for special times when my side starts to ache and my legs collapse and the water gets into my nose.

JIM: We can get you a doctor but you have to get up.

(She collapses on the floor and stays very still with JIM standing over her.)

Come on. I'll take you into town.

MAID: But once it's over it isn't bad at all. Once you get over the shock of having water all around and dragonflies and water lilies floating by and little silver fish flashing around you. Once that's past and you get all used to your flippers and your fins and your new skin, then it comes very easy.

(She stands slowly with no concerns at all for her cramps and gathers together all the dirty laundry as she continues to talk.)

You move through the water like you were born in that very same place and never even knew what land was like. You dive and float and sometimes rest on the bank and maybe chew on some watercress. And the family in town forgets where you went and the swimming coach forgets who you are and *you* forget all about swimming lessons and just swim without knowing how and before you know it the winter has come and the lake has frozen and you sit on the bank staring at the ice. You don't move at all. You just sit very still staring at the ice until you don't feel a thing. Until your flippers freeze to the ground and your tail freezes to the grass and you stay like that for a very long time until summer comes around.

(She glances at JIM *and then exits out the door with the linen;* JIM *stares after her for a second, then rushes toward the door.)*

JIM: Hey! I could drive you home!

(He opens the door and looks out.)

Hey! Do you want a lift!

(He shuts the door, then turns downstage; he pauses, then rushes to his pants, he starts to put his pants on hurriedly, he gets them halfway on and CAROL *enters, she is carrying a bag of groceries and wearing glasses, the door slams behind her,* JIM *looks at her for a second, then finishes putting on his pants,* CAROL *sets the groceries down on the stage-left bed.)*

CAROL: Well. Guess what. A funny little thing. A very funny thing. I'm in the grocery store, see. I'm standing there looking for bread or something and guess what?
JIM: What?
CAROL: I start itching.

(She crosses down right; JIM *stands center with his back to the audience, staring at the door.)*

Not just a simple itch but a burn. A searing kind of thing. A biting, scratching thing that's tearing at me, see.

*(*JIM *crosses slowly upstage and stands looking out the screen door.)*

Well I'm paralyzed. I don't know what to do because it's all up my legs and under my arms.

(She walks back and forth downstage.)

I can't start scratching my private zones right in the middle of a grocery store. So I run to the bathroom. I make a beeline for the bathroom and I lock the door and I rip my clothes off. I literally tear them off my body. And I look. And do you know what it is? Bugs! Bugs all over me. Buried in my skin. Little tiny itty bitty bugs, clawing and biting at me. They're all in my hair and everything. Sucking my blood, Jim! They're actually in my skin. I've been carrying them around with me. And do you know what? I have a sneaking suspicion that they're in this room. I picked them up from being in this room. I'll bet they're right inside here. In the beds even.

(She goes to the stage-right bed and rips off the bedspread and sheets.)

They're breeding in these beds. I'll bet you any amount of money. These cabins are so old and filthy. I bet they've been here for years without anybody checking. Bedbugs are no joke, Jim. I mean they suck your blood and everything.

(She goes to the other bed and tears it apart.)

I can't stand it. Just thinking about it upsets me. We'll have to get another room. That's all there is to it. Either that or go back home. I really can't take it. It's awful. Jim!

(JIM turns to her slowly, there is a stream of blood running down his forehead.)

JIM: What?
CAROL: What happened?
JIM: When?

BLACKOUT

Cowboys #2

Cowboys #2 was first performed at the Mark Taper Forum, Los Angeles, in November 1967, as part of an evening of plays entitled *The Scene*, with the following cast:

STU:	Gary Hanes
CHET:	Philip Austin
MAN NUMBER ONE:	Lucian Baker
MAN NUMBER TWO:	John Rose

It was directed by Edward Parone.

SCENE

The setting is a bare stage, very dimly lit. Upstage center is a sawhorse with a yellow caution light mounted on it. The light blinks on and off throughout the play. On each side of the sawhorse is a YOUNG MAN *seated against the upstage wall. They both wear black pants, black shirts and vests, and black hats. They seem to be sleeping. Offstage is the sound of a single cricket, which lasts throughout the play. As the curtain rises there is a long pause, then a saw is heard offstage, then a hammer, then the saw again.*

MAN NUMBER ONE: *(Off left)* It's going to rain.

STU: Do you think so?

CHET: What?

STU: Uh, rain?

CHET: Oh . . . sure. Maybe.

STU: Could be.

CHET: Let's see.

(MAN NUMBER ONE *whistles as if calling a dog off left. Pause.*)

STU: It wouldn't be bad for my clothes.

CHET: Clothes?

STU: It'd be good for my clothes, I said. It'd be like taking a bath with my clothes on.

CHET: Sure. It'd be the same for me, I guess.

STU: Sure. Why don't you go over there and see if you can see any cloud formations?

(*He points downstage.* CHET *gets up and crosses downstage like an old man. He stands center and looks up at the sky, then speaks like an old man.*)

CHET: Well, well, well, well. I tell ya', boy. I tell ya'. Them's some dark ones, Mel. Them's really some dark ones.

STU: *(Talking like an old man)* Dark, eh? How long's it been since ya' seen 'em dark as that?

CHET: How long's it been? Long? How long?

STU: Yeah. How long a time, Clem?

CHET: Long a time? Well, it's been a piece. A piece a' time. Say maybe, off a year or so. Maybe that.

STU: A year, eh?

CHET: Yep. Could be longer.

STU: Longer?

CHET: Yep. Could be two or three year since I seen 'em all dark like that.

STU: That's a piece a' time, Clem. That's for sure.

CHET: Yep! Yep! *(He whistles loudly and starts doing a dance like an old man.)*

STU: *(Normal voice)* Hey! Come back!

(CHET stops short. He walks back upstage like an old man and sits in his original position. MAN NUMBER TWO whistles from off right. CHET and STU look in the direction of whistling, then at each other.)

You know what?

CHET: What?

STU: I think I'll take a look.

CHET: Okay.

(STU stands and walks downstage like an old man. He looks up at the sky and speaks like an old man.)

STU: By jingo! Them really is some dark ones.

CHET: Sure.

STU: Them's really dark like ya' said, Mel!

CHET: Dark as they come.

STU: All dark and puckery like—like—

CHET: Like what?

STU: Well . . .

CHET: Like what?

STU: *(To CHET, in a normal voice)* Would you give me a chance?

CHET: Like what?

STU: Give me a chance to figure like what. I haven't even thought of it yet. So give me a chance.

CHET: Okay.

(STU *turns back and looks at the sky; he looks for a while.*)

Have you decided?

(STU *turns back to* CHET.)

I'm sorry.

STU: Are you going to give me a chance or aren't you?

CHET: I said I'm sorry. So go ahead.

(STU *turns back and looks at the sky again.*)

STU: *(Old man)* By jingo, them's really some dark ones, eh, Mel?

CHET: Fuck.

STU: *(Turning suddenly to* CHET) Goddamn you!

CHET: Well, shit, why don't you say it? I'm not going to sit here all day.

STU: All right! *(He turns back very fast to the audience and looks at the sky; he says the lines rapidly).* By jingo, them's really some dark ones, eh, Mel? I haven't probably seen clouds as dark as them myself.

CHET: *(Stands and yells at* STU) So!

STU: *(Still facing the audience)* So it's important! Ya' got to notice things like that! It's important!

CHET: So!

STU: So ya' can stay alive or something. Ya' got to notice things like that.

CHET: Why?

STU: So ya' can tell when it's gonna' rain! So ya' can tell when it's gonna' snow. So ya' can tell when—when—so ya' can tell!

CHET: I seen 'em already!

STU: Good!

CHET: I seen 'em lots a' times in Utah and in other places.

STU: *(Turns to* CHET) So?

CHET: So I already seen 'em. If I already seen 'em, there ain't no point in me lookin' agin.

(CHET sits abruptly. There is a pause, then STU starts doing jumping calisthenics, clapping his hands over his head. He faces CHET as he does this.)

STU: Clap, clap, clap. Clapping, clapping. Clap.

CHET: What are you doing?

STU: This?

CHET: That.

STU: Oh. Well, you remember yesterday?

CHET: Yesterday what?

STU: Remember yesterday when I was sitting and my feet fell asleep?

CHET: Yeah.

STU: Well, this is for that.

CHET: Oh. To get the blood going and circulating?

STU: Yes. To get the blood going the way it should.

CHET: So it runs.

STU: So it runs.

CHET: So it doesn't stop and get clogged up?

STU: Right.

CHET: You know, you may have something like, uh, diabetes.

STU: *(Stops and looks at CHET)* Diabetes?

CHET: Yes. It may be a low sugar content.

STU: No. That's diabetes.

CHET: Yes.

STU: Well, that's what I don't have. *(He starts jumping again.)*

CHET: You don't know. You can't really tell.

(CHET gets up and crosses to STU. He walks around STU in a circle, talking to him as STU continues jumping.)

Diabetes is a strange thing. Very strange. It's been known to lie dormant for years, then one day it just pops up. And there you are.

(STU stops as CHET continues to walk around him.)

STU: Where?

CHET: There you are, lying in bed or sitting on a subway or walking down the street or eating a hamburger or drinking a Coke or smoking a cigarette.

STU: There I am.

CHET: There you are and you fall over.

(CHET *falls on the ground.* STU *stands looking down at him.*)

You fall out. You breathe harder and you get weaker and weaker. There was this kid I remember in junior high school. He had it. He collapsed one day right in math class. Just fell out of his chair and collapsed on the floor. Well, we had to bring him sugar. That's what it takes. Sugar. Each one of us had to go to the cafeteria and bring him back a bowl full of sugar. Each one of us.

STU: How did he do?

CHET: What?

STU: How did he pull through?

CHET: Oh. Shh!

STU: What?

CHET: Shh! Listen.

(CHET *stands slowly. They both stand facing the audience and listening. The sound of rain is heard faintly offstage; it builds as they continue the scene.*)

STU: Is it?

CHET: Sounds like it.

(*Smiling, they look up at the sky.*)

STU: I think it is.

(*They start doing a dance and laughing, slowly building and getting more hysterical.*)

CHET: It's them clouds!

STU: Rain! Rain, mother!

(*They take off their hats and wave them over their heads.*)

CHET: It's comin' down.

(*They become the old men again.*)

STU: Here we go!
CHET: Look at it!
STU: Rain, bitch! Rain!

(They laugh hysterically.)

CHET: My clothes!
STU: You could tell by them fuckin' clouds!
CHET: Rain on me!
STU: Come on, baby!
CHET: It's like the great flood of 1683!
STU: Everything's wet!
CHET: Wet all over!
STU: Look at the mud!
CHET: Mud!

(They fall on the floor and roll around in the imaginary mud.)

STU: Mud! You're beautiful!
CHET: All this mud!
STU: Mud all over!
CHET: Kiss me, mud!
STU: Dirty mud!
CHET: *Aaah!*
STU: Muddy, muddy!
CHET: Dirty gook!

(They kiss the floor and throw mud on each other.)

STU: Muck and slime!
CHET: *Aaah,* mud!
STU: Fucky, fuck!
CHET: Mud and guck!

(The rain sound stops suddenly.)

STU: Oh, mud.
CHET: Mud.
STU: Mud.

(They slowly stop laughing and roll over on their backs. They stare at the ceiling.)

CHET: You know, some girl asked me about the Big Dipper and I couldn't tell her.

STU: You couldn't tell her what?

CHET: I couldn't tell her anything about it. The big one.

STU: Is that the big one? *(He points to the ceiling.)*

CHET: That's what she asked me and I couldn't tell her, so how can I tell you?

STU: Is that the big one or the little one? *(A pause.)* Is that the big one or the little one?

CHET: It looks like the little one to me.

STU: Can't you tell? *(A pause.)* Can't you tell?

(CHET stands suddenly and walks upstage looking at the ceiling.)

You don't know?

CHET: I said before that it looks like the little one. I said that. Now what?

STU: Then it is the little one, isn't it?

CHET: I guess! Yes! Why not?

(STU stands and walks up to CHET. CHET walks around the stage looking up at the ceiling as STU follows close behind him.)

STU: It should be the little one, if you say it's the little one.

CHET: I guess.

STU: I guess it is, Chet.

CHET: I guess it is, Stu.

STU: You're probably right. I've never seen either one really, so I can't tell.

CHET: I've never seen them together.

STU: They don't come out together, do they?

CHET: I don't know.

STU: That's the only way to compare them. To see them together.

CHET: I guess.

STU: That looks like the little one though.

(CHET turns suddenly to STU; they stare at each other. MAN NUMBER ONE and MAN NUMBER TWO whistle back and forth across the stage, then stop.)

CHET: *(Old man's voice)* Clem, I thought we was in the Red Valley.
STU: *(Old man's voice)* Red Valley? That's right, Mel. This here's the Red Valley area.
CHET: Is that right?
STU: That's right, boy. Come on down here.

(STU leads CHET downstage center. They look out over the audience.)

CHET: What?
STU: Come on. Now see that? *(He points off in the distance.)*
CHET: What?
STU: See all that out there? That area all out in there?
CHET: Yep.
STU: That's it, Clem.
CHET: This whole area's the Red Valley?

(The sound of horses running can be heard faintly offstage.)

STU: That's right, Mel.
CHET: This here's the same Red Valley you was referrin' to back in Des Moines?
STU: This here's the very same area.

(The horses get louder.)

CHET: The very same place? Clem, I think you was either lyin' to me or you was misinformed somehow.
STU: How's that, Mel?
CHET: Listen.

(The horses get louder.)

STU: What's that?
CHET: Well, that's what I mean.
STU: What?
CHET: That.

(He points in the distance. The sound of Indians screaming joins in with the horses and becomes very loud.)

STU: Damn.

CHET: We got to do somethin', boy.

STU: Get down behind them barrels and get out yer rifle.

(They kneel down and hold imaginary rifles.)

CHET: Sure is a lot of 'em, Clem.

STU: Well, we can hold 'em for a while.

CHET: Don't have much ammo . . .

STU: We'll fight 'em with our rifle butts after that.

(The sound offstage gets very loud and is joined by gunfire.)

CHET: Wait till they get up close.

STU: Okay.

CHET: Okay. Fire!

(They make gun noises and fire at imaginary Indians.)

STU: Fire!

CHET: Fire!

STU: Damn! Look like Apaches!

CHET: Some of 'em's Comanches, Clem!

STU: Fire!

CHET: Good boy, ya' got him!

STU: Fire!

CHET: Got him again. One shot apiece, Clem.

STU: Get 'em, Mel.

CHET: Fire! Got me a brave! Got me a brave!

STU: Good boy!

CHET: Thought he was fancy, ridin' a pinto.

STU: Your left, Clem. Got him! Tore him up!

CHET: Good boy. Got him in the head that time. Right in the head. Watch it!

STU: Fire!

CHET: 'Atta baby!

(STU grabs his shoulder, screams and falls back. CHET stands and yells out at the audience, firing his rifle.)

You lousy redskinned punks! Think you can injure my buddy? Lousy red assholes! Come back and fight!

(The sound fades out. CHET *pulls* STU *upstage and props him up against the wall.)*

STU: My arm . . .

CHET: Ya' okay, boy?

STU: Got me in the arm.

CHET: Take it easy. Easy. I'll take care a' ya', boy. Take it easy.

STU: Redskins all over.

CHET: Red Valley area. (CHET *rolls* STU's *sleeve up and breaks off an imaginary arrow.)* Easy, boy.

STU: My arm . . .

CHET: I'll get it. Gonna' be okay.

STU: Bad arm.

CHET: Bloody, blood.

STU: Mud.

*(*CHET *crosses downstage center. He kneels down on the edge of the stage and takes his hat off. He dips his hat in an imaginary stream as though the edge of the stage were the bank.)*

CHET: Water. Gonna' get ya' some a' this. *(He pours water on his head from the hat. He dips his hat again and pours more water on his head.)* Good water. *Aaah.* All sweet and everything.

(He dips his hat again and carries the hat carefully upstage. He throws the water in STU's *face.* STU *jumps up. They talk in normal voices.)*

STU: What the fuck are you doing!

CHET: I was—I was trying to cool you off.

STU: Thanks.

CHET: Okay.

STU: I don't need it.

CHET: Oh.

STU: I'm cool already.

CHET: Oh.

STU: So thanks anyway.

CHET: That's all right.

(STU crosses downstage center and sits. He takes off his shoes and socks and puts his feet in the stream. He sits on the edge of the stage. A pause. CHET remains upstage looking at STU.)

STU: Nice.

CHET: What?

STU: Air.

CHET: Air?

STU: Yep. Used to be lots of orange orchards around here, you know.

CHET: Really?

STU: Yep. Lots. All over. You could smell them.

CHET: I guess. I'm sorry about the water.

STU: They were all over. Then they cut them all down, one at a time. Every one. Built schools for kids and homes for old flabby ladies and halls for heroes and streets for cars and houses for people.

CHET: I was trying to cool you off, Stu.

STU: Then buses for kids to go to the schools and buses to take them back. Peacocks. Peacocks for mansions. For gardens. Peacocks screaming like mothers and daughters. Peacocks screwing on top of people's houses. Peacocks shitting in people's driveways. On people's cars. They can hardly fly. Fat, ugly birds with no wings and overlong tails. Tail feathers that people put in vases and set on top of fireplaces and dust collects on them. They dust them off. Green feathers with eyes in the middle. Blue eyes in the middle of green feathers. You can't eat peacocks. They're too tough.

CHET: I'm sorry, Stu.

STU: Pheasant is the thing they eat.

CHET: Stu?

(Car horns are heard offstage. STU stands and looks out over the audience.)

STU: Bird of paradise. That's a flower. They grow like that. Acres full of bird of paradise. Truck comes by in the morning and picks them up.. They take them to another town and sell them. They go in vases, too. Peacock feathers and bird of paradise. They just leave them in vases and let the stems rot and the water gets all smelly and green.

(He picks up his shoes and socks and crosses slowly upstage. He walks backward looking at the audience; as he does this CHET *slowly crosses downstage, also looking out at the audience.)*

They have turtles, too. Turtles, with painted shells from the county fair. A dozen turtles in bowls and pans, with water and rocks and turtle food floating around. Then the turtles die and the water gets all green and slimy and smells. The whole house starts smelling from dead turtles and rotten stems and slimy water. Pens full of sheep and lambs. Chicken coops with chicken-do hanging in the wire. The chickens walk all over it and through it. Their feet rot after a while from walking in their own crap so much.

(Car horns are heard offstage.)

They start eating it after a while, and it gets inside them and infects their throat and their liver. Their livers rot and their feathers fall out. Their skin gets all blue and pus starts coming out their noses. They bleed from the mouth and can't control their bowels. It just runs out of them like water. They lie there in a pool of shit and pus and feathers and cluck. It's a little cluck in the back of their throat. Their wings throb and they make this clucking sound and they just lie there.

*(*CHET *sits on the edge of the stage.* STU *lies down on his back upstage. The car horns continue. There is a long pause.)*

CHET: It's a nice morning though. *(He takes off his shoes and socks and puts his feet in the stream.)*

STU: Hm.

CHET: I like mornings. Any kind of morning. You know what I like best about mornings? Hey, Stu!

STU: Hm?

CHET: Do you know what I like about mornings more than anything?

STU: What?

CHET: Food. All the different kinds of food.

STU: Food's food.

CHET: Not in the morning. Food is more than food in the morning.

STU: It's breakfast food.

CHET: I wasn't talking about any kind of food. I was talking about food being different in the morning because you're most hungry in the morning.

STU: Why?

CHET: Because you haven't eaten all night. So when you get up, you're really hungry.

STU: I see.

CHET: You know, I could go for some breakfast.

STU: Already?

CHET: Yep. Some scrambled eggs and hot chocolate and toast. Rye toast.

STU: This early?

CHET: Sure. Some farina. Hot farina with cold milk and prune juice. Maybe some pancakes, with butter and maple syrup and powdered sugar. About ten pancakes on top of each other. You know, they have all different kinds of cereals here. Cold and hot. Cornflakes, Rice Krispies, oatmeal, Sugar Corn Pops, farina, Malto-Meal, Nutrina, Purina, and many others.

(Car horns sound offstage. While CHET *continues speaking,* MAN NUMBER ONE *and* MAN NUMBER TWO *carry on their conversation. They are unseen.)*

CHET: And eggs. Poached eggs on toast, with hot milk and butter, and when you break the yolks the yellow part drips down into the hot milk and mixes with the toast. Salt and pepper and coffee and hot chocolate. Then just something plain on the side. A little sour cream maybe, on the eggs. Then some sausage. Bacon. Or eggs sunny side up and turned over lightly. Some hashbrown potatoes fried in deep butter. A tall glass of milk with water on the outside of the glass. Then two glasses of water and another cup of coffee and some cigarettes.

MAN NUMBER ONE: The rent's down to a dollar a month now.

MAN NUMBER TWO: Oh yeah? How did you manage that?

MAN NUMBER ONE: Something about the City Health Department or Rent Commission.

MAN NUMBER TWO: Well, that's good.

MAN NUMBER ONE: I guess so.

MAN NUMBER TWO: We got enough food to last for a while.

MAN NUMBER ONE: Sure.

MAN NUMBER TWO: Don't take much to live on.

MAN NUMBER ONE: A buck a month.

(More car horns. CHET sits looking out over the audience. He smells his armpits, then his feet.)

You know, Stu, we really stink. We really do. My feet smell like cheese. Blue cheese. It's really strong.

(He picks his toes.)

MAN NUMBER TWO: That's as cheap as you can get.

MAN NUMBER ONE: I guess so.

MAN NUMBER TWO: I guess for free would be cheaper.

It's toe-jam. That's what they call it. That's what stinks. It's not our feet. It's the toe-jam. Whew! *(He lies back.)* It's in our clothes, too. My clothes smell just like my body smells, only worse. Sweat. *(He sits up and looks at the sky.)* We're going to go on sweating, too. In this sun we're going to go on sweating and smelling more and more. *(He squints his eyes and looks at the sun.)* It's just morning and look at the sun. It's really early. *(He stands suddenly still, looking out.)* Hey, Stu! It's morning and look at the sun already. What time is it, Stu? *(He turns upstage.)* Stu!

(He turns back very slowly toward the audience and becomes an old man again, shielding his eyes from the sun. MAN NUMBER ONE and MAN NUMBER TWO whistle back and forth, then stop.)

Well, well, well. The sun's up already and it ain't even time. It's early yet. It's comin' down, boy. That heat. It's gettin' hot, Mel. I seen it like this before. *(He turns and runs upstage to STU.)* Mel, ya' got to get up, boy. Ya' got to get up now. *(He shakes STU by the shoulder.)* Enough sleep! We got to look for some water, boy! *(He turns to the audience.)* You don't seem to realize the situation, Mel. We're in fer some heat. We're in fer some hot days now, and we got to find water. All right! All right! I'll look fer the water and you sleep. Don't move, boy. Just sleep and I'll get the water. *(He pulls his vest up over his head and wanders around the stage searching.)* Where shall we look? Can't exert. Got to save our strength. *(He paces back and forth.)* Good thing we got a lot a' clothes, otherwise we'd be sunburned to death. Oh, it's really hot. It's really hot. I wonder how hot it is right now. Must be ninety at least.

What if it's ninety, Mel? If it's ninety that means it could get up to a hundred or a hundred and ten or a hundred and twenty. We'll be scorched and boiled. We got to find some shade. Mel! *(He switches to his normal voice.)* Okay, Stu, this isn't funny. I don't think it's funny. You're going to sleep all day while I bust my ass looking for shade? Come on. I'll get you into some shade.

(He drags STU slowly downstage as the lights come up very slowly; the lights should reach their full brightness at the end of the play. Car horns are heard softly offstage.)

Come on down here. There's better shade down here. Come on, boy. That's it. Let me get ya' some water. *(He dips his hat in the stream and pours it over STU's face; he does the same to himself. He looks up at the sky, then stands slowly. He talks like an old man.)* By jingo, looky there. We're really in trouble, Mel. Them birds. See them birds, Mel? See what they're doing? I seen them things in Utah. Vultures. Condors or somethin'. Mean, nasty birds. They eat cows, Mel. I seen 'em eat a whole goddamn cow like it weren't nothin'. Come on, come on. *(He drags STU back upstage.)* Got to get ya' back. Get ya' in the other shade.

(The horses and Indians join with car horns offstage and build in volume to the end of the play.)

Better shade back here. Gettin' worse, Mel. Can't feel my tongue no more. Worse. Need some shelter, boy. *(He stands and yells at the birds.)* Get away from here, you mothers! This ain't funny! *(He runs downstage, waving his hat at the birds.)* This ain't no joke, you shitty birds! What do ya' think this is? TV or somethin'? I ain't gettin' et by no vultures. Get out!

(He runs upstage and drags STU back downstage again. As he does this MAN NUMBER ONE and MAN NUMBER TWO come on from opposite sides of the stage with scripts in their hands. They are both dressed in suits and are the same age as CHET and STU. They read from the scripts in monotone, starting from the beginning of the play. The sound builds to its full loudness; the lights come up all the way as CHET continues.)

Better shade, boy. Shade down here. Take it easy. Easy. Come on, boy. *(He takes off his shirt and vest and covers* STU's *head with them. He kneels, looking out at the audience.)* Keep the sun off. Got to keep it off. Sunburn. Tongue's cracked down the middle. All around the edges, Stu. Get away, birds! Get outa' here! This ain't the place! Go look fer some cows! Get out! Get out!

(The sound offstage stops suddenly. CHET *stares at the sky.* MAN NUMBER ONE *and* MAN NUMBER TWO *continue reading in monotone as the lights dim down.)*

CURTAIN

Forensic & the Navigators

Forensic & the Navigators was first produced at Theatre Genesis on December 29, 1967, with the following cast:

FORENSIC:	Bob Schlee
EMMET:	Lee Kissman
OOLAN:	O-Lan Johnson-Shepard
1ST EXTERMINATOR:	Walter Hadler
2ND EXTERMINATOR:	Beeson Carroll

The production was directed by Ralph Cook.

SCENE

Black space. A small table center stage with a long white linen tablecloth that goes almost to the floor. An old-fashioned oil lamp in the center of the table. Two office-type swivel chairs at opposite ends of the table facing each other. FORENSIC *sits in the stage-right chair with a notepad and pen in front of him. He has long blond hair, a brown cowboy hat, a long red scarf, a black leather vest, jeans and moccasins.* EMMET *sits at the other end of the table with a small portable typewriter in front of him with paper in it. He has long black hair, a green Cherokee headband, beads around his neck, a serape, jeans, and cowboy boots. An elaborate Indian peace pipe sits in the center of the table in a large glass ashtray. The stage is black. Sound of* EMMET's *typewriter clacking. Silence. Whole cast sing in the dark.*

WHOLE CAST:
    We gonna be born again. Oh Lord.
    We gonna get born again. Good Lord.
    We gonna be born again.
    Lord have mercy now.

    We gonna be saved tonight. Oh Lord.
    We gonna get saved tonight. Good Lord.
    We gonna be saved tonight.
    Lord have mercy now.

(They sing both verses three times through, then stop short. Silence. Sound of EMMET's *typewriter. The oil lamp slowly glows and becomes brighter. The light comes up full. As the characters become visible, they both relax from their writing and lean back in the chairs like executives. They stare at each other.)*

FORENSIC: Where's that woman, Emmet? Ya' can't count on her to get ya' a hot meal on the table afore six A.M., then could ya' tell me what kinda' good is she? Tell me that one, Emmet.

(EMMET *just stares at* FORENSIC, *then begins to type.*)

So far as you're concerned we're really cutting out of here. I take it that that's the story so far. Do I take it right, Emmet? Right or wrong? Do I take it right or wrong?

(*He stands and slams his fist on the table.* EMMET *stops typing and looks at* FORENSIC.)

Boy, I'll cut you down! Answer me right or wrong!

EMMET: If you have to be stubborn, do it outside, Forensic. I'm writing a letter.

FORENSIC: Who to then? Tell me that much. Jesus, I feel so far out of what's going on since you and everyone else decides we ain't goin' through with a whole plan that's been goin' on since we was ten years old.

EMMET: Sit.

(FORENSIC *sits.*)

Now, I'm writing to my mother and for me to do that I have to have my wits. Would you like a smoke?

FORENSIC: Your mother. Jesus. All right. I'll light it.

(*He picks up the peace pipe and lights it.*)

EMMET: It's no good being disappointed, Forensic. We've been through that. We have to just lay low for a while. We need you a lot so don't go feeling left out of things. Right now we have to take care of certain business. We have to transfer the guns and the equipment. We have to individually escape. We have to be quiet. We have to do these things before we make any moves. If we make any other moves we're screwed and that's the end of that. We have to switch our sensibilities so that we're not even pretending. So that we are transformed for a time and see no difference in the way we are from the way we were. We have to believe ourselves.

FORENSIC: Here.

(He hands the pipe to EMMET, *who smokes it.)*

It's just chicken, Emmet, and you know it. It's downright yellow and cowardly. We could blow that whole place up in less time than it would take to go through a sensibility switch. Besides, there's people in there now who are really trapped for real. What about them? We're out here switching disguises while they only think of ways to escape. We could blow that whole motherfucker sky high and you know it.

EMMET: Here.

(He hands the pipe to FORENSIC, *who smokes.)*

Don't talk like a dumb kid, Forensic. You got any idea whatsoever what this project looks like from the outside, objectively, without emotion? Why, it looks overwhelming, Forensic. It's a fucking desert fortress is what it amounts to. They've rebuilt it since the time of the Japanese, you know. It's not the same camp at all. New plumbing, double inlaid wire fencing that fronts a steel wall thirty feet high without doors.

FORENSIC: How do they get in, then, and what difference does the plumbing make?

EMMET: By helicopter and the plumbing difference is that since its reconstruction we have no idea what the design is underground, which makes internal explosions almost out of the question.

FORENSIC: Then bomb the motherfucker.

EMMET: And kill all the inmates. RIGHT! BOMB THE MOTHERFUCKER AND KILL ALL THE INMATES! THAT'S WHAT YOU'RE SAYING! THAT'S WHAT YOU'RE SAYING, FORENSIC! OUT OF MY SIGHT! GET OUT OF MY SIGHT! I DON'T WANT TO SEE YOU EVER AGAIN!

(He stands and lunges for FORENSIC *as* OOLAN *enters wearing a white hospital gown such as is worn by the insane, and sandals on her feet. She holds a frying pan with a single pancake in it. She circles the table flipping the pancake and catching it in the pan.)*

OOLAN: You boys should have told me what hour it was getting to be. Why, my goodness sakes, I look at the clock and the time is getting to be way past the time for you boys' breakfast. And you both know how uptight the two of you get when breakfast isn't just exactly when you get the most hungry. So here it is. Hot and ready.

(She flips pancake onto the table. FORENSIC and EMMET stare at the pancake as OOLAN smiles. EMMET sits back in his chair. OOLAN picks up the pipe and smokes it.)

EMMET: How many times I gotta' tell you I don't eat that buckwheat Aunt Jemima middle-class bullshit. I want Rice Krispies and nothing else. Is that clear?

FORENSIC: Get that pancake off the conference table, you stupid girl.

OOLAN: Here.

(She hands the pipe to FORENSIC, then picks up the pancake and eats it slowly as she watches them.)

FORENSIC: Emmet, you're as soft and flabby as you say your enemies are.

EMMET: You're pretty much of a shit yourself. Shit face.

(A loud knock that sounds like somebody banging on a steel door with a sledgehammer. EMMET and FORENSIC stand suddenly and pull out small ray guns they have concealed in their crotches. EMMET motions to OOLAN to answer.)

OOLAN: I can't, my mouth is full.

(Another loud knock. EMMET motions again, more angry this time. OOLAN forces the pancake down and fixes her hair. She faces upstage and answers.)

Who is it? Just one moment, please.

(Another loud knock. EMMET motions again, really mad. OOLAN crosses upstage.)

Yes. Hello. Who is it, please?

EXTERMINATOR'S VOICE: IT'S THE EXTERMINATOR, LADY!

(She looks at EMMET, *who waves his ray gun and shakes his head.)*

OOLAN: Um—we don't want any. Thank you anyway.

EXTERMINATOR'S VOICE: DON'T WANT ANY WHAT? IT'S THE EX-
TERMINATOR. OPEN UP!

OOLAN: OK. Wait just a second.

(She turns to EMMET *and shrugs her shoulders.* EMMET *and* FORENSIC *duck under the tablecloth and disappear. Another loud knock.)*

Coming! Just hold tight.

(Two huge men appear in the light. They are dressed like California Highway Patrolmen, with gold helmets, gas masks, khaki pants and shirts, badges, boots, gloves, and pistols. They carry large tanks on their backs with hose and nozzle attachments which they hold in their hands. They just stand there and look around the room.)

Um—we haven't had any rats here since last February, March, around in there.

1ST EXTERMINATOR: Well, they told us to cover the place from top to bottom.

2ND EXTERMINATOR: You'll have to leave, ma'am.

OOLAN: Fuck you. This is my home.

*(*EMMET'S VOICE *is heard from under the table.)*

EMMET'S VOICE: Cool it, Oolan.

(The EXTERMINATORS *wander around, casing the joint.)*

OOLAN: Um—don't you think you had better check it out with your home
office and see if you got the right place? I mean it would be awful if
you got the wrong place. Don't you think? What do you think, fellas?

1ST EXTERMINATOR: This is exactly the place, little girl.

2ND EXTERMINATOR: The table gives it away. Without the table or with
the table in another place maybe it would be cause to call the home
office. But with the table in the place it is and looking the way it does
there is absolutely no doubt we have the right place.

(They both turn upstage to adjust nozzles and synchronize watches. As they do this FORENSIC and EMMET lift the table from underneath and move it upstage right so the table looks as though it moves by itself.)

1ST EXTERMINATOR: Now we have to synchronize our watches and adjust our nozzles and get ourselves ready.

2ND EXTERMINATOR: You'd better get out of here, lady. Without a gas mask you're as good as dead.

(FORENSIC'S VOICE is heard from under the table.)

FORENSIC'S VOICE: Sing something, Oolan.

OOLAN: What?

EMMET: Anything.

(OOLAN starts singing "Ahab the Arab" and looking at the audience. The EXTERMINATORS turn and cross to OOLAN. She keeps singing and smiles at them. They see the table and cross up right and stare at it. They cross back to OOLAN and stare at her, then back to the table. This happens several times as OOLAN sings:)

AHAB THE ARAB

Well, let me tell you 'bout Ahab the Arab, the sheik of the burning
    sands,
He had emeralds and rubies just a drippin' offa' him and a ring on
    every finger of his hand.
He wore a big old turban wrapped around his head and a scimitar
    by his side,
And every evening about midnight he'd jump on his camel named
    Clyde.

And he'd ride,
Thru the desert night, to the Sultan's tent
Where he would secretly make love to Fatima of the seventh veil.
And as he rode, he sang:
Yodli yadli yidli i o,
Nyodli nyadli i o.
Which is Arabic for "Whoa, Clyde."

And Clyde, he say:
Nghee hgraargh norchghhh hargghh
(grunting noises)
Which is camel for "OK, baby."

Well, he brought his camel to a screeching halt
In the rear of Fatima's tent.
Jumped off Clyde, ducked around the corner,
And into the tent he went.

There he saw Fatima,
Layin' on a zebra skin rug.
With rings on her fingers and bells on her toes,
And a bone in her nose. Ho-Ho . . .

by RAY STEVENS

1ST EXTERMINATOR: ALL RIGHT, STOP THAT SINGING!

(OOLAN stops and giggles.)

Now what happened to that table, lady?

(OOLAN turns around and looks at the table.)

OOLAN: Oh my god!

(She faints in the arms of the 2ND EXTERMINATOR, who catches her.)

2ND EXTERMINATOR: Great.

1ST EXTERMINATOR: Well, put her down, you dope.

(He lets OOLAN fall to the floor.)

2ND EXTERMINATOR: We gotta think fast, Forensic, or we're screwed.

1ST EXTERMINATOR: What did you call me? Forensic? Is that what you
called me? What kind of name is that?

2ND EXTERMINATOR: I don't know. I don't know what came over me.

1ST EXTERMINATOR: Now look. Didn't you and I both see that table over
here when we first came in here?

2ND EXTERMINATOR: Gee, I don't know.

1ST EXTERMINATOR: What do you mean? Wasn't it you that said we could tell we were in the right place on account of the table being where it was, which was right here, not over there. Wasn't it you who said that to her? Answer me, mushmouth. Was it me or you?

2ND EXTERMINATOR: It was me, but it still seems like the right place even with the table over there.

1ST EXTERMINATOR: But we can't be sure now. Before, we could be absolutely sure, but now there's some doubt. Am I right? Am I right or wrong!

2ND EXTERMINATOR: I guess.

1ST EXTERMINATOR: So that means we'll have to call the home office before we can make another move. Am I right? Where's your phone, lady?

2ND EXTERMINATOR: She's fainted or something.

(EMMET'S VOICE *is heard from under the table.*)

EMMET'S VOICE: There's a pay phone just down the road.

1ST EXTERMINATOR: There's probably a pay phone just down the road, so why don't you go down there and call while I stay here?

2ND EXTERMINATOR: Down the road?

1ST EXTERMINATOR: Yeah. Now hurry up! I'm going to be right here waiting. Just ask them if it makes any difference where the table is.

2ND EXTERMINATOR: OK. You're going to wait here?

1ST EXTERMINATOR: Yeah. Now move!

(2ND EXTERMINATOR *exits.* 1ST EXTERMINATOR *looks around, then moves over to* OOLAN, *who is still on the floor. He stares at her, then takes off his helmet and gas mask. He takes off the tank and then kneels down beside* OOLAN *with his back to the table. He stares at* OOLAN's *face for a while, then touches her shoulder. The table suddenly moves downstage, right behind* 1ST EXTERMINATOR. *He kisses* OOLAN *on the forehead, then takes off his gun belt and holster. He lies down beside* OOLAN *and stares at her, then puts his arm around her.* FORENSIC *and* EMMET *come out from under the table very quietly and slowly.* 1ST EXTERMINATOR *kisses* OOLAN *on the lips.* FORENSIC *picks up the tank and gas mask.* EMMET *picks up the gun and holster.* 1ST EXTERMINATOR *pulls* OOLAN *close to him and hugs her.* EMMET *puts on the gun while* FORENSIC *puts on the tank and gas mask. This all happens while* 1ST EXTERMINATOR *squeezes* OOLAN *and kisses her and strokes her hair.*)

Oh my darling. You mustn't worry now. We'll get you out. I'll get you far away to a safe place where we can be quiet and you won't even know. Just relax. All you'll see is smoke filling up the valley. We'll be very high up. Don't you worry about that. It was a tree house but now it's a fort. It's very strong and beautiful. You can trust it to keep you safe and sound. It's colored just like the trees. Orange and yellow and green and blue. And it makes sounds like birds and dogs and wild boar. Really. If anyone comes you can see them from two miles off. You can signal to me if I'm not around. But I always will be. I'll never leave for a second. You can count on me. If you could only see me now I know you'd believe me. If you could wake up in my arms and act like I was supposed to be here. Like I was always here and always will be. If you could wake up like that then we could go away from here now. Right this very minute. We could leave and live in the trees.

(EMMET *has the gun on* 1ST EXTERMINATOR. FORENSIC *points the nozzle at him.*)

EMMET: All right, Big Bopper, on your feet.

(1ST EXTERMINATOR *jumps to his feet and raises his hands.* OOLAN *gets up.*)

OOLAN: What a nasty rotten trick.
FORENSIC: Shut up!

(FORENSIC *crosses to* 1ST EXTERMINATOR, *holding the nozzle on him.*)

So you're a lover in disguise. Is that it, Big Bopper? You're really full of pizzazz but you just got led astray. Is that the story?
1ST EXTERMINATOR: Don't press that nozzle!
EMMET: Just keep your hands raised up there.
OOLAN: Don't press that nozzle! We'll all go up in flame!
FORENSIC: It's not a torch. It's gas. Toxic gas. Highly poison toxic gas that when you breathe it you're dead right away.
1ST EXTERMINATOR: Don't be ridiculous.

FORENSIC: WHAT! WHAT DID YOU SAY, SMART ALECK! DON'T GET SMART, MISTER, OR I'LL GAS YOUR ASS!

EMMET: Take it easy, Forensic.

FORENSIC: Well, he's a wise guy.

1ST EXTERMINATOR: That gas is for roaches, rats and varmints. Not people. It just gets you sick and makes your eyes water.

FORENSIC: What?

EMMET: Wait a minute. Now just take it easy.

FORENSIC: He's trying to come off like a killer of pests and bugs.

EMMET: Just don't get excited. We might find out something. Are you hungry, mister?

1ST EXTERMINATOR: No.

EMMET: Well, I am. Would you mind if the two of us sat down at the table and I ate some Rice Krispies while I ask you some questions?

1ST EXTERMINATOR: All right.

FORENSIC: What is this?

EMMET: Go fetch the Rice Krispies, Oolan.

OOLAN: You know he has a friend somewhere out there in a phone booth who's going to come back here.

EMMET: Just get the Krispies, woman!

OOLAN: Jesus.

(She exits.)

EMMET: Now set yourself down here, mister. Come on. Just fold your hands on top of your head.

(1ST EXTERMINATOR clasps his hands on top of his head and sits in the stage-left chair. EMMET keeps the gun on him and sits in the stage-right chair.)

FORENSIC: Now what am I supposed to do, goddammit?

EMMET: Now then, mister, I take it you've come a long way. Not just from down the block or down the road.

1ST EXTERMINATOR: Well, yes. I mean, that depends.

EMMET: I take it you have certain tools at your disposal which provide photographs and details of our layout here. Like table positions, et cetera.

1ST EXTERMINATOR: That goes without saying. What's the name of that girl?

EMMET: I'll give you a hint. It sounds like it might have something to do
with tea but it doesn't.

FORENSIC: What the fuck am I supposed to do?

1ST EXTERMINATOR: Darjeeling?

EMMET: Now your home office must be getting pretty edgy to send a couple toughs like you, all equipped and everything. Hot and ready.
They must suspect a move on our part but the amazement is that we
have no idea they had any interest in our project whatsoever. I mean
you just show up out of the clear blue sky. We don't even have any
dogs.

1ST EXTERMINATOR: Dogs?

EMMET: Doberman pinschers, German shepherds, wire-haired pointing
griffons circling the place, sniffing for trouble, ready to tear out a
throat on those that smell of a different turf. Do you understand? No
young blond dopey muscle boys practicing jujitsu on the front lawn.
We're vulnerable as all get-out. We've left ourselves with our drawers
down. That gives you all the room to plunge in and you have. Which
means for us that we temporarily have to abandon the idea of temporarily abandoning the project and throw ourselves once again into
the meat of the game. You've forced our hand, as it were.

(1ST EXTERMINATOR *takes his hands down.* FORENSIC *starts circling the stage
restlessly with the gas mask and tank still on.*)

EMMET: Keep up those hands.

FORENSIC: We don't need this. I'm telling you. We're not going to find out
anything more or better by interrogation than we are by going out
there and seeing for ourselves what the place looks like. What its po-
tentials are for collapsing. We can't sit around all abstracted out of
shape while they lie stacked up on top of each other behind steel
doors. It just isn't fair.

1ST EXTERMINATOR: What's her approximate age?

EMMET: Thirty-two, twenty-one, thirty.

1ST EXTERMINATOR: Does she see many boys? Young ones? Do they come
to her door? Do they sit outside in the driveway honking in their Co-
bras with their right arm coaxing and kneading and fondling the tuck
and roll and their left hand pumping, squeezing on the wheel?

EMMET: Do you have a master's degree, mister?

1ST EXTERMINATOR: Not at all.

EMMET: What qualifies you then for a job in the line of gassing?

1ST EXTERMINATOR: I'm past my prime.

FORENSIC: So he goes for the skirt, does he? Perhaps we could make a deal.

EMMET: Forget it, Forensic. We got her out of there once, or don't you remember? Now you want to start the whole thing over. Put her in a position for being taken back. You don't think clearly. BOMB THE MOTHERFUCKERS! We got her out and she stays out and she ain't going back for no kind of deal. Not even for the most precise, delicate ground plan of the new plumbing system that they just recently put in. Not even for that.

1ST EXTERMINATOR: You mean to say that you'd consider some sort of trade? Some information for her inspiration. I'll do it, by jove. I'll do it just as sure as you're standing there.

EMMET: Keep those hands up.

(FORENSIC *tears off the gas mask and the tank and lays them on the floor. He goes to the table.*)

FORENSIC: Now you're talking.

(EMMET *stands and paces around.* FORENSIC *takes his place in the chair facing* 1ST EXTERMINATOR, *who takes his hands down and slowly begins to stroke himself and grope his own crotch.*)

EMMET: Out of the question. Absolutely out of the question. We can't jeopardize her position. It's ridiculous. She'd be right back in solitary or something worse. She'd be stacked up right along with the rest of them.

FORENSIC: Big Bopper, you are on the brink of having for your very own the hottest little discotheque mama ever to come on the set.

(OOLAN *enters with a bowl, milk and a box of Rice Krispies. She crosses to the table.*)

EMMET: Oh good. It's about time. Bring it down here.

(*He crosses down right and sits cross-legged on the floor.* OOLAN *goes and stands beside him.*)

1ST EXTERMINATOR: Oh that's fantastic. I'll tell you anything.

FORENSIC: OK, first off, do you have a map of the plant?

1ST EXTERMINATOR: Map? Map. Yes I do. Of course I do. But I don't think the plumbing is included in the detail. I mean . . .

(He pulls out a map and hands it across the table to FORENSIC, *then goes on groping himself as he watches* OOLAN.*)*

FORENSIC: Let me see it. Come on, come on.

*(*FORENSIC *opens the map and spreads it on the table in front of him.)*

OOLAN: Emmet, you'll never in a million years guess what I just a little while ago figured out in the kitchen.

EMMET: Come on, come on. Krispies, woman. Gimme Krispies.

OOLAN: I know, but it's about that. It's about Krispies and the complaint you've had against them all these years. The complaint being that you always lose a few of them because as soon as you add milk to a full bowl they rise up and overflow the bowl and fall on the floor. So what you've had to do all this time is fill the bowl half-full, add the milk, mush the half-filled bowl down into the milk so they get soggy and don't rise, then add more fresh Krispies on top of those and then a little more milk and then mush the fresh ones down so that the whole bowl is soggy and then finally add the sugar and then finally you get to taste the very first spoonful after having gone through that long painful process.

EMMET: Yes, I know, I know. That why I always have good woman fix Krispies so that man not have to go through so much pain.

OOLAN: I know, but what I'm saying is that I've solved that whole problem.

EMMET: Good, good.

OOLAN: I'll show you how to do it.

EMMET: Good.

OOLAN: OK, now first I pour the Krispies in. All the way full.

(She fills the bowl with Rice Krispies.)

Now I put both my hands gently but firmly on top of the Krispies like this.

(She puts her hands on the Krispies and looks at EMMET.)

EMMET: Yeah?

OOLAN: Now you pour the milk.

EMMET: Over your hands?

OOLAN: Yes. Go ahead. Don't be afraid.

EMMET: I don't want somebody's grimy hands in my cereal.

OOLAN: Just pour the milk.

(EMMET picks up the milk and pours it over OOLAN's hands. She smiles at him.
He sets down the milk and looks at her. She takes her hands off the cereal.)

See?

(EMMET picks up a spoon and starts eating ravenously as FORENSIC speaks.)

FORENSIC: Listen here, this is no use to us. It's all in some sort of code or
something. Everything's mixed up, according to this. Hey, what are
you doing? Hey! Hands above the table, mister. HANDS ABOVE
THE TABLE!

(1ST EXTERMINATOR quickly puts his hands on the table and faces FORENSIC.)

Look, you're going to have to earn this woman, mister. This map
doesn't show anything whatsoever where the central stockade is,
where the ammunition's kept, where the officers stay, where the
guard towers are, where the electric source is, not to mention food
and what means of transportation they have in case of a pursuit.
None of that's down here. How do you account for that? What's this
map for?

1ST EXTERMINATOR: I don't know. They hand it to us. The first day we get
uniforms, helmets, guns, tanks, gas, and they hand us that map. One
apiece. We each get one to study when we go home. We each are told
to memorize the details of this map and to make sure we have them
by the next morning because we are going to be thoroughly tested
and retested on these details. But we never are. Each morning we're
never tested and each evening we're threatened that we will be tested
the next morning. But we never are.

(He puts his hands down and starts groping again.)

FORENSIC: Ah ha! I get the picture.

(He picks up the map, stands, walks around the table to 1ST EXTERMINATOR and begins interrogating him. OOLAN just watches EMMET as he devours the Rice Krispies. Each time he finishes a bowlful she fills the bowl again and he goes on eating.)

Let's just see what kind of homework you claim you've been doing then. You wouldn't mind that, I'm sure. After all, you've studied so hard night after night and each morning you've been disappointed. So it's about time you had a chance to show your stuff. Don't you think?

1ST EXTERMINATOR: Does she care about things like popularity and letter-men's jackets?

FORENSIC: Now pay attention, swabbie!

(1ST EXTERMINATOR snaps to attention in his seat. He salutes and puts his hands on the table. FORENSIC circles him with the map in his hands.)

EMMET: Good. Krispies. Good.

FORENSIC: What's the capital of the state of Arizona!

1ST EXTERMINATOR: Phoenix.

FORENSIC: How much barbed wire does it take to encircle four hundred acres!

1ST EXTERMINATOR: Nine thousand two hundred and seventy square yards.

FORENSIC: How many guns on the east wall facing the western barricade?

1ST EXTERMINATOR: Forty-five.

FORENSIC: On which side are the women kept!

1ST EXTERMINATOR: Southwest corner and northeast.

FORENSIC: Two parts? The women are split in two parts?

1ST EXTERMINATOR: Yes, sir.

FORENSIC: Which two again? Again! Which two!

1ST EXTERMINATOR: Northeast and southwest.

FORENSIC: And the men!

1ST EXTERMINATOR: Northwest and southeast.

FORENSIC: And the dogs!

1ST EXTERMINATOR: Right in the middle and all around the edges.

FORENSIC: Which edges! Make yourself clear, Forensic: Which edges!

1ST EXTERMINATOR: Every edge. All the way around.

FORENSIC: On the sides then. All around the sides. Wouldn't that be a
better way to put it?

1ST EXTERMINATOR: Yes.

FORENSIC: And are they chained, tied, on leashes attached to men, running wild, vicious, kind, what kind of dogs?

1ST EXTERMINATOR: Dobermans, shepherds. Griffons.

FORENSIC: Where's the light source now? Where does it come from?
How much wattage? What kind of lamps?

1ST EXTERMINATOR: Three million kilowatts, underground, double spots,
ninety-inch strobes . . .

FORENSIC: Wait a minute. Underground? Underground! What's underground?

1ST EXTERMINATOR: Light source, sir.

FORENSIC: Underground light source. How? What kind? How is that possible?

1ST EXTERMINATOR: Underground streams, sir.

FORENSIC: Water?

1ST EXTERMINATOR: Yes, sir. That's right, sir. Water.

FORENSIC: I'll be damned. How deep?

1ST EXTERMINATOR: What?

FORENSIC: How deep down! The water! How many feet?

1ST EXTERMINATOR: Oh. I can't reveal that kind of information, sir. That's
not part of the test.

FORENSIC: Ah ha!

*(He grabs the pen off the table and makes a big check on the map, then sets
down the pen.)*

Not part of the test indeed! You were doing so well for so long.

1ST EXTERMINATOR: What do you mean? That's not part of the test, how
deep.

FORENSIC: All right, all right. We'll go on. Now then, how many guards
are standing on the right wall facing the embankment overlooking
the pond?

1ST EXTERMINATOR: Wait a minute. I know how deep it is but I'm not supposed to tell.

FORENSIC: Never mind. How many guards?

1ST EXTERMINATOR: Don't you want to know how deep?

FORENSIC: How many guards!

(EMMET gorges himself faster and faster as the interrogation gets more intense. OOLAN keeps filling the bowl. FORENSIC paces around the table.)

1ST EXTERMINATOR: Sixty feet deep!

FORENSIC: AH HA! What kind of pumps! Hydraulic, electric, gas! What kind of pumps!

1ST EXTERMINATOR: Vacuum, sir.

FORENSIC: They run on air then. DO THEY RUN ON AIR!

1ST EXTERMINATOR: Yes, sir.

FORENSIC: AND IF THE AIR WERE TO BE CUT OFF WHERE WOULD IT BE CUT OFF AT!

1ST EXTERMINATOR: At the throttle, sir.

FORENSIC: AT THE THROTTLE! WHAT DOES THAT MEAN, AT THE THROTTLE? DON'T YOU MEAN AT THE THROAT? CUT IT OFF AT THE THROAT! DON'T YOU MEAN THAT? ANSWER YES OR NO!

1ST EXTERMINATOR: Yes.

FORENSIC: THEN HOW DO WE GET TO THE THROAT, FOREN-SIC!

1ST EXTERMINATOR: Through the back, sir.

(Loud banging again as before. EMMET jumps to his feet with the package of Rice Krispies clutched to his chest. 1ST EXTERMINATOR jumps up and grabs OOLAN, holding her tightly as though a bomb is about to drop. EMMET and FORENSIC rush around the stage not knowing what to do.)

EMMET: Hide the Krispies! Hide the Krispies! What'll we do?

FORENSIC: Under the table, Emmet!

EMMET: Oolan!

1ST EXTERMINATOR: Leave her alone!

FORENSIC: Under the table, Oolan!

EMMET: Take the Krispies! Take the Krispies!

(OOLAN grabs the Krispies from EMMET and hides under the table. 1ST EXTER-MINATOR follows her. Another loud knock.)

FORENSIC: Not him! Just her! Just Oolan!

1ST EXTERMINATOR: Leave her alone!

EMMET: Yes! Who is it, please!

(2ND EXTERMINATOR's VOICE *over a microphone.*)

2ND EXTERMINATOR: IT'S THE EXTERMINATOR, LADY!

EMMET: I'm no lady, mister! I'm a man!

FORENSIC: Don't talk like a dumb kid, Forensic. Open the door.

EMMET: Fuck you. This is my home. Give me that gun.

FORENSIC: Stand back, Emmet, or I'll blow you wide open.

(EMMET *lunges at* FORENSIC *and grabs the gun. They struggle with the gun. Another loud knock.*)

2ND EXTERMINATOR: OPEN THIS DOOR OR I'LL BREAK IT DOWN!

(EMMET *and* FORENSIC *struggle all over the stage with the gun. Long loud ripping sound of door being crashed in. At the end of the sound,* 2ND EXTERMINATOR *falls onto the stage. He is still dressed in the uniform but without gas mask and tank. A pause as* EMMET *and* FORENSIC *look at the* 2ND EXTERMINATOR. *They both have hold of the gun and neither of them lets go until the end of the play. The* 2ND EXTERMINATOR *gets up slowly and brushes himself off. He looks around the stage.*)

2ND EXTERMINATOR: Boy, is it ever weird out there. Have you guys ever been out there?

FORENSIC: Out where?

2ND EXTERMINATOR: Out there. You haven't got much time, though. I should tell you that right away. Fair warning and all that sort of stuff. Now what's happened to Forensic?

(*He starts looking around as* EMMET *and* FORENSIC *tug at the gun.*)

EMMET: What's weird out there, mister? I've been out there before and there hasn't been anything weird. What's so weird?

2ND EXTERMINATOR: The whole thing. The road and everything. The phone booth. The road. Do you suppose he left or something? I suppose so. It's better, I guess.

FORENSIC: What's better? What's weird about the road? Make yourself clear!

2ND EXTERMINATOR: Especially the road. Just walking along in a gas mask and looking the way I look and everything. I mean there's not many people, but if you run across anybody while you're out there it's really weird. But you'd better get out before it's too late. They'll be here before you can say Jack Robinson.

EMMET: Who?

2ND EXTERMINATOR: I suppose what he did was he just decided to quit the whole business. I suppose that's it. He just got tired of waiting around. Left his gear and everything. In fact we must have decided the very same thing at the very same time but we just happened to be in different places is all. That's it, I'll bet. I'll bet that's what happened. Just as I put down the receiver and folded the glass door open and stepped outside and looked down at the tank and the mask leaning up against the tree trunk and a semi roaring by, just as he, standing around his table, hears the same semi roaring by and takes off the mask and sets down the tank, just as I leave the tank and the mask leaning up against the tree trunk and start following the semi down the road, just as he leaves the room with the tank and the mask sitting here on the floor and starts walking toward—We must have passed each other somewhere. That's it. I'll bet that's what happened. He starts walking toward the phone booth and I start back toward the house and we missed each other on the road. I'll bet you that's the way it happened. But you guys had better get out. They're going to gas this place once and for all.

(Very slowly blue smoke starts drifting onto the stage. It keeps up until the stage is completely covered and all you can hear are the voices of the actors. It gradually pours over into the audience and fills up the entire theater by the end of the play. It could change colors in the course of filling the place up, from blue to pink to yellow to green.)

FORENSIC: Who is? You're out of your mind! Gimme the gun, Emmet.

EMMET: He's lying, Forensic. Can't you see that? He's not in any hurry to get out, so why should we be?

2ND EXTERMINATOR: I suppose if I just wait around he's bound to turn up. Fat chance of finding him this time of night, walking along in the

dark. Barely see your own nose in front of your own face. Nice place
you boys have.

*(He sits in the stage-left chair, puts his feet on the table and leans back with his
hands folded behind his head.* EMMET *and* FORENSIC *tug at the gun.)*

FORENSIC: He's not either lying. He's called the home office and found
out where the table's supposed to be and they're sending men out to
help him. He's waiting around for his men. Now gimme the gun,
Emmet.

EMMET: He just told you that he left all his gear back at the phone booth
and he came back to meet his buddy. They're deserters, Forensic!

2ND EXTERMINATOR: Yep. A place like this could get a man dreaming
about settling down. Finding some roots. A kind of headquarters. A
place to come back to.

FORENSIC: This is our home!

2ND EXTERMINATOR: Where's that woman, Emmet?

EMMET: What?

2ND EXTERMINATOR: That woman you had here before.

*(*OOLAN *giggles under the table; nobody hears.)*

EMMET: Oh she . . .

FORENSIC: Don't tell! Don't you tell him anything!

2ND EXTERMINATOR: The trouble is, what if he arrived at the phone
booth, found my tank and mask leaning up against the tree trunk and
thought the same thing as me at the very same time but in two different places? What if he's set himself down inside the phone booth or
up against the tree and he's waiting for me thinking the same thing as
me; that it's too damn dark to go walking back on that road at this
time of night. What if that's the way it is?

EMMET: Then you'd better walk back and get him.

2ND EXTERMINATOR: No, no. You don't understand. If either one of us
makes another move like the moves we've already made then the
whole thing could go on forever. Now is a very crucial time. We have
to each think individually what the other one is going to do or we'll
just miss each other again and again and we'll finally give up and go
our separate ways. Do you get what I mean?

FORENSIC: Maybe he doesn't even want to meet you, though. Did you ever think of that?

EMMET: Shut up!

2ND EXTERMINATOR: Maybe you're right, Forensic. Maybe you're absolutely right. Maybe he doesn't. That means he could be somewhere altogether different from the phone booth. That means he could be anywhere.

FORENSIC: That means he could be right under the table even.

EMMET: Will you shut up!

2ND EXTERMINATOR: He most certainly could be, Forensic. He most certainly could. Right under my very nose. Right under the table. But that means I'm right then. That both of us are thinking the very same thing at the very same time. But if he's under the table then we're also in the very same place. I hardly think that could be true, Forensic, because if it were then it could mean only one thing. That he not only doesn't want to meet *me* but he also doesn't want *me* to meet *him*.

(1ST EXTERMINATOR's VOICE *is heard from under the table.*)

1ST EXTERMINATOR'S VOICE: Now you got the picture.

(OOLAN *giggles.* EMMET *and* FORENSIC *tug at the gun.* 2ND EXTERMINATOR *stands and paces around the table. He addresses the table.*)

2ND EXTERMINATOR: Then I take it the whole thing's off. Do I take it right? Do I take it right or wrong?

1ST EXTERMINATOR'S VOICE: Right! You take it absolutely right.

2ND EXTERMINATOR: Then we just split up and go our different ways.

1ST EXTERMINATOR'S VOICE: That's up to you. I'm staying here.

EMMET: Will you give me the gun!

2ND EXTERMINATOR: I called the home office, you know.

1ST EXTERMINATOR'S VOICE: I know, I know.

2ND EXTERMINATOR: Then I take it you know what's going to happen.

1ST EXTERMINATOR'S VOICE: You take it right.

FORENSIC: What's going to happen?

2ND EXTERMINATOR: And even so you're willing to stay. Even knowing what's going to happen. You're going to stay here.

1ST EXTERMINATOR'S VOICE: Yes, I am. I've fallen in love.

EMMET: What's going to happen?

2ND EXTERMINATOR: You don't care if we win or lose, then. You don't care if I stay or go. You just don't care. YOU JUST DON'T CARE, FORENSIC!

FORENSIC: Yes, I do! What's going to happen?

1ST EXTERMINATOR'S VOICE: Why don't you leave? You don't have to stay.

2ND EXTERMINATOR: Me? Alone? You want me to go running out there alone and go skipping up to them in my fancy new uniform and wave and throw kisses maybe and say hey fellas you've got the wrong house, you've got the wrong farm, you've got the wrong lawn. There's nothing here to exterminate. It's just us. It's just us and a few of our gang. Really. Try the next ranch. Try next door or down the road a piece. Down where they've got all the dogs. Down where you hear all the screaming till late in the night. We don't even play the phonograph after eleven o'clock. You can ask them if you like. Just down the road there. They'll tell you. Not a complaint in over thirty-five years. You can come in and look but it's just like I say. It's just a bunch of friends not knowing what else to do. Having breakfast now and then. It's pretty dirty but come right on in. Sure, search wherever you like. You won't find a thing. What do you think we are? Patsies or something? What do you think? Sure, tear up the bed, tear off the sheets, rip out the drawers, tear off our clothes. You won't find a thing. Guns? Guns? You think we have guns? Not on your life. Where would we hide guns? Under the floor? Under the floor! You hit the nail right on the old head. Guns under the floor. Under the table. Guns all over the place. See for yourselves. Every turn you make there's another gun. Automatics, elephant guns, Marlin four hundreds. Knock yourselves out. Well, I'm not going to do that, Forensic. I'm not going out there ever again. I'm staying right here!

(Loud banging is heard as before. The smoke by this time has filled up the stage and poured over into the audience. The banging keeps up at short intervals and develops a kind of mounting rhythm. This lasts for quite a while as the smoke gradually begins to thin out. Finally, as the smoke disappears, the actors, table and chairs are all gone so that the audience is looking at empty space at the end.)

The Holy Ghostly

The Holy Ghostly was first performed by the New Troupe at the McCarter Theatre, Princeton, New Jersey, in January 1970, with the following cast:

POP:	Peter Craig
ICE:	Ben Vereen
CHINDI'S OLE LADY:	Jeanette Ertelt
CHINDI:	Richard Wexler
COMPANY:	Edward Barton, Jerry Cunliffe, Theodore De Colo, Victor Lipari, Cleve Roller, Leah Scott, Joyce Stanton, Harris Weiner, Michael Meadows, Michael Warren Powell, Alan Braunstein, Deatra Lambert, Hedy Sontag

It was directed by Tom O'Horgan with music by Mr. O'Horgan.

SCENE

The desert at night. A large campfire glows in the center, the audience sits around it in a circle. POP, *in his late fifties, is sleeping face up with a hat over his face in a sleeping bag.* ICE, *his son, in his twenties, is squatting by the fire roasting marshmallows. He wears a hat, blue jeans, boots, vest and a blanket thrown over his shoulders. Around the fire are various cooking utensils, packs and empty cans. It looks as though they've been living there for a while. Blue light fades up slowly.*

ICE: *(Singing softly)*
> Oh didn't he ramble. Rambled all around.
> Rambled 'round the town. Oh didn't he ramble.
>   Rambled all around.
> Rambled 'round the town. Oh didn't he ramble.
>   Rambled all around.
> Rambled 'round the town. Oh boy didn't he ever
>   ramble. Rambled
> 'round the town. Rambled all around. That boy
>   sure did ramble.
> Rambled all around. Lookin' at the ground. Oh
>   didn't he ramble.
> Rambled all around. Rambled 'round the town. Oh
>   didn't he ramble.
> Rambled all around. All around the town.

(He takes the marshmallow out of the fire and tests it with his tongue, then sticks it back in the fire.)

> Oh didn't he ramble. Rambled all around. All
>   around the town.

Oh didn't he ramble. Rambled all around. All
around the town.

(POP *sits up fast, pulling a gun out from under his pillow and aiming it at* ICE, *who sits there coolly.*)

I've been trying to get that particular toasty golden brown that you like, Pop, but it sure takes a long time. So much easier just to stick it directly in the flames and let her burn.

POP: What do ya' think I am, a cannibal or somethin'. I like 'em cooked proper or not at all.

ICE: Well, you just lay back there and take a load off and I'll let you know.

POP: You seen the Chindi?

ICE: Now if I had, do you think I'd be sitting here toasting marshmallows and worrying whether or not they're getting too brown or too black?

POP: Just don't go gettin' confident on me. He's a sneaky devil.

ICE: Go to sleep.

POP: I have an idea you probably think yer old man's teched in the head. You probably do.

ICE: Go to sleep.

POP: You do, don't ya'? Don't ya'?

ICE: If I did, do you really think I'd have dropped everything I had going for myself in New York City, grabbed the nearest Greyhound bus and wound up out here in the Badlands with you?

POP: All what you had going in New York City? All what? My ass. You were just another bug in the rug, boy. Gimme that marshmallow and stop playin' with it.

(POP *reaches over and grabs the marshmallow off the end of the stick. He pops it in his mouth.* ICE *takes another one out of a bag and puts it on the stick.*)

Now listen to me. I could care less whether or not you believe in ghosts and phantoms. The reason I asked ya' out here weren't for sympathy and it sure as hell weren't for yer instincts. Lord knows those a' been shot to shit in that damn city. I plain and simple need an extra gun.

ICE: Then why didn't you hire one?

POP: Not to be trusted! None of 'em. Get an old man like me out here in the desert alone and right away they'd take me for everything I got.

ICE: Which is exactly what? Let me see. A fishing knife, a John B. Stetson circa 1890, a Colt forty-five, a Browning over and under . . .

POP: Yer so smart! Yer so goddamn smart! Look at ya'! Just look at ya'!

ICE: Spittin' image of his old man. Yessir. Why if it weren't for the age separatin' 'em you'd think they was the same person.

POP: Yer no son a' mine. No son a' mine woulda' gone and changed his name and dressed his self up like a hillbilly.

ICE: Well, I didn't know we were in a fashion show.

POP: Yer so goddamn smart, aren't ya'.

ICE: Well, I had me some good teachers. Sheep ranchers and horse thieves and what all. Taught me everything I know.

POP: I'm tellin' you, boy, you don't know what fear's all about. You ain't even begun to taste it.

ICE: How's the marshmallow?

POP: Fair to middlin'.

ICE: They say men make better cooks than women.

POP: Do they now.

ICE: Why don't you stop coming on like a hard-on? I'm the only company you've got.

POP: That's what you think. That's really what you think, ain't it? What if I was to tell you there was a Chindi out there with more faces and more arms and legs than the two of us put together? You really think we're alone, don't ya', boy? You think we're just a sittin' out here in the starry night passin' the time a' day and roastin' marshmallows like a couple a' Boy Scouts away from their mothers.

ICE: You told me he looked just like you.

POP: Who?

ICE: The Chindi.

POP: Sometimes he does. Sometimes he does that just to trick me. Trick me into believin' it's all a figment a' my imagination. But I know better. I know he's out there waitin'. Waitin' for me to make a wrong move. Bidin' his time. Smellin' my campfires. Pushin' his toe into the holes my body made when it was asleep.

ICE: Listen, I got an idea. You say he's out there waiting for us and we're here waiting for him. Right?

POP: That's about the size of it.

ICE: Then why don't we push him? Lean on him a little. Ghosts don't count on that. They count on fear. We might scare the shit out of him if we went after his ass.

POP: And how do you figure on trackin' him, smart boy? Ever seen a ghost make tracks?

ICE: We could pretend we were leaving. He'd come after us and then we'd get him. If we split up, one of us behind, me behind and you in front. We'd get him in the middle.

POP: Go to sleep.

ICE: Look, Pop, I gotta' get back to the city. All my friends are there. I can't be diddling around here in the desert forever.

POP: Important business. Big man. Big important man. Go ahead then! Go on! Go off and leave yer old dad. Go ahead!

(He rolls back into the sleeping bag and puts the hat back over his face.)

ICE: Will the radio bother you? Pop?

(No answer from POP. ICE takes a transistor out of his bedroll and turns it on softly to a rock station.)

POP: I'm not in show business, ya' know. There's some people likes to sleep at night. I need my rest. Ice? I said this ain't goddamn New York City where ya' can be playin' the radio at all hours of the goddamn day. Ice!

(A shrieking, screeching howl is heard. They both jump to their feet with their guns out. Silence. Except for the radio.)

He's there.

ICE: Come on. Now's our chance.

(ICE goes running off. POP stays frozen.)

POP: Ice! Come back here, boy! Come back here! Ice!

(POP goes to the radio and shuts it off. He turns in a tight circle with his gun out looking into the night.)

I ain't afraid to die. I just want ya' to know that much. I ain't afraid. I had my day.

(The sound of bells jingling on someone's ankles as he walks. POP starts in the direction of the sound.)

I hear ya'. Now look. I don't rightly know what this is all about. I really don't. I figure that somewhere in yer mind you got this idea that I done somethin' to deserve yer comin' after me and torturin' me and maybe killin' me or somethin', but—

(The voice of the CHINDI is heard in the dark. He moves onto the stage slowly. A tall figure dressed in black blankets with bells around his ankles, eagle feathers around the wrists and neck and coming out of his head. The face is all white, the rest of the body jet black.)

CHINDI: You're already dead, Mr. Moss.

POP: How do you know my name?

(The CHINDI darts across the stage behind POP. POP wheels around and fires. The CHINDI sways from side to side and clacks his teeth.)

CHINDI: Did you change it?

POP: No, I didn't change it. I got some pride in tradition. That's my son yer thinkin' of. Ice. He changed his name to Ice. What do ya' think of that? From Stanley Hewitt Moss the seventh to Ice. What do ya' think a' that? It's him yer thinkin' of. Maybe it's him yer after? Is it him yer after?

CHINDI: I'm not after nobody, Mr. Moss.

(The CHINDI darts again to another part of the stage. POP wheels and fires twice. The CHINDI shakes his feet and slaps his hands on his thighs.)

POP: I done nothin' to deserve this. What've I done! I got a right to live out the rest a' my life in peace. Lord knows I've had a struggle.

CHINDI: The Lord knows nothin', Stanley.

(The CHINDI darts again. POP fires. The CHINDI smacks his lips.)

POP: Don't go givin' me none a' yer highfalutin esoteric gobbledygook, Buster Brown. Just 'cause ya' struck off fer the big city on yer own and made a big splash when ya' was just a whippersnapper don't mean ya' can humiliate an old man.

CHINDI: Why don't you face up to it, Mr. Moss. You're dead.

POP: Get away form me! Stand back! Stand back or I'll blow ya' to kingdom come!

CHINDI: Come with me, Stanley.

(The CHINDI *reaches out his hand for* POP. POP *fires. The* CHINDI *darts to another part of the stage and blows on the back of his hand.)*

POP: I don't know what you think you're trying to prove, Ice, but I ain't fallin' for it. Cheap theatrics. That's all! That getup don't fool yer old dad for a minute. I suppose ya' thought I'd drop over dead outa' sheer fright. I suppose ya' thought that. You'd like that, wouldn't ya'! Wouldn't ya'! Then with yer old man outa' the way you could step right in and take over the ranch, lock, stock, and barrel. All six hundred acres and the sheep to boot. Well, I ain't fallin' for it! Ya' hear me! You hear me, boy!

CHINDI: You're a fool, Mr. Moss.

(The CHINDI *darts offstage and leaves* POP *standing there.)*

POP: Now you come back here! Ice! Come back here, ya' damn ingrate! This here has gone further than far enough! I'm yer pa! There's no reason we can't see this thing out eye to eye! All right! All right, you asked for it. There ain't been any feudin' in the family since 1884 but if that's the way you want it that's the way you'll get it.

(POP goes to the sleeping bag and pulls it away. Underneath is a bazooka. He hoists it up on his shoulder and takes it over near the campfire. He sets it down and goes back to the sleeping bag and pulls out some shells. The sound of an Indian drum steadily beating is heard offstage. POP *looks out.)*

Ice?

(He goes to the bazooka and loads a shell into it. The drum keeps drumming.)

Ice! You damn fool! They won't even be able to tell the difference between you and the sand if this thing goes off. Listen to reason, boy.

(POP *mounts the bazooka up on his shoulder and gets it ready to fire.*)

I always liked to think of the two of us as blood brothers. Ya' know what I mean? Not father and son but brothers. I mean ever since you was old enough to learn how to shoot a thirty-thirty. The way we used to go out in the jeep late at night and flash the headlights on them jackrabbits. Blastin' them damn jackrabbits all up against the cactus. Remember that, Ice? Them jackrabbits was as big as puppies. Not enough left to even make a decent stew out of by the time we was through. And that old gun. The way that old Winchester used to kick ya' so hard it'd throw ya' right into the back seat. Yessir. Shadow Mountain that was. Those was rich days, boy. We was close as sticky socks back then.

(*The drum gets closer.*)

What do ya' want to throw all that away for, Stanley? I know ya' set out to hurt me. Right from the start I knowed that. Like the way ya' changed yer name and all. That was rotten, Stanley. I give ya' that name 'cause that was my name and my pappy gave me that name and his pappy before him. That name was handed down for seven generations, boy. Now ain't no time to throw it away. What's gonna' happen when you have yerself a son? What's gonna' happen to him with a name like Ice? He'll get laughed right outa' school. How's he gonna' play football with a name like that? You gotta' think on the future, son.

(*The drum continues to get closer.*)

I know ya' probably think I was rough on ya' and the truth is I was. But I tried to show ya' the ropes. Tried to give ya' some breaks too. Me, I never had no real breaks. My old man was a dairy farmer. Started hittin' the bottle and lost the whole farm. Things started goin' downhill from that point on. Next thing he got himself a job sellin' Hershey bars door to door. Never saw much a' Pa then. Travelin' all around. Chicago, Detroit, Des Moines, Tucumcari, Boise. Then we found out that Pa got his self so drunk in a hotel room that he fell asleep with a cigar burning in his hand. Burned the whole hotel right to the ground with him in it. So I had to go to work. Support the whole family.

(The drum continues through the speech.)

Then my brother Jaimie comes home one day complainin' of a bad pain. Take him to the doctor and come to find out he's got himself a case a' polio and they're gonna' have to take his leg off. The whole damn leg from the hip down. That was right around the time a' the Great Depression. 'Course you don't remember them days. So me, I'm workin' night and day in Macy's downtown Chicago and bringin' home the bacon once a week so Ma can buy the groceries. By the time Jaimie gets old enough to work I'm startin' to think on marrying yer mother. 'Course Jamie was a cripple but strong as an ox from the waist up. That come from hoistin' himself up and down stairs since he was just a squirt. So right away Jaimie goes out and decides he wants to become a truck driver. Yessir. That old boy had some real spunk. Walks right up to Bekins Van and Storage and asks 'em fer a job. Well, they could see right off that he only had but one good leg and the other one wood but he figured he was just as good as the next man. So they sent him to a special school where he learned how to use that wooden leg a' his. First thing ya' know he's out there in the real world drivin' a goddamn Bekins truck with a wooden leg. So me, I get myself hitched to yer mother and get all set to take off fer college and get myself a diploma so's I could make me a heap a' money, when lo and behold if old Uncle Sam don't decide it's come my time to serve my country. So off I goes to learn how to fly B-24s and B-17s and drop bombs and whatall. Italy, Holland, Germany, England, the whole shebang. Then I come back with nothin' to show for it but some Jap rifles and Kraut helmets and little red bombs cut on my leather jacket with a Gillette Blue Blade. Each one showing mission accomplished. Each one showin' I got back alive. But I was feelin' all right 'cause about that time I got myself something to look forward to Stateside. I'm comin' home to my little woman in Rapid City, South Dakota, and she's got one hell of a package waiting for me. She's got me a son. A son with my name and my eyes and my nose and my mouth. My own flesh and blood, boy. My son, Stanley Hewitt Moss the seventh.

(ICE *appears. He has white war paint stripes on his face and an Indian drum in his hand which he beats in a slow steady rhythm.*)

ICE: Hi, Pop.

POP: Don't call me none a' yer family names.

(ICE *stops beating the drum.*)

ICE: I saw the Chindi, Pop.

POP: I'll bet you did. I'll bet you could tell me exactly what he looks like too. What he has for breakfast and which side of his crotch he hangs his dick on.

ICE: When are you going to stop talking like a dirt farmer? You're an intelligent, mature adult with a lot of potential. Stop putting yourself down.

POP: Ya' see this here?

ICE: The bazooka?

POP: It ain't no bazooka. It's a rifle grenade. Made it myself.

ICE: Nice work.

POP: Thanks. I was gonna' blow yer damn head off fer pullin' that stunt on me, but now I figure it's all fer the best. Ya' helped bolster my courage for when the real thing comes.

ICE: You know what he told me? He told me that you were dead and you don't even know it.

(He *sits and plays the drum softly with his hands.*)

POP: Now we've carried this damn fiasco far enough, boy! I don't know what kind a' fool plan you've got in yer head but if yer tryin' to scare me yer gonna' have to go. . . .

ICE: Go fuck yourself, you old prick! I'm going back to New York and you can stay here and jerk yourself off forever on this desert!

(ICE *starts to leave.* POP *jumps up and grabs* ICE *around the shoulders.* POP *drops his accent.*)

POP: All right. All right, Stanley, look. . . .

ICE: My name's Ice.

POP: All right. OK, Ice. Look, we don't have to fight. We really don't. We can be calm and sensible. But all these games you've been . . .

ICE: What games? You call me up person-to-person collect and I can barely understand you because you're so hysterical, and you tell me there's a ghost after your ass and I believe you although it seems a bit farfetched and I drop everything and come whaling out here to meet you and pull you together and now . . .

POP: I was kidding, though. Just kidding around. I mean . . .

ICE: Kidding? You jive motherfucker! I should blow your head off right here and now.

POP: Wait a minute, Stanley!

ICE: GODDAMMIT! You make that mistake again and I'll cut you in half!

POP: I'm sorry! I'm sorry! I just haven't gotten used to it. The sound of it. It doesn't make any sense to me. I'm an old man, son. I'm not used to . . .

ICE: Well, get used to it! Get used to another thing too while you're at it. For eighteen years I was your slave. I worked for you hand and foot. Shearing the sheep, irrigating the trees, listening to your bullshit about "improve your mind, you'll never get ahead, learn how to lose, hard work and guts and never say die" and now I suppose you want me to bring you back to life. You pathetic creep. Hire yourself a professional mourner, Jim. I'm splitting.

POP: No! No, Stanley!

ICE: That's it! That's it. I told you. One more time, old man.

(ICE *starts stalking* POP.)

POP: Now wait a minute, son.

ICE: I'm no son a' yours. Remember? You better go for yer gun, boy. I'm gonna' kill you once and for all. The difference this time is that you'll know that you're dead.

POP: Ice! Don't be a fool! I always taught you never to play around with a weapon. You have to have respect for a gun!

ICE: Draw, old-timer.

POP: Ice! Have you lost your good sense! I'm your father! Your own flesh and blood!

ICE: Abandon the creeping meatball!

POP: You can't turn against your own kind! We're civilized human beings! Just because we don't see things eye to eye on certain political opinions.

ICE: Pop, the oppressor's cherry!

POP: I always saw to it that you had a hot meal on the table and a roof over your head. It's just that I'm lonely, Ice. I missed you. Ever since your mother passed on, I've had the most terrible nightmares. Visions of demons and goblins chasing me and taunting me.

ICE: Poor baby. Does him do-do-do and pee-pee in his um's bed too?

POP: And you know about my stomach. Ever since the war. I keep seeing slanty-eyed faces of faces I never saw. Any minute it could burst and eat into the intestines and then I could die.

ICE: You're already dead, dope. You're a ghost.

POP: Be kind, Ice. It's not asking much.

ICE: It's asking too much. It's asking the world, Bozo, and I ain't got it to give.

POP: Let's just be friends. Let bygones be bygones, son. Why can't we be friends?

(A white WITCH appears with POP's corpse on her back, carrying it piggyback style. The corpse is dressed exactly the same as POP, and has a chalk-white face. The WITCH is dressed in white robes with black feathers on her wrists and neck and coming out of her head. Her face is painted black, with long black hair. She sets the corpse down near the fire facing the flames and warms herself by the flames. The corpse is in a squatting position.)

WITCH: Lovely evening.

ICE: Yeah. Howdy.

POP: Who are you?

WITCH: I'm the Chindi's old lady. And you're Bozo the Clown.

(She cackles and laughs like the Witch in The Wizard of Oz.*)*

POP: What's that thing? It's disgusting. It gives off a stench.

WITCH: That's your body, Bozo.

POP: Stop calling me that! My name's Stanley Hewitt Moss the sixth.

WITCH: Far out.

POP: Would you kindly warm yourself up and then remove that stinking mound of flesh and be on your way?

WITCH: Didn't you tell him, Ice?

ICE: I didn't get a chance to. We started arguing.

WITCH: That's a drag.

POP: What in God's name is going on here? Do you two know each other?

ICE: More or less.

WITCH: Your son's a ballin' fool, Mr. Moss.

POP: Is this another part of your scheme to scare me into admitting I lied to you, Ice? I already admitted that. What more do you want?

ICE: To admit that you're dead.

POP: But I'm not dead! I can see! I can touch! I can smell! I can feel! I'm alive!

WITCH: The Chindi is coming back for you, Mr. Moss.

POP: Well, that's nice. And what am I supposed to do when he comes?

WITCH: You're to go with him. He'll take you away.

POP: And what if I don't want to go?

ICE: You got no choice, Pop. Finally you've got no choice.

WITCH: You're a ghost, Mr. Moss. Do you know what a ghost is?

POP: I don't know and I don't care. I've never been inclined toward hocus-pocus and I'll be damned if I'll start now.

WITCH: A ghost is one who has died without finishing what he had to do on the earth. Sometimes because they were cut short, like baby ghosts. Sometimes because they never found out what they were here for, like you, Mr. Moss. A ghost is hung up between being dead and being alive because he doesn't know where he's at. We're here to show you exactly where you're at.

PQP: You presumptuous little cunt. I have a good mind to take you over my knee and spank you.

WITCH: Try it.

POP: I'm not a man of violence. I never have been.

ICE: Never?

POP: Well, not when I could help it. I was only doing my job. You can't hold that against me.

WITCH: The Chindi asked me to tell you that you have a certain amount of time between now and when you're going to have to reckon with him. That time is going to be measured by this body, Mr. Moss. Your own body. Which you left and abandoned and tried to get back inside of. By the time rigor mortis completely sets into the body, by the time the body stiffens out straight as a board, the Chindi will be back to take you with him.

POP: And where are we supposedly going?

WITCH: To a place you'll never come back from.

ICE: Never?

WITCH: Not this time. He had his chance.

ICE: Looks like curtains, Pop.

WITCH: It's better this way, Mr. Moss. Imagine hanging around for eternity in the state of mind you're in now. Strung out between right and wrong, good and evil, the right and the left, the high and the low, the hot and the cold, the old and the young, the weak and the strong, the body and the spirit. You're a fucking mess. We're going to put you back together again. A whole man. One whole thing. How about it? You'll never be the same again.

POP: *(He goes back into accent)* No soap, Snow White. And you can tell your Chindi friend that he'd better bring a six-shooter if he's aimin' to bring in Stanley Hewitt Moss the sixth!

WITCH: Well, thanks for the fire, Ice.

ICE: 'Bye.

(The white WITCH *disappears in the night.* POP *is back into his dirt-farmer image.)*

POP: Well, at least we know where we stand now, boy. Least we know who the enemy is. Better dig yourself in there, boy. They'll be acomin' before long.

*(*POP *goes back to the bazooka and lies down behind it, mounting it on his shoulders and trying to dig in like a marine, using the pack and sleeping bags as a foxhole.* ICE *sits by the fire and starts beating on the drum. He stares into the eyes of the corpse. The corpse, from this point on, almost imperceptibly stiffens from a sitting position to lying straight out on the ground on his back. Something like a slow-motion self-immolation.)*

Thing I couldn't get straight was whether or not it was real or not. Know what I mean, boy? Like whether I was just scarin' myself fer no good reason. Hallucinatin' and what not. Well, now we know, I guess. Don't we? I mean now we know it's real. The ghost. Stop playin' that damn fool drum and talk to yer pa!

(ICE *keeps playing the drum. When he talks to* POP *he directs his speech to the corpse.*)

ICE: (*His voice changes to a little boy's.*) You're the one who taught me, Daddy. You said practice, practice, practice. That's the only way to do the best.

POP: Well, that's right. It stands to reason. Just look at Gene Krupa, Buddy Rich—how do you think they got where they are today?

ICE: Well, look at Sonny Murray, Keith Moon. What about them?

POP: Never heard of 'em. Upstarts. The whole bunch. It takes more than gulldanged imagination to be a great drummer. It takes guts. That's the thing you never learned. You gotta' build up yer strength. You gotta' work on that left hand so hard you can do a triple paradiddle with yer right hand tied behind yer back. Ya' gotta' get yer right foot so strong it's like steel. Work with that ankle so hard that it feels like it's gonna' break off. Then when ya' reach that point where ya' can hardly stand the pain of it—that's when you start yer real practicin'. That's when yer work begins. Separate all the pieces. Two arms, two hands, two wrists, two legs, two ankles, two feet. Everything in pairs. Break it all down in pairs. Make the pairs work together, with each other. Then make 'em work against each other, independent. Do some cymbal work, just use the ride, then the sizzle, then the splash, then yer high hat. Feel out all the sounds you got at yer disposal, all the tones in a good set a' tubs. Yer high toms, yer lows.

ICE: What about cowbells?

POP: Well, if you go fer that Latin hand-drum sound, that's all right too. Congas and bongos and timbalis and Dholaks and Dumbaks. All them catchy calypso, mambo, cha-cha-cha rhythms they got. Helps ya' keep on yer toes. Teaches ya' a lot about what's behind a rhythm structure. Offbeats and such. That offbeat stuff. 'Course all the technique in the world ain't gonna mean yer a genius. No sir. Ya' can only go so far with learning the essentials, then the rest is up to you and God.

ICE: Were you a genius, Pop?

POP: Me? Naw. Damn good though. One of the two or three fastest in the country. 'Course them were the days of Dixieland and Cajun music. Don't hear much a' that anymore. Mind if I turn the radio on?

ICE: I'm not asleep.

POP: I know. But ya' always ask me before you turn it on so I thought I'd extend ya' the same courtesy.

(POP *turns the radio on soft.*)

ICE: It's just that I know how you hate rock and roll.

POP: Now that ain't true, boy. Not a bit. That kinda' music come outa' good roots. Rhythm and blues and country music, Western music. Them's good roots. My gripe was and always has been that it got into the wrong hands. A bunch of teenage morons. That's all. All that "doo, wa, doo, wa, doo, wa, ditty, talk about the girls from New York City." Stuff like that. Like a bunch a' morons. Grates against a man's ears who's played with the best. Why, if I was young today I'd probably be playin' rock and roll myself, right along with the rest of 'em. Can't says I'd go in fer all this transvestite malarkey that's been goin' on though. I'd keep my self-respect. But I'd probably figure in the picture somewhere.

ICE: You probably would.

POP: Ya' sound far away, boy. What're ya' thinkin'?

ICE: Just dreamin' on the fire. You can see the whole world in a fire.

(*Pause.* POP *sings. During the song he becomes like a little boy.* ICE *becomes like his father.*)

POP: (*Sings*)

A beautiful bird in a gilded cage
A beautiful sight to see.
You may think she's happy and free from fear
She's not though she seems to be

She flew from the hills at a tender age
She flew from the family tree
You may think she got to the promised land
But she's not where she wants to be.

POP: Ice?

ICE: Yeah.

POP: Ice, could you tell me a story? I feel lonely.

ICE: Sure. Turn the radio off and come on over here.

(POP *turns off the radio and crawls over to* ICE *and curls up in his lap.* ICE *strokes his forehead and tells him a story. He stops beating the drum. The corpse keeps stiffening through all this.*)

ICE: Once upon a time millions and millions of years ago, before man was ever around, there was a huge, huge fiery ball of fire.

POP: Like the sun?

ICE: Sort of—but much huger and hotter than our sun. A super sun. At the same time, somewhere in space, there was a giant planet made out of cosmic ice.

POP: What's cosmic ice?

ICE: Of, or pertaining to, the cosmos.

POP: What's the cosmos?

ICE: Everything.

POP: Then what happened?

ICE: For millions of years the super sun and the giant ice planet traveled through space, spinning and spinning and spinning. Then one day they collided with each other and the giant ice planet penetrated deep inside to the center of the super sun and buried itself. For hundreds of thousands of years nothing happened until one day suddenly the accumulating steam from the melting ice planet caused an enormous explosion inside the super sun. Fragments of the sun were blown out into outer space. Other fragments fell back on the ice planet. Still other fragments were projected into an intermediate zone.

POP: What's intermediate?

ICE: Something in between. These intermediate fragments are what we call the planets in our system. There were thirty fragments which gradually became covered with ice. The moon, Jupiter, and Saturn are made out of ice. The canals on Mars are cracks in the ice. The only fragment that wasn't completely ice was the one we're riding on right now. The earth. Ever since then the earth has been carrying on a constant struggle between fire and ice. At the same time as this great explosion, at a distance three times that of Neptune from the earth, there was an enormous band of ice. It's still there and you can see it tonight.

POP: Where?

ICE: *(Pointing to the sky)* Right up there. Astronomers call it the Milky Way because stars shine through it from the other side.

POP: It must be really cold up there.

ICE: It is.

POP: But we're nice and warm.

ICE: Well, we're by the fire.

POP: Won't the ice ever melt though?

ICE: Sometimes it does. That's why it rains. Look at the moon.

POP: It seems really close.

ICE: It's getting closer all the time. One day it's going to collide with the earth and another battle will go on between fire and ice. It's happened before.

POP: With the moon?

ICE: Not this moon but other ones. Three other moons came before this one. And three times the earth was destroyed and made over again.

POP: And it's going to happen again?

ICE: Yes.

(POP jumps up and goes to the bazooka.)

POP: Bull pukey! You really expect me to believe that hocus-pocus?

(POP switches on the radio again.)

ICE: No.

POP: The earth ain't no more made outa' ice than the sun is. Who filled yer brain with that hogwash anyhow? I'll tell ya' who's gonna' make and break this planet, boy. We are! You and me and nothing else! We're gonna' set this world on fire, boy. Soon's we blow up this Chindi fella and that two-bit whore a' his, we'll be on our way. I'll show ya' a thing or two about fire and ice. I'll show ya' how to make the world spin!

ICE: How're you gonna' blow him up, Pa?

POP: You'll see. Soon's he sets foot in this camp he's a dead man.

ICE: But he's already dead and so are you. You can't kill a dead man.

POP: More hogwash! Fairy tales! What's real is real and there ain't no way around it.

ICE: You won't even see him this time. He'll just come for you and take you away and you won't even know he's there.

POP: Why don't you go down by the crick and wash that damn makeup off yer face? If ya' weren't my own son I'd say you was a sissy.

(ICE *stands up.*)

ICE: I think I will. I think I'll walk to the crick and keep right on walking.

POP: No! Ice! You can't leave me now. There's not much more time. Look at that corpse. It's gettin' stiffer by the minute.

ICE: Tell you what. As soon as you blow up the Chindi come straight to Rapid City and we'll meet up there.

POP: No! I need your help!

ICE: Really? What for? To load your bazooka?

POP: There must have been some time once when you needed me and I helped you out.

ICE: There must have been.

POP: Well, now you can pay me back.

ICE: Right.

(*He draws his gun and shoots* POP *in the stomach, then walks off.*)

POP: Ice! Ice! Stanley!

(POP *grabs his stomach and staggers around the stage. The corpse is almost completely stiffened out by now.*)

Stanley! You can have the ranch! The sheep! The station wagon! The Dodge half-ton! The spring tooth harrow! The barbeque pit! The house! You can take it! Take it! I'm not kidding, Stanley! This is no way to leave yer pa after all these years! (*To himself*) The moon's getting closer. I can make out the craters. All of the craters. It's a marvelous thing, Stanley! This is a remarkable time we're living in when a man can look from behind the moon, over his shoulder, past the ice and see that warm, greenish blue planet spinning around and around with its cargo of little people. Don't you think? I agree with you, Stanley! I agree with your philosophy and your political point of view, only don't leave me now! We can argue! That's part of the fun. Ya' can't expect me to make an omelet without breaking a few eggs! Conflict's a good thing! It keeps ya' on yer toes! Stanley! Yer pa is dying!

(Again the screeching howl. The bells of the CHINDI *are heard as before, getting louder and louder; the corpse is completely stiff.* POP *stops and listens; he runs to the radio and shuts it off.)*

So yer really gonna' try it after all. Yer really gonna' try bringin' in Stanley Hewitt Moss the sixth. Well, come on! Come on then!

(He goes to the bazooka and mounts it on his shoulder. More bells are heard from other parts of the theater. It should be a live sound, not recorded.)

Come on, ya' weasely little no-count! Sneakin' around in the dark. I can remember the time when wars was fought out in the open field. Hand-to-hand combat. Teddy Roosevelt style. None a' this sneaky guerrilla stuff that's come into fashion. Hit-and-run perverts! Throw a grenade and run the other way. Never even see the faces of the dead. Well, I got one shot and I'm gonna' make it count. Stanley! That old Chindi thinks he's come to take a patsy off!

*(*POP *pulls his hand away from his stomach and looks at it. It's dripping with blood.)*

Wait a minute. Wait a darn minute.

(He crawls over to the fire on his hands and knees. He holds his hand up to the flames so the light shines on it.)

If that don't beat all.

(He rubs his stomach again and holds his hand to the light.)

No blood. A bloodless critter. Not a speck a blood. They was right the whole time. Wait a minute! Stanley! You was right!

(He pulls up his sleeve and slowly, carefully sticks his whole arm into the flames and holds it there.)

No pain. There's no pain!

(He breaks into loud laughter and jumps up. He dances in circles and shouts.)

No pain and no blood! No pain and no blood! No pain and no blood! No pain and no blood!

(He stops for a second and looks into the fire. The sound of the drum starts up again. More bells all over the house in a steady rhythm.)

(In the corpse's face) You're a dead man, Stanley. You're a dead man.

(He looks at the corpse.)

A dead body.

(He walks into the centre of the campfire and laughs. He dances in the fire.)

Oh didn't he ramble. Rambled all around. All around the town. Oh didn't he ramble. Rambled all around. All around the town. All around the town. He sure did ramble. Rambled all around. All around the town. Boy, didn't he ramble.

(He stops and runs out of the fire. He goes to the bazooka and lifts it up, then throws it into the fire. He keeps up the talk as he goes around the stage throwing everything into the fire: sleeping bags, cans, blankets, guns, hats, radio. He leaves the corpse for last. As he throws more and more things into the fire the flames grow higher and spread outside the circle. This could be done with a projector and film loop above the audience. POP is in a manic state. He talks to the corpse, himself, an imaginary ICE and ghosts he doesn't see.)

Boy, if my boy could see me now! If my boy Stanley was here to see me now! He wouldn't believe it. The change in his old man. A changed man. Believe you me, Stanley, he wouldn't believe it! Imagine me, crawlin' off into the Badlands like an old alley cat, knowin' he's dyin', dyin' alone. Tryin' to save pain. Save face. Keep the family calm. No sense in them seeing their man of the house in his last moment on earth. It's a long moment, Stanley! Boy, don't you know if there was a phone booth out here I'd sure make a collect call to that boy and have him hightail it out here to see his old man now! Yessir! That boy would be so proud! He'd fall on his knees to kiss the earth my boots stomp on. It's been a long time. A long, long time. Wonder what he's lookin' like now. A grown man. My boy, a grown man. And his old man, a boy. You're as old as ya' feel, Stanley! And I feel as old as forever! I've never been more alive in my life, son! Never been more full a' fire and brimstone. All that useless fear. All them years yelpin' like a pup, afraid to look the eagle in the eyeball. It's never like ya' think it's gonna' be, Stanley! Never! Never endless and lonely and no end in sight. Just goin' on and on without a stop. It's right here, boy, in the fire. Ya' take the fire in yer hand, boy, in both hands. And ya' squeeze it to death! Ya' squeeze the life out of it. Ya' make it bleed! Ya' whip it and make it dance for ya'. Ya' make it do its dance. Ya' make it scream like a woman with the pain and joy all wrapped up together! Ya' send it beyond fear, beyond death, beyond doubt. There's no end to its possibilities.

(He looks the corpse in the eye.)

(To the corpse) And what're you doin'?

CORPSE: Nothin'.

POP: Don't do nothin' in the kingdom a' God! Burn! Burn! Burn! Burn! Burn! Burn! Burn! Burn!

(He picks up the corpse, holds it over his head and spins it around in circles, then throws it into the fire. The drums and bells increase, the flames flicker all over the audience. The whole theater is consumed in flames as POP screams over and over and dances in the fire.)

BURN! BURN! BURN! BURN! BURN! BURN! BURN! BURN!

BLACKOUT

Operation Sidewinder

A PLAY IN TWO ACTS

Dedicated to the following for their keen inspiration:
Michelangelo Antonioni
Dapper Tommy Thompson
Crazy Horse
The Stones
The Holy Modal Rounders
The Hopi
Nancy
Gabby Hayes
Old Oraibi
Mickey Free
1968
O-Lan

Operation Sidewinder was first produced on March 12, 1970, at the Repertory Theater of Lincoln Center/Vivian Beaumont Theater, New York City, with the following cast, in order of appearance:

DUKIE:	Robert Phalen
HONEY:	Barbara eda-Young
MECHANIC:	Michael Miller
YOUNG MAN:	Andy Robinson
FOREST RANGER:	Robert Riggs
BILLY:	Roberts Blossom
COLONEL WARNER:	Joseph Mascolo
CAPTAIN:	Robert Phalen
CADET:	Gus Fleming

MICKEY FREE:	Don Plumley
1ST COHORT TO MICKEY FREE:	Ralph Drischell
2ND COHORT TO MICKEY FREE:	Arthur Sellers
CARHOP:	Catherine Burns
BLOOD:	Garrett Morris
BLADE:	Paul Benjamin
DUDE:	Charles Pegues
GENERAL BROWSER:	Paul Sparer
DOCTOR VECTOR:	Ray Fry
SPIDER LADY:	Michael Levin
EDITH:	Joan Pringle
CAPTAIN BOVINE:	Philip Bosco
INDIANS:	José Barrera,
	Paul Benjamin,
	Gregory Borst,
	Gus Fleming,
	Robert Keesler,
	Michael Levin,
	Clark Luis,
	Richard Mason,
	Muriel Miguel,
	Louis Mofsie,
	Santos Morales,
	Garrett Morris,
	Jean-Daniel Noland,
	Joan Pringle,
	Barbara Spiegel
1ST DESERT TACTICAL TROOP:	Robert Priggs
2ND DESERT TACTICAL TROOP:	Robert Phalen
3RD DESERT TACTICAL TROOP:	Michael Miller

The production was directed by Michael A. Schultz and Jules Irving.

Act One

The houselights come down. The stage is black. The sound of a rattlesnake rattling.
A coyote in the distance. The rattle grows louder. A soft blue light fills the ceiling of
the stage then flashes off. A bright flash of yellow light from the center of the stage
floor then black again. The blue light comes on and goes out. Again the yellow light
flashes, then comes on again slowly and glows brightly, with the rest of the stage
dark. It forms almost a perfect circle. In the center of the circle can be seen a very
large sidewinder rattlesnake, coiled and ready to strike. The light seems to be coming
from the snake itself. When stretched to its full length the sidewinder measures over
six feet and looks like it weighs over thirty pounds. The eyes are ruby red and blink
on and off. The tongue spits. The rattle rattles. The snake's skin is bright yellow with
black diamonds. It undulates in a mechanical rhythm. Its hissing grows louder and
the rattle too. The head sways from side to side. Sound of a jet going across the sky
very loudly, then into silence, then a sonic boom. Silence. Sound of a car passing on
a highway. A MAN'S VOICE *is heard.*

MAN'S VOICE: Look, Honey!

> *(Sound of car screeching to stop, then backing up, then stopping again. Sound*
> *of car door slamming. Bright yellow desert light comes up and fills the stage,*
> *making it hard to see the snake except for the black diamonds and the ruby*
> *eyes. The snake keeps up its rhythmic rattle, sway, blink, hiss as the* MAN *enters*
> *from stage left with a fancy-looking movie camera, straw cowboy hat, open*
> *shirt, hairy chest, Bermuda shorts, and Hush Puppies. He yells back off left.)*

MAN: Bring the tripod, Honey! Hurry up!

> *(He starts focusing his camera on the sidewinder and inching in on it, taking*
> *his eyes away from the view finder once in a while to make sure he's not getting*

too close. HONEY, *a very sexy chick with long blond hair and tight pants, high heels, etc., comes running on from left with a tripod.)*

Take it easy! Not so fast! We don't want to get him aggravated.
HONEY: Boy, what a monster! I've never seen one so huge.

(She hands him the tripod. The MAN *sets up the camera on the tripod and moves in for a close shot.)*

Be careful, Dukie. They're deadly poisonous. I read it in one of those desert manuals. They're the only thing to really be afraid of out here.
MAN: Don't worry. I didn't spend the best part of my years in the Philippines for nothing you know.

*(*HONEY *makes a wide circle around the sidewinder as she talks and the sound of the camera whirring is heard as the* MAN *shoots. The sidewinder just keeps up his tense rhythm.)*

HONEY: He's actually kind of beautiful when you look at him close. I was always taught to be afraid of snakes but actually they're not so bad. I mean he's just out here trying to get a suntan or something. There's nothing awful about that. He looks kind of tense but I'll bet he'd loosen up in no time at all if he got the right kind of attention. You know what I mean, Dukie? Little mice and stuff. I'll bet he'd make a nice pet.

(The MAN *straightens up from his camera.)*

MAN: Maybe we oughta' aggravate him a little, Honey. He blends right into the background when he's not moving. I don't want to waste any more film than I have to.
HONEY: OK.

(She stomps her foot and hisses at the sidewinder.)

MAN: Now wait a minute! For crying out loud! Not like that.
HONEY: Well how then?
MAN: Well I don't know. Aren't there some stones around we could throw at him?

HONEY: Nope. Just sand.

MAN: Well how about a stick then?

HONEY: I don't see any.

(Suddenly the sidewinder leaps out and grabs HONEY around the neck and pulls her to the ground. She screams. The MAN jumps and crashes into his camera; it smashes to pieces. He falls on the ground and frantically scrambles away as the snake coils around HONEY's body. She screams and kicks but the sidewinder coils tighter so that it's completely wrapped around her from her neck to her feet. The MAN watches on his hands and knees as the eyes of the sidewinder blink, the tongue spits and hisses, and the rattle rattles.)

MAN: Now, Honey, take it easy! Don't fight it. You'll just make him madder than he already is. Just relax and I'll go try to find a Forest Ranger.

HONEY: Oh fuck! He's really got me. Don't leave! Dukie!

MAN: I'll be right back. Try to relax, Honey. Don't make a move until I get back.

(He runs off right.)

BLACKOUT

(The song "Do It Girl" comes on in the BLACKOUT. The red eyes of the sidewinder blink in the dark.)

DO IT GIRL

Everytime I see you wanna do it girl
Right out in the street I wanna do it girl
In front of everybody wanna do it girl
I'm losing my control I feel it in my soul

I wanna do it I wanna do it
I wanna do it, do it, do it, do it,
do it, do it, do it, do it, do it

Like a reindeer in the tundra
Wanna do it girl
Like a reptile on a mesa

Wanna do it girl
Like a tiger in the jungle
Wanna do it girl
So lay it on the line
I need you all the time

I wanna do it I wanna do it
I wanna do it, do it, do it, do it,
do it, do it, do it, do it, do it

I know you're going to love the
Way I do it girl
I know you're going to bless the day
I do it girl
There really isn't much to say
But do it girl
The time is going fast, so let the
Good times last

I wanna do it I wanna do it
I wanna do it, do it, do it, do it,
do it, do it, do it, do it, do it

by PETER STAMPFEL & ANTONIA
Music by HOLY MODAL ROUNDERS

SCENE TWO

The song fades out. The blinking red eyes turn to yellow lights and slowly rise about ten feet off the ground. Voices are heard in the dark as the lights fade up and reveal a small Volkswagen in the air on a hydraulic lift with the tail end facing the audience, its yellow tail lights blinking on and off. Below the car is a MECHANIC *dressed in greasy coveralls holding a wrench, rag, and oil can. Next to him is a* YOUNG MAN *with long blond hair down to his shoulders, a bright purple T-shirt, tight leather pants, and bare feet. They are both looking up underneath the car with their backs turned toward the audience as they talk.*

MECHANIC: So for no reason at all they just all of a sudden started blinkin' on and off?

YOUNG MAN: Well it seemed like the whole car shook for a second and then they started to blink. All the lights.

MECHANIC: Well, it could be your voltage regulator or the generator. I'll just check out yer wiring here to make sure.

YOUNG MAN: Thanks.

MECHANIC: Could've picked yerself a better time to make a movie ya' know. Days get pretty hot and long this time a' year.

YOUNG MAN: Yeah. I know.

MECHANIC: Even the all-year-arounders usually leave 'round about now. They migrate around May or June at the latest, then come back toward the tail end of September.

YOUNG MAN: Where do they go?

MECHANIC: Oh, some move into the San Berdoo Valley, some even go to Hollywood, L.A., around in there.

YOUNG MAN: No kidding.

MECHANIC: Yeah. You come here from there and they go there from here. Crazy.

YOUNG MAN: Crazy.

MECHANIC: I suppose what with all the earthquake scares and riots and all there's gonna' be a lot more folks movin' out here in the desert.

YOUNG MAN: Yeah. I suppose.

(The MECHANIC *fiddles around with some wires under the car. The* YOUNG MAN *is getting impatient.)*

MECHANIC: Well, you're gettin' paid good for your work so why should you care. How much do you get for a movie anyway?

YOUNG MAN: It depends.

MECHANIC: At least a thousand, right?

YOUNG MAN: At least.

MECHANIC: Where'd you go to college?

YOUNG MAN: I didn't.

MECHANIC: Me neither. I'm in the wrong racket though. You know how many months I gotta' work to clear a thousand? Take a guess.

YOUNG MAN: A million months. Look, what about my car? Can I get going pretty soon?

MECHANIC: Sure, sure . . .

(A pistol falls from under the car onto the ground. The MECHANIC *looks at it, then at the* YOUNG MAN. *The* YOUNG MAN *bends down and picks it up.)*

Say, you better hadn't let the Ranger catch you with that thing, son. No firearms allowed in the National Monument.

YOUNG MAN: Oh, it's all right. It's not mine. I'm taking it to a friend of mine who lives on the desert. It's his. I had it cleaned for him and put a new chamber in. He's a prospector so he never gets a chance to come into town much. So I told him I'd do it for him.

MECHANIC: Well I never heard of no prospector using a weapon like that.

(Sound of a car coming up fast and screeching to a stop. The YOUNG MAN *tries to hide the gun in his pants but it won't fit so he just sticks his hand inside his shirt with the pistol bulging out. The* MAN *from the first scene rushes on from stage right.)*

MAN: Oh—oh—I need some help. Anyone. You've got to come quick. Help—

MECHANIC: Take her easy there, mister. Catch your breath. I'll get you something to set on.

(The MECHANIC *goes off right and comes back with a wooden crate. The* MAN *is panting and looking at the* YOUNG MAN *who is getting uptight. The* MECHANIC *sets down the crate and sits the* MAN *down.)*

Here now. Here. Sit down for a second and get your breath back.

MAN: Oh—you've got to send help.

MECHANIC: What's the problem now?

MAN: My wife. Honey. My wife. She—

YOUNG MAN: What about my car!

MECHANIC: What *about* your wife?

MAN: She's—she's been attacked.

MECHANIC: Attacked?

YOUNG MAN: Come off it.

MAN: By a snake.

MECHANIC: You mean she got bit? Was it a rattler?

MAN: A huge snake.

MECHANIC: Now calm down and try to tell me where she was bit. It's important.

MAN: In the neck. Then—all over. All over.

(The YOUNG MAN *whips out the pistol and holds it on the* MECHANIC.*)*

YOUNG MAN: Now stop fucking around and fix my car, you dumb grease monkey!

MECHANIC: Now just a second, kid.

MAN: You've got to help me. My wife's going to die!

(The MAN *becomes hysterical and jumps up from the crate, rushing toward the* YOUNG MAN *who fires the pistol hitting the* MAN *in the stomach and sending him backward. He lies in a heap, dead. The* MECHANIC *moves toward him. The* YOUNG MAN *stops him with the gun.)*

YOUNG MAN: Hold it! Get my car down off the rack! Hurry up! Get it down!

MECHANIC: You're in some pickle now, son.

YOUNG MAN: Don't say anything. Just get my car down!

MECHANIC: And what if I don't?

YOUNG MAN: Then *I'll* get it down!

(He fires again, hitting the MECHANIC *in the stomach. The* MECHANIC *falls back on top of the* MAN's *body. The* YOUNG MAN *rushes to a lever under the lift and pulls it. Nothing happens. He yanks it to the right and left. Nothing happens. He kicks the lever. Still nothing.)*

YOUNG MAN: Come on, come on! Work, motherfucker! Work! Why won't you work! Work! Please work! Please! Pretty please! Work. Oh work! Please work! Work! Work! Work! Work! Work!

(Sound of bell in gas station and car pulling up and stopping off left. The YOUNG MAN *runs off right leaving the car up on the rack. Sound of jet passing overhead. Silence. A man is heard whistling off left.)*

VOICE: Shorty! Anybody home?

(A FOREST RANGER *comes on from left, dressed in uniform and sipping a Coke. He just wanders onstage without seeing the bodies and glancing up at the car.)*

BLACKOUT

("Pipeline" by the HOLY MODAL ROUNDERS *comes on in the dark.)*

FLOAT ME DOWN YOUR PIPELINE

Float me down your pipeline sometime
I came here with my guidebook
With my license in hand
But the landing field keeps slipping out of line
And this ain't what they told me I'd find
The biggest laugh around here
Is the changing ground here
Down in the alley
When the game gets fast
There ain't no piece of paper
Gonna save your ass
So float me down your pipeline sometime

I need to find a guideline sometime
These old concentric circles
Are spinning me out
And everything I do goes down in doubt
So won't you show me which way is out
I guess this is the moment
When I might need a friend
Backwater waiting for my mind to break
Guess you're the only chance that's left to take
So float me down your pipeline sometime.

by ANTONIA
Music by HOLY MODAL ROUNDERS

SCENE THREE

The song fades into the sound of the sidewinder's rattle. The blinking red eyes are seen in the dark. The lights come up on BILLY, *an old prospector with a long gray beard, floppy hat, yellow shirt, red bandanna, overalls with suspenders, long boots, pots and pans attached to his waist so they clang when he walks, and a pack on the floor beside him. He is sitting on his haunches directly behind* HONEY *who is lying frozen in the same position with the snake coiled around her body.* BILLY *talks to her in a calm soothing voice. The snake continues its rhythms.*

BILLY: Well, that was just about nineteen-o-six when they was a-gettin' all het up about the area. Yep. If you'd a' told any one a' them ten thousand folks back then that their boom town weren't a' gonna' have nothin' left but a shanty and some wild burros come nineteen-seventy-one, why there wouldn't a' been a one of 'em would a' paid ya' no never mind. No sir. They smelled that gold pumpin' through the rhyolite and there weren't no one gonna' stop that town from boomin'. 'Course there's still a few old tough ones like myself and Death Valley Smiley and Wheelburro Tex and Dapper Tommy Thompson and some a' the others. Still loco enough to believe them old yarns.

(HONEY *makes a low groaning sound and starts to undulate with the sidewinder. She seems to get more and more turned on as* BILLY *tries to calm her.*)

BILLY: Now, ya' don't want to move around much there, miss. I've seen these here critters strike so fast it'd make yer head swim. 'Course now this one's a bit extra sized. Can't say fer certain when I ever did see such a big one. If it weren't the middle of the American desert here I'd even be prone to say she was a boa constrictor. Like they have in Africa and such. 'Course that's a tad farfetched. Never can tell though. Them Air Force boys pull some mighty funny stunts out here. There's a bunch of 'em stationed just close by here ya' know. Over at Fort George. Maybe you seen 'em roarin' by. Roarin' by. Testin' the sky fer holes or somethin'. Nothin' else to do. Could be one a' them fellas dropped this big feller right outa' the sky. Ain't likely. I mean, first off they'd have to fly off to Africa to get the damned thing in the first place. Then fly it back out here. Ain't likely. Could just be though. They get so galldarned bored I'll betcha'. Testin' all the time. Sure. Nothin' else to do but fly around makin' explosions. Droppin' snakes. Probably think it's funny. Get a big charge outa' trappin' young ladies. I'll betcha'.

(HONEY has an orgasm as the YOUNG MAN comes running on from right. BILLY smiles and stands up, his arms outstretched. The YOUNG MAN crosses down left paying no attention to HONEY or the sidewinder.)

BILLY: Jimmy boy! Right on time. Just like clockwork. Look what I found here, Danny. Just lyin' here while I was a-waitin'. Come by to wait and here she was, all bound up and chokin' to death. So I tried to tell her a thing or two about the desert and snakes and such.

YOUNG MAN: Come here, Billy.

BILLY: What ya' got there, Johnny? I been a-waitin' like ya' told me. I don't ferget.

(BILLY crosses down to the YOUNG MAN who takes out the gun and runs his hands over it. The YOUNG MAN turns to BILLY and holds out the gun for him to see. BILLY takes it.)

BILLY: Oh, now Jimmy, ya' shore got a nice one. Ya' needn't a' got such a nice rod fer that half-breed. He don't know the difference 'tween a B.B. gun and a thirty-odd-six.

YOUNG MAN: I want him to have this one. You'll see that he gets it, Billy?

BILLY: Shore. I'll hand it right over. No trouble 'tall.

YOUNG MAN: Now listen carefully. I've run into some trouble so I'm going to have to do some doubling back. Now tell Mickey Free to meet me right here tomorrow at sunrise. You got that?

BILLY: Sunrise tomorrow.

YOUNG MAN: Right. Now tell him to come alone and not to bring the gun. I'll explain the rest when he gets here.

BILLY: Alone and no iron. I savvy, Johnny.

YOUNG MAN: OK. Now get going.

BILLY: What about the lady?

YOUNG MAN: What lady?

(BILLY motions to HONEY who again has become rigid as the sidewinder blinks and spits and rattles.)

She's got nothing to do with me. Now get going and remember what I just told you.

BILLY: OK, Danny. Adios!

(The YOUNG MAN hurries off right. BILLY walks up to HONEY and around behind her. He picks up his pack and slings it over his shoulder. He bends over and looks into HONEY's face. Her eyes are into a blank stare. BILLY shakes his head and goes off left twirling the pistol and singing softly)

"A beautiful bird in a gilded cage.
A beautiful sight to see.
You may think she's happy and free from fear.
She ain't though she seems to be."

(The lights fade to BLACKOUT as BILLY exits.)

("Generalonely" is heard in the BLACKOUT.)

GENERALONELY

Sad news has come to town, the blues it came in
Right up through my front door, looked like it was staying
My aide de camp replied, "What's that it's saying"
The blues has come to town looks like it's staying

A General am I and a General only
Generally I'm generally lonely
A General am I and a General only
Generally I'm generally lonely

Generally I'm generally lonely
Generally but a General only
Then my aide de camp replied, "The legal tenderly
And now we are all registered blues members"

by STEVE WEBER
Music by HOLY MODAL ROUNDERS

SCENE FOUR

The song fades out as the lights come up on an Air Force COLONEL seated behind his desk with a glass of brandy and a cigar, his foot up on his desk. Across from him is a

CAPTAIN, *also sipping brandy but slightly drunker than the* COLONEL. *Behind them is a huge colorful U.S. Air Force insignia map of the American eagle. Photographs of jets in flight. Trophies on the desk.*

COLONEL: Trouble with that bitch was, you just didn't get her out in the world enough, Henry. A young bitch like that's gotta' come in contact with a whole lotta' people and noise. Otherwise you'll just never get her cured. There's a world of difference between your dog and your bitch. A lot of breeders forget that. Just like people. Now a woman's just naturally gonna' be more sensitive than a man. No two ways about it. Same with a dog.

CAPTAIN: I don't know about that, Warner. I've seen some pretty spooky males in my day.

COLONEL: Sure! You're gonna' get your share of gun-shy males too. No way around it. That's that old argument. That heredity and environment thing. I wouldn't be the one to take sides for either. They both got their strong points. But I'll tell you this much. You can't expect a young pup, male or female, to grow up into a healthy bird dog if he's had a bad surrounding when he was little. Like a pup who's been around a lot of little brats pestering him all the time and making loud noises right in his ear. He's not gonna' grow up as brave as the pup who had a quiet peaceful home. Have some more brandy, Henry.

CAPTAIN: No. No thanks.

COLONEL: Aw, go on. Don't cost me nothin'.

CAPTAIN: All right.

(The COLONEL *pours him another drink.)*

Say, Warner, you know that big stud dog you got? The one with the speckled chest?

COLONEL: Bruce. Sure. Oh no. I'm reading your mind right now, Captain.

CAPTAIN: What?

COLONEL: I suppose you want to breed that gun-shy bitch of yours to my male.

CAPTAIN: Well her conformation makes up for her temperament. You gotta' admit that much. She's got one of the best heads you'll see in a long time.

COLONEL: A pretty head don't mean she can smell birds. Some of the best hunting dogs I've seen have been ugly as sin. Now come on, Henry. You don't want my Bruce to go getting a trauma right off the bat. He's only sired two litters so far, and if she gives him a bad bite he might never get over it. I mean I gotta' think of his future too.

CAPTAIN: She's not gonna' go biting your male, Warner. Besides, we could muzzle her.

COLONEL: Oh no. Absolutely not! I never muzzled a dog in my life and I never will. I don't care if it's the meanest dog around. That's something you just don't do to an animal. I saw a dog almost suffocate on its own saliva once. Just from that very same thing.

CAPTAIN: Well we wouldn't go off and leave them alone. I'd stand right there and hold her.

COLONEL: I'm sorry, Henry. It's just not the way I like to breed my dogs. It's a very touchy game. You're dealing with living animals, not machines.

(A loud knock on the door.)

Come in!

(A CADET enters and salutes stiffly.)

At ease.

CADET: Colonel, sir. Your presence is requested immediately at the laboratory, sir. It seems the sidewinder computer has escaped.

(The COLONEL stands abruptly, knocking over his brandy glass. The CAPTAIN tries to get out of his seat but he's too drunk.)

COLONEL: Escaped! What do you mean escaped! It's under strict surveillance!

CADET: I'm not sure, sir. That was the message from General Browser, sir.

COLONEL: How could a computer escape? Answer me that!

CADET: I have no idea, sir. That was the whole message, sir. General Browser and Dr. Vector are waiting in the lab, sir.

COLONEL: Tell them I'm on my way. Go on!

CADET: Yes sir!

(The CADET *salutes and exits.)*

COLONEL: Of all the goddamned nerve! Escaped!

BLACKOUT

("Catch Me" comes on in the dark.)

CATCH ME

Catch me if you can while I last 'cause there's nothin' to keep me
    around
Touch me with a ten-foot pole and I'll make both your feet leave the
    ground
Watch me if you can't come along 'cause I got enough here for us
    both
It's eating me inside out but I know that it won't stunt my growth

It doesn't matter what you try it's all about take and give
It doesn't matter how you die but only how you live

I'm burning up ninety-nine pounds of rubber up here in the sky
I don't know just how I got wheels or why it's so easy to fly
I can't see for millions of miles it looks like a fog up ahead
Catch me if I crash to the ground and make sure I don't land on my
    head

It doesn't matter what you try it's all about take and give
It doesn't matter how you die but only how you live

by SAM SHEPARD
Music by HOLY MODAL ROUNDERS

SCENE FIVE

*The song fades into the rattle of the sidewinder. The blinking red eyes. Hissing. The
lights come up on* HONEY, *still entangled by the sidewinder. Three men are standing
behind her, watching the sidewinder intently.* MICKEY FREE *is in the middle with two*

Apache INDIANS *standing slightly behind him, on either side. All three have long flowing black hair which falls down over their shoulders. The two* INDIANS *are very dark-skinned and dressed in the renegade Apache costume of the late eighteen hundreds, but unique from each other. Knee-length moccasin boots, rawhide pants, long loin cloths with Mexican-type designs, heavy shirts, suit jackets captured from wayward whites, tooth and bone necklaces, straight-brimmed black hats with Mexican silver coin headbands, two wide belts of ammunition crisscrossing from shoulder to waist, knives sticking out of the tops of their moccasins, and 30.30 rifles from the cavalry times.* MICKEY FREE *is a half-breed: Mexican, Irish, Apache; his skin is lighter but he looks Indian. He's half-blind in his right eye so he squints it constantly and moves his head in strange ways. He is dressed like the Apaches but flashier in spots and more heavily armed. His prize weapon is a huge Bowie knife with a turquoise and silver handle which he keeps in a beaded deerskin sheath which hangs down over his crotch, like a cock piece. All three of them watch* HONEY *and the sidewinder in silence as she goes through throes of agony-ecstasy with the sidewinder continuing his relentless moves and rhythms. Finally her eyes open and she looks up at* MICKEY FREE.*

HONEY: Help me.

(The INDIANS *are silent.* MICKEY FREE *stares at her with his one good eye.)*

Please. Help me.

*(*MICKEY *turns to the* INDIANS. *The* INDIANS *speak to him in Apache. The language should sound like a mixture of Spanish and Oriental.)*

1ST INDIAN: Natcha la oot. Gracha om laate.
2ND INDIAN: No me ta santo. Esta un gran mal muerta.

*(*MICKEY FREE *is silent. He turns back to* HONEY *and looks down at her.)*

HONEY: Please, help me. Please. Help me.

*(*MICKEY *takes out his huge Bowie knife and kneels down beside* HONEY. *He strokes the head of the sidewinder with his left hand very gently and makes a soothing sound in his throat. Suddenly his left hand seizes the neck of the sidewinder and squeezes it. The jaws pop open revealing huge fangs. He makes one sudden slash with the knife and the head comes off, leaving the body*

writhing and squirming on HONEY, *who screams and goes into hysteria. She flings the body downstage and collapses. The body writhes as* MICKEY *slowly stands up still holding the head with eyes still blinking. The* INDIANS *make sounds of approval and touch the snake's head.* MICKEY *smiles and wipes the knife off on his pants, then puts it back in the sheath. He drops the head into a beaded pouch which he wears on his waist. The body stops writhing. The* VOICE *of the* YOUNG MAN *is heard off right.)*

YOUNG MAN'S VOICE: Mickey? That you, Mickey?

*(*MICKEY *and the* INDIANS *look off right.* HONEY *is in a delirium daze.)*

HONEY: Dukie?

(The YOUNG MAN *comes on from right.)*

YOUNG MAN: Mickey! You made it!
I see you're free now. Why don't you split.

*(*HONEY *looks bewildered. The* YOUNG MAN *moves center downstage.* MICKEY *follows with the* INDIANS *close behind. The* YOUNG MAN *takes two plasticene bags filled with white powder out of his crotch and sets them on the ground. He sits down cross-legged.* MICKEY *sits beside him with the bags between them. The* INDIANS *stand behind.)*

YOUNG MAN: Did Billy give you the gun?
MICKEY: Yes.
YOUNG MAN: Is it all right?
MICKEY: Yes.
YOUNG MAN: Good. Now—
MICKEY: I'll need more than one gun.
YOUNG MAN: OK. I'll see what I can do. How many do you want?
MICKEY: Two more.
YOUNG MAN: OK. I'll get them by next week. How's that?
MICKEY: Good. Give them to Billy.
YOUNG MAN: Yeah. Now . . .
MICKEY: You have a ready roll?
YOUNG MAN: Sure.

(He takes out a cigarette and hands it to MICKEY.*)*

MICKEY: You have two more?

(The YOUNG MAN *offers the pack to the two* INDIANS.*)*

YOUNG MAN: Here. Keep the pack.

(The INDIANS *take the pack and take out cigarettes.* MICKEY *puts out his hand to the* INDIANS. *They give the pack to* MICKEY *who puts it in the top of his moccasin.* MICKEY *takes out a butane lighter from his other moccasin and lights his cigarette, then he lights the* INDIANS'.*)*

YOUNG MAN: Now, this is the stuff. It's more than enough to do the trick.
MICKEY: Trick?
YOUNG MAN: Yeah. Trick, job.
MICKEY: Job.
YOUNG MAN: Now your job is very easy but you have to pull it off without fail. There's a lot of people counting on you. People you've never seen before. You're going to mean a lot to them if everything works the way we have it run down. Now the reason we've come to you is because you know the layout of Fort George probably better than anyone in the desert, mainly because you helped them get it started.
MICKEY: Yes. I find them low ground.
YOUNG MAN: Right. And that's valuable to us because now you can take these bags directly to their reservoir and dump them without anyone getting suspicious. Now here's the plan: tomorrow, you and your friends ride into the fort at high noon. You go straight to the commanding officer's headquarters and ask to speak to General Browser. They'll ask you what you want to see him about and you tell them that you're looking for work.
MICKEY: Work!
YOUNG MAN: Yeah. Work, job. You need a job. And then they'll tell you they're very sorry but they have no work, come back some other time, and you say all right and start to leave. Then you ask them if it's all right if you water your horses out at the reservoir because you've been riding all day and they're really wiped out. Then they'll probably give you a pass to enter the reservoir area. If they don't then ask them for

one. Then you take the pass, get back on your horses, with the dope in your saddlebags.

MICKEY: Dope?

YOUNG MAN: Yeah, the stuff! And ride into the reservoir area. I doubt if they'll have a guard on duty there but if they do I'm sure you can handle him. Just show him the pass and play dumb. When you get to the reservoir, dismount and water your horses. Then just take the dope out of the saddlebags and cut the bags open and let all the powder fall into the water. Be sure to put the empty plastic bags in your saddlebags. Don't leave them at the reservoir. Then just get back on your horse and ride away. You got it?

MICKEY: Yes.

YOUNG MAN: Good.

MICKEY: I have more friends who wish to help too. They say anything that will make the silver birds leave the skies will be pleasing to the Spider Woman.

YOUNG MAN: Tell them to wait. Anything can happen. We'll let them know.

(MICKEY *gives an order to the* INDIANS.)

MICKEY: Nanza nienta paz. Para los caballos.

(*The* INDIANS *go to the plasticene bags. One of them has a leather saddlebag which he opens while the other one puts the bags inside.* MICKEY *stands up with the* YOUNG MAN. *They shake hands by clasping each other's wrists.*)

YOUNG MAN: I'll come to your place next week and let you know how things went.

MICKEY: Good.

YOUNG MAN: Good luck.

MICKEY: Hasta luego.

(*The three of them go off stage left. The* YOUNG MAN *looks at* HONEY *who is staring at him with a blank gaze.*)

YOUNG MAN: What're you looking at?

(He reaches into his pocket and pulls out a small leather pouch with a zipper. He sits down and zips it open. He takes out a needle, an eye-dropper syringe and a small vial of liquid. He lifts up his T-shirt and feels for his belt. He notices he's not wearing one.)

Hey! Do you have a belt on you? Or a tie?
HONEY: Belt? No.

(He looks around the stage angrily. He sees the sidewinder's body. He reaches for it and grabs the rattle end, pulling it close to him. He fixes up the needle, opens the vial and draws the liquid up into the syringe.)

Do you have any water?
YOUNG MAN: Yeah. It's in the canteen.

(HONEY scrambles to the canteen, opens it and takes a long drink. The YOUNG MAN struggles with the snake's body, trying to tie it as a tourniquet around his left arm.)

HONEY: What are you doing?
YOUNG MAN: Trying to get off. What does it look like. Fuck! Would you come here for a second.
HONEY What?
YOUNG MAN: Just come here. I'm not going to bite you.

(HONEY crawls to him on her hands and knees.)

Would you wrap this tight around my arm and just hold it.
HONEY: Are you crazy? That thing almost strangled me to death.
YOUNG MAN: Well now it's your turn to strangle it. Come on. Look. He's dead.

(He shakes the sidewinder's body in her face. She jumps back.)

Dead! Just do it for a favor. OK? Please? Come on. Be a sport.

(She takes the snake and wraps it around his left arm.)

Pull. Now just hold on to it. Don't let go.

(HONEY pulls the snake tight. The YOUNG MAN rubs his vein and jabs the needle in. HONEY makes a shriek and jumps back, letting the snake go. The YOUNG MAN lets out a yell.)

Oh fuck! You stupid cunt! You almost broke my point! My last point! You almost ripped out my vein! Jesus Christ!

(He rubs his arm in agony.)

HONEY: I'm sorry. I didn't know you were gonna' poke yourself.
YOUNG MAN: I told you not to let go. Now would you wrap it tight and hold on this time.
HONEY: All right.

(She goes through the same thing again with the snake. He jabs the needle in this time and gets a hit.)

YOUNG MAN: All right. Now let go slowly. Slowly. Easy. That's it.

(She slowly releases her grip on the sidewinder. It falls to the floor. The YOUNG MAN relaxes and smiles at HONEY.)

Now. That wasn't so bad, was it?
HONEY: Are you a diabetic?
YOUNG MAN: Yeah. I need lots of sugar.
HONEY: Could I have some?
YOUNG MAN: You think you need it?
HONEY: I can't seem to get up any energy. I mean you use it for energy, don't you? That darn snake knocked the wind out of me.
YOUNG MAN: I suppose I could spare some. Just to get you up on your feet. Don't come asking me for more though.
HONEY: Oh, I won't. I just need a boost. Boy, I'm really glad you came along. You know? I thought I was gonna' be stuck out here forever. There's a lot of creepy people out here. You're the first decent person I've seen.

(He wraps the snake around her right arm.)

YOUNG MAN: All right. Now grab both ends and pull tight. Close your eyes and don't look. OK?

(She follows his orders as the YOUNG MAN *fills the syringe and* HONEY *talks with her eyes closed. The lights fade out to* BLACK *as the* YOUNG MAN *shoots her up.)*

HONEY: It's not going to hurt, is it? I've had enough pain for one day. I just have to get up enough energy to look for Dukie. He's my husband. He just all of a sudden ran off someplace to get some help and I haven't seen him since. We were on our way to Las Vegas to get a divorce. It's not that we weren't happy or anything. We were very happy. We just needed a change you know. A sort of vacation from each other. So we decided to make it a vacation together. You know what I mean. I mean so long as we were getting divorced we might as well make it a vacation. Kill two birds with one stone. Then this snake got me and I don't even know what happened. One minute we were together and the next minute we were separated. Just like that. I guess this desert does funny things to your brain or something. It's not going to hurt me, is it?

BLACKOUT

*(*HONEY *screams. "Euphoria" is heard in the dark.)*

EUPHORIA
   Ma's out here switchin' in the kitchen
   And dad's in the living room grousin' and a bitchin'
   And I'm out here kicking the gong for "Euphoria"

   Euphoria when your mind goes wheelin' and a walkin'
   Your inside voices go squealin' and a squawkin'
   Floating around on a belladonna cloud
   Singing Euphoria

   There's a man in the corner underneath a table
   He sat makin' faces at a union label
   He pitched his ears and then he rolled his eyes
   And whispered "Euphoria"

Euphoria when your mind goes wheelin' and a walkin'
Your inside voices go squealin' and a squawkin'
Floating around on a belladonna cloud
Singing Euphoria

I went for a walk and just got back
I saw a junkie mother boosting Similac
She had her baby on her back and her works in her hand
She hollered "Euphoria"

Euphoria when your mind goes wheelin' and a walkin'
Your inside voices go squealin' and a squawkin'
Floating around on a belladonna cloud
Singing Euphoria

Pinched Eve on the bottom, patted Adam on the back
Smiled at the serpent and it winked back
Took a bite from the apple with two bites gone
And hollered "Euphoria"

Euphoria when your mind goes wheelin' and a walkin'
Your inside voices go squealin' and a squawkin'
Floating around on a belladonna cloud
Singing Euphoria

by ROBIN REMAILY
Copyright—Windfall Music 1968
Music by HOLY MODAL ROUNDERS

SCENE SIX

The song fades out. The lights slowly come up on a '57 Chevy convertible. Three Blacks are sitting in the car. BLOOD *is driving.* BLADE *and* DUDE *sit in the back. Above them hanging in midair is a huge hot-dog sign. A* CARHOP *enters from left and walks up to the car. She is young and dressed in a stupid white mini outfit with a funny hat, a checkbook and pencil.*

CARHOP: Can I help you guys?

BLOOD: *(To the two in back)* What do you want?

BLADE: Let me have a cheeseburger, a chocolate malt and a order a' fries.

DUDE: Yeah. Same thing for me except make it vanilla.

CARHOP: The malt?

BLOOD: Right.

CARHOP: Say, are you guys with the Panthers?

DUDE: No, we're with the Rams.

BLOOD: Let me have a B.L.T. on whole wheat toast with mayo.

CARHOP: A B.L.T. on whole wheat.

BLOOD: And a large milk.

CARHOP: Sure. You know I've been wanting to talk to some of your people for a long time. I go to City College and it seems like there's this whole gap in dialogue between what we're trying to do and what you're trying to do. You know what I mean? Like I can really dig this whole unity thing that you guys are into but it seems like we could be doing something to help bind it all together. You know. I mean you people have such a groovy thing going.

BLOOD: Yeah, right.

CARHOP: I mean all this shit about the pigs, man. I mean fuck the pigs. Forget all those gray people. We're not going to turn on any of those zombies. We gotta' find our own people. Turn ourselves on. Make something happen for us.

DUDE: For us?

CARHOP: Yeah, us. You and me. Fuck them. All that festering bullshit is just going to collapse anyway. I mean I gotta' work to pay for my school but once that's over, man, I'm gone. You know? I mean I'm going to go out and help organize, help get it together. Because if we don't get it together pretty soon we're gonna' be had. Am I right?

BLADE: Right.

CARHOP: And I'm not just doing a rap to make myself feel good either. Because I got nothing to lose. Least of all this shitty job. I mean I can see where things are at. With you guys it's all laid out. With me it's different. I got a lot of guessing to do. With you it's armed struggle. I'm for that. I think it's a necessary step. A revolution begins when a faction seizes power and begins to use it to change society. Armed struggle comes before the revolution. Armed struggle begins when the oppressed people pick up guns and are willing to die for the revolution.

I'm willing. I know you guys are. I got a gun right in my house, man, and I'm ready to use it too.

BLOOD: Good. What kind is it?

CARHOP: What? The gun? I'm not sure. A thirty-eight or something. But listen, we can't afford to compromise anymore. Some people are saying all they want is a piece of the American pie. Well we can't have a piece of that pie because that pie exploits our brothers in Vietnam, in Latin America and in Africa.

BLOOD: Let me have a piece of cherry pie with that too.

CARHOP: Cherry pie?

BLOOD: Yeah. With the B.L.T.

CARHOP: Oh. OK. All right. One cherry pie. Right. I'll be right back.

(She writes it down on her checkbook and exits right.)

BLOOD: Now, down to business.

DUDE: Yeah, what's the story with this flower child in the desert? You really trust him to deliver the goods?

BLOOD: Don't worry, once that dope takes hold the Air Force is going to be doing some mighty funny things.

BLADE: How's it supposed to work anyway?

BLOOD: Mickey Free makes the drop. Right?

BLADE: Right.

BLOOD: The pilots get a good taste of supersonic water. They start feeling funny. They hear voices. They see things in the air. They hear music. They get stoned like they never been before in their lives.

DUDE: Then what?

BLOOD: In the middle of the night they all get up in unison like Dracula and his sisters and walk straight out into the night. They climb into their sleek super duper F-one-elevens and take off. They fly straight for a little island just south of Miami whereupon they land and await further instructions.

DUDE: Sounds pretty shaky to me.

BLOOD: How come?

DUDE: I don't know, it's just like James Bond or something. Why don't we just go in and take the thing over.

BLADE: Yeah, I can't see getting involved with this hippie cat, Blood. His mind's been burned out. The drug thing just isn't going to pull it off.

BLOOD: We gotta' give it some time. It's just a step.

DUDE: Watch it, here comes the S.D.S.

(The CARHOP *enters again with their order. She walks up to them.)*

CARHOP: Say listen I'm sorry I got so carried away before but I really meant what I said.

BLOOD: Right. You got the milk?

CARHOP: Milk? Oh. Yeah. Here it is. I mean we can't debate whether we want revolution or whether we don't want revolution because for our survival we're going to have to make revolution. Right? I mean I guess you guys already know that.

BLADE: Pass the french fries.

BLACKOUT

("Synergy" is heard.)

SYNERGY
  CHORUS

  Superman's on the can contemplating synergy
  Lone ranger on the range and Dr. Strange got synergy
  Cool heads certainly agree concerning synergy
  Likewise Liberace's momma
  Donald Duck and Dalai Lama
  Yes sir!

  Come along, sing with me sing a song of synergy
  Find that peace in your soul
  We're all one and heaven is our goal

  CHORUS

  Synergy will get us all and it's going to be a ball
  Kick that gong, ring that bell, synergy will save us all from hell

  CHORUS

  Be a friend, lend a hand, try your best to understand
  We are all born alone, but the light of love can lead us home

CHORUS

Get undressed, plant a tree, make love to machinery
Throw away all the locks, open up the jails and stop the clocks

CHORUS

We can have paradise right now at a bargain price
Heaven is ours to make, peace on earth is there for us to take

CHORUS

by PETER STAMPFEL & ANTONIA
Music by HOLY MODAL ROUNDERS

SCENE SEVEN

The Air Force Laboratory at Fort George. Test tubes, vials, Bunsen burners, a general clutter of chemical and electronic gadgets. In the middle of all this DOCTOR VECTOR, *sitting in a wheelchair, dressed in a white chemist's smock. He is very tiny and his entire body is twisted and bent. He wears extra-thick dark glasses and elevator shoes and speaks with a weird shifting accent. When he wants to move his wheelchair he presses a button on one of the arms and the chair propels itself electronically. On either side of him are* GENERAL BROWSER, *obviously pissed off but trying to keep his cool, and* COLONEL WARNER *who goes into fits of temper but snaps out of it by the* GENERAL's *presence.*

COLONEL: I've never in my whole career in the United States Air Force heard of such a half-cocked idea as this one! I mean freedom to experiment to my mind has always meant for the experimenter, I mean the person or persons doing the experiment, not the goddamn experiment itself! Now that's just never ever been done before, Doctor Vector, and I for one . . .

GENERAL: Now settle down, Warner. I'm sure the doctor had his reasons for allowing this to happen. What's done is done. The fact is that I should have personally seen to it that the arrangements for Operation Sidewinder were made more clear to everyone involved. Including myself. I certainly had no idea you were off on a tangent like this, Doctor Vector.

DR. VECTOR: What tangent? No tangent. This now is marking the beginning of the stage I had so long awaited. You should both be beaming with the joy I now feel. The sidewinder computer has now chosen to go off on its own accord. It has chosen to be free and exist on its own. For weeks I have watched it writhing and squirming with its wonderful powerful body. Sidewinding its way around its little artificial desert. Searching for a way out. Searching every corner. Its magnificent head straining toward the top of the glass then back down to the bottom. Knowing that all around, outside, out in the real world was a desert and sky so vast and so free. A captive with more cosmic secrets than a man could learn from the whole of history. Finally I saw the decision lay in my hands, gentlemen. In my hands. It was up to me to either keep this creature in its cage and continue to feed it my steady diet of limited knowledge or to set it free and have it discover its true potential. Do you realize the magnitude of this action? It means for the first time ever we can begin to study the effects of the machine's own decisions on its own survival. For the first time in history we shall see if it is possible to produce a machine with its own brain and its own synthetic form of life and have it survive on its own without our constant presence and supervision. All this and still have it retain the willingness to achieve the purpose for which it was programmed. Oh sure, you say it's already been done before. Some biochemist in New Jersey might maybe come up with some small germ of plastic bacteria that he says is life. All year they watch it under glass and give it injections and change the light and switch around the soils but so what! That is no experiment! Not like the sidewinder! The sidewinder computer this very minute is surviving on one of the most inhospitable deserts in the world! Surviving by its own synthetic wits! And you two talk as though we have thrown away a lifetime! Bah! The Army should never have nothing to do with Science!

COLONEL: This is the Air Force, Doctor! And it's not a lifetime that you've thrown away but almost two billion dollars! How does that grab you?

GENERAL: Now wait a minute, Colonel. The doctor seems to feel that his sidewinder computer will perform better and reveal more information to us if left on its own. That's all well and good. However, I'm left with certain uncertainties, Doctor.

DR. VECTOR: Yah, General?

GENERAL: From a purely pragmatic point of view, now that the computer has escaped, or in your words ventured off on its own, how is it possible for you to program it or even trace its existence, if in fact it is still alive. I mean . . .

COLONEL: Alive! Judas Priest!

DR. VECTOR: Gentlemen, gentlemen! Operation Sidewinder was begun by the government in late 1964 Yah? (Yah!) in an effort to produce a tracing computer which would help to solve the questions of whether or not unidentified flying objects actually existed. Oui? (Oui!) Since that time we have discovered that they do in fact exist Dah? (Dah!) and the next step, as you both are well aware, was of course to trace their flight patterns in an effort to learn their trade routes and possibly the planet or star from where they are living.

COLONEL: Now come off it, Doc. We all know that Constellation Pegasus has . . .

GENERAL: Please, Colonel! Let the doctor finish.

DR. VECTOR: At this stage it became apparent to me that all manmade efforts to produce this type of information were useless and that a much more sophisticated form of intelligence was necessary. A form of intelligence which, being triggered from the mind of man, would eventually, if allowed to exist on its own, transcend the barriers of human thought and penetrate an extraterrestrial consciousness. This is when I began my studies of the Western rattlesnakes and experimenting with the possibilities of their rhythmic movements being directly connected with the movements of the planets and the flight patterns of the UFOs. These studies resulted in the initial design for my sidewinder computer. Now, whether or not the sidewinder will be able to attain this realm of extraterrestrial consciousness is something none of us will know until we are ready. One thing is for certain, the sidewinder must have complete freedom to discover this realm for itself. And gentlemen, if it succeeds we will be the first to know. Think of it, gentlemen! We will be in direct contact with these flying objects and eventually with those who operate and control them!

COLONEL: What a bunch a' horse shit.

BLACKOUT

("Dusty Fustchuns" comes on in the dark.)

DUSTY FUSTCHUNS

> Don't leave me dying in the desert
> Don't leave me dangling in the dust
> I don't wanna live here with these here lizards
> They look at me with a cold and hungry lust
> Big bird circlin' in the sky is a buzzard
> Think he got his eye on me
> The ever shiftin' sand is the only sound I hear
> And that mirage over there is the only water near
>
> I got a pound of sand in my navel
> When night comes I turn into ice
> At high noon brains melt like butter
> No one to talk to but the toads and the mice
>
> Devil take away these damn sand dunes
> Devil take away this sun
> Devil take away this dry dusty hole
> This is all a mistake and
> I'm cooked till overdone

(Coyote howls for last verse)

by ROBIN REMAILY
Music by HOLY MODAL ROUNDERS

SCENE EIGHT

The song fades into the sound of crickets. A coyote howls. A full moon glows in the dark. Stars come out. The lights fade up slowly to bluish moonlight. The YOUNG MAN *and* HONEY *are lying on their backs upstage staring at the night sky. The body of the sidewinder is downstage left.* HONEY *moves voluptuously around on her back, stretching and unbuttoning her blouse. The* YOUNG MAN *just stares at the sky.*

HONEY: Oh, it's so gorgeous. A full moon. And the stars. I never felt so good in my whole life. Everything smells so wild out here. Smell the yucca. It's so peaceful and nice. Hey, what's your name anyway? Do

you have a name? My name's Honey. That's because my husband
called me that. He said it was because of my honey hair. My yellow
honey hair. Dukie said it even smelled like honey. You wanna' smell
my hair? You can smell it if you want. Sometimes I even smell it. I
used to all the time. When I was a little girl. I'd go in the closet and
smell it. I never cut it because my mama said that sometime . . .
someday I'd make my living from my hair. That's what she told me.
That I should come to Hollywood and the very next day, just from
walking around the streets and everything, that someone would see
my hair and ask me to come and get a screen test. And that before
very long I'd be famous and rich and everything. I'd never have to
worry about a man supporting me or anything because I'd have
enough to support myself. And then I met Dukie and . . .

*(A shock of blue light goes off above the stage, like a huge flash bulb. Then a
beam of white light goes across the sky behind them from left to right and disappears.* HONEY *sits up. The* YOUNG MAN *stays relaxed on his back.* HONEY
stares up at the sky.)

HONEY: Hey! Did you see that!
YOUNG MAN: Shooting stars.
HONEY: Boy. I never saw one before. It looks like it's still there.
YOUNG MAN: Why should it go away?
HONEY: Well, don't they just fall and then . . . Look! Look at the way it's
   moving. Sideways. I'm scared.
YOUNG MAN: Why be scared of a star?
HONEY: What if it's not a star? What if it's one of those creepy saucer
   things?
YOUNG MAN: What if it is?
HONEY: Boy, you don't get very excited about anything, do you?

(She lies back down next to the YOUNG MAN *moving closer and trying to turn
him on.)*

YOUNG MAN: Only when it counts.
HONEY: I'll bet you're really something when you get excited. How come
   you don't get a haircut?
YOUNG MAN: 'Cause my pappy told me that one day I'd make my living
   from my hair.

HONEY: Are you making fun of me?

YOUNG MAN: No. It's true. My pappy was way ahead of his time. He said, son, in a few years all a young man'll have to do to make a few bucks is just grow his hair long and set on a street corner and things'll start happening to him. Like magic.

HONEY: Do you believe in magic?

YOUNG MAN: I used to. I walked through the crowd. I saw my best friends there. Real friends. I felt such a warm bond between us. Like we were all in the same place at the same time for the same reason.

HONEY: What are you talking about?

YOUNG MAN: And suddenly I felt free, my mind was lifting up, up, up in flight. Not like that thirteen-year-old, wild, crazy, out-of-the-house-on-Friday-night feeling but something much deeper. Like nothing could hurt me. Nothing could touch my peace.

HONEY: Boy, you're really weird.

YOUNG MAN: It was like all that oppression from the month before had suddenly cracked open and left me in space. The election oppression: Nixon, Wallace, Humphrey. The headline oppression every morning with one of their names on it. The radio news broadcast, TV oppression. And every other advertisement with their names and faces and voices and haircuts and suits and collars and ties and lies. And I was all set to watch "Mission: Impossible" when Humphrey's flabby face shows up for another hour's alienation session. Oh please say something kind to us, something soft, something human, something different, something real, something—so we can believe again. His squirmy little voice answers me, "You can't always have everything your way." And the oppression of my fellow students becoming depressed. Depressed. Despaired. Running out of gas. "We're not going to win. There's nothing we can do to win." This is how it begins, I see. We become so depressed we don't fight anymore. We're only losing a little, we say. It could be so much worse. The soldiers are dying, the Blacks are dying, the children are dying. It could be so much worse. Everything must be considered in light of the political situation. No getting around it. It could be so much worse.

HONEY: Think about something nice.

YOUNG MAN: Let's wait till four years from now when we can take over the Democratic party. Teddy Kennedy is still alive. Let's not do anything at all. It can only get worse. Let's give up. And then I walked through the crowd of smiling people. They were loving and happy, alive and free. You can't win all the time. You can't always have everything your own way. You'll be arrested. You'll be arrested, accosted, molested, tested and retested. You'll be beaten, you'll be jailed, you'll be thrown out of school. You'll be spanked, you'll be whipped and chained. But I am whipped. I am chained. I am prisoner to all your oppression. I am depressed, deranged, decapitated, dehumanized, defoliated, demented and damned! I can't get out. You can get out. You can smile and laugh and kiss and cry. I am! I am! I am! I am! I am! I am! I am! I am! I am! I am! I am! Tonight. In this desert. In this space. I am.

(Another flash of blue light that seems more prolonged this time. Again the beam of light goes across the sky from stage left to stage right. At the same time the body of the sidewinder lights up green and jumps. The rattle rattles and the end of the tail begins to twitch. HONEY screams and cuddles close to the YOUNG MAN who sits up slightly.)

YOUNG MAN: What's the matter now?

HONEY: That snake! It's still alive! It moved!

YOUNG MAN: Bullshit.

HONEY: It did! It lit up green and moved. There! Look at it! It twitched! Didn't you see it!

YOUNG MAN: You're just hallucinating. Relax.

HONEY: I swear it moved. Listen! Can't you hear it? It's rattling. It's still alive! Sit up and look at it!

(The YOUNG MAN lies on his back and stares at the sky. The sidewinder moves again. As HONEY watches it and talks, the sidewinder body slowly inches its way across the stage.)

HONEY: Well I don't want to get strangled again. Once is enough. It's moving again! Hey! Hey!

YOUNG MAN: Take it easy. It's all in your mind.

HONEY: It's not in my mind! It's right there! It's moving and rattling and I'm looking right at it! Why don't you look and see for yourself. Please look at it. You're scaring me. I know I'm not going crazy! Who are you anyway! Hey! Talk to me. I've told you everything about me and you haven't told me one thing. Hey!

(The YOUNG MAN *suddenly grabs her and pulls her to the ground then rolls over on top of her. He kisses her and feels her up.* HONEY *screams and squirms. Another flash of light from above. The beam of light across the sky. The sidewinder lights up red and twitches wildly. The rattle grows louder as it inches its way across the stage.)*

HONEY: What are you doing! Let go of me! Let me go! Stop! Stop it! Get off! Get off of me! My husband's going to get you for this! Dukie! Help! Help! Somebody!

(The YOUNG MAN *rips off her blouse and starts kissing her tits and stomach.* HONEY *gets turned on and runs her fingers through his hair.)*

Oh. Oh. OOOOOOOOH. Yes. Yes. Oh. Lick me. Lick me. Yes. Oh. You're fantastic. Oh. Yes. Yes. Yes. Lick me! Lick me!

(The YOUNG MAN *stops suddenly and stands up, straddling* HONEY *with his legs.)*

What's the matter? You can kiss me. It's all right. What's wrong? You're really weird, mister. I'm leaving. I want to leave!

The YOUNG MAN *looks up at the sky with his back to the audience and stares.* HONEY *begins to panic. From this point on there are more frequent blasts of blue light. Each time the sidewinder lights up alternately green and red and the rattling grows louder as he slithers and inches across the stage.)*

YOUNG MAN: It's all going to happen now.
HONEY: What is? I'm leaving here!

(She tries to leave. The YOUNG MAN *puts his foot gently on her chest and pushes her back down.)*

YOUNG MAN: You can't. We're caught. We're captured.
HONEY: Not me! Nobody's capturing me or kidnapping me or anything else! I'm free! I can come and go anywhere I like! You can't make me stay here!
YOUNG MAN: You're right.

(He lets her up. She stands but can't move. She seems almost hypnotized.)

HONEY: Wait a minute. Wait . . . What did you give me anyway? What was in that needle? You're not diabetic! I've seen diabetics before and you're not one of them! Who are you anyway? How did you get here? Where are you from?

YOUNG MAN: I am from the planet Crypton. No. I am from the Hollywood Hills. No. I am from Freak City. That's where I was raised anyway. A small town. A town like any other town. A town like Mama used to make with lace doilies and apple pie and incest and graft. No. It's not true. I am an American though. Despite what they say. In spite of the scandal. I am truly an American. I was made in America. Born, bred and raised. I have American blood. I dream American dreams. I fuck American girls. I devour the planet. I'm an earth eater. No. I'm a lover of peace. A peace maker. A flower child, burned by the times. Burned out. A speed freak. A Tootsie Roll, an Abazaba. I came to infect the continent. To spread my disease. To make my mark, to make myself known. To cut down the trees, to dig out the gold, to shoot down the deer, to capture the wind. But now I'm myself. Now I'm here. And it's all going to happen now. Right now. It's all going to happen.

(HONEY collapses.)

BLACKOUT

(Bright flash of light. Beams of light go back and forth across the sky. Then back to blackness. A sonic boom. Above the proscenium a large neon "Intermission" sign in red blinks on and off continuously as the song "Alien Song" comes on.)

ALIEN SONG

You don't have to do me no favors
You don't have to tell me no lies
Just tell me what happened to my neighbors
When all I can see is black flies

It wasn't so long that I wandered
It wasn't so long I was gone
But now I come back and there's no wooden shack
And the turnips I grew are all gone

You don't look to me like a native
The way that you move is so strange
I wish I was feeling creative
But maybe it's time for a change

Maybe I took the wrong highway
Maybe I made a mistake
But this is the creek where I caught pollywogs
And I know 'cause I just took a drink

Maybe we could make conversation
I see that your lips have no skin
There must be a simple explanation
But how come you're wearing a grin

I couldn't go back where I came from
'Cause that would just bring me back here
And this is the place I was born, bred and raised
And it doesn't seem like I was ever here

It looks like your forehead's on fire
But maybe I'm losing my grip
It sounds like your voice is a choir
And now both my feet seem to slip

Now I can see my whole body
Stranded way down by the creek
It looks so alone while it looks for its home
And it doesn't hear me while I shriek

by SAM SHEPARD
Music by HOLY MODAL ROUNDERS

Act Two

Black stage. The houselights go down. The sun glows onstage and becomes brighter and brighter revealing the '57 Chevy seen in Act One, center stage. The three Blacks are seated inside. They are on the desert. The radio in the car is blaring Booker T.

and the M.G.s' "Green Onions." The Blacks sit motionless and listen to the tune for a full sixty seconds. Then BLOOD *turns the radio off with a sharp snap.* DUDE *and* BLADE *slowly open their doors on either side and get out of the car. They slam the doors shut and walk to the back of the car as* BLOOD *sits motionless behind the wheel staring straight ahead.*

DUDE: Keys, Blood!

(BLOOD *takes the keys out of the ignition and, without looking back, puts his arm out the window and tosses them back to* DUDE, *who catches them.* DUDE *unlocks the trunk and raises it. Inside are the* YOUNG MAN *and* HONEY *with their hands tied behind their backs and gags in their mouths.* DUDE *and* BLADE *lift them out of the trunk and pull them around to the downstage side of the car and slam them up against it. The* YOUNG MAN *and* HONEY *make muffled screams and protests as* DUDE *and* BLADE *pull out guns and level them at their heads, as though to execute the two of them.)*

BLOOD: Hold it!

(BLOOD *opens his door and slides out. He walks up to* HONEY *and the* YOUNG MAN *and stares at them, them reaches up simultaneously with both hands to grab their gags and yanks them out of their mouths.)*

YOUNG MAN: Hey Blood, what's . . .
BLOOD: Shut up!
HONEY: You guys better not hurt us. They got Forest Rangers out here. They make the round every half-hour.
YOUNG MAN: What's going on, Blood? Did something go wrong?
BLOOD: Yeah, something went wrong. Your friend Mickey Free didn't make the drop.
YOUNG MAN: What? Why not? What happened?
BLOOD: You tell me.
YOUNG MAN: I left him with the dope. I trusted him completely.
BLOOD: Seems as though he took off into the desert with a very valuable computer and just forgot all about our plan.
YOUNG MAN: I don't know anything about a computer.
BLOOD: It also seems like there's a couple dead men in a garage somewhere who can easily be traced to a Volkswagen which can be easily traced to us.

YOUNG MAN: I had to shoot them. They were slowing me down.

HONEY: You shot somebody? You never told me you shot anybody.

YOUNG MAN: Shut up!

BLOOD: One thing I figured sure was that we could shape a psychedelic head any which way once we gave it the proper injections. Once we set it straight on a few political scores. 'Course there might be such a thing as an overdose of that technique. I mean I can dig it. The revolution looks old-fashioned once you seen the universe. Ain't I right now. I mean all them lovelies floatin' around the street lookin' for a taste of acid pants and some insights into their karma and the right sign to match up to theirs. I mean there ain't much of a choice between balling all day and getting high or becoming a responsible revolutionary. Now ain't that the truth. I mean shoot, you didn't spend all them years fightin' the draft just to get the same bullshit from a bunch of crazy Blackmen.

YOUNG MAN: OK man, look.

BLOOD: Oh, now he's calling me man! He's speakin' my language! Yeah, brother! Bring on the chitlins! You gonna' have to be a whole lot hipper than hip to get out of this mess, chump.

YOUNG MAN: I'm trying to talk to you!

BLOOD: Rap!

YOUNG MAN: I ran into a jam at a garage. The car was doing weird things. So I went into this garage to get it checked out. I was there for a couple hours trying to get it fixed. Then this crazy comes running into the gas station saying his wife got bit by a huge snake or something.

HONEY: When was that? You never told me about that.

YOUNG MAN: Just shut up!

HONEY: That was me he was talking about.

YOUNG MAN: Shut up! So this guy comes running in and gets the mechanic all hung up in his thing. So I shot him. I shot them both.

HONEY: That was Dukie! That was my Dukie! You shot him! You shot my Dukie!

(HONEY *starts screaming and kicking at the* YOUNG MAN. BLOOD *gives a command and* BLADE *steps in and jams the gag back in* HONEY'*s mouth. She goes on sobbing and kicking.*)

BLOOD: *(To young man):* You're real stupid. You know that?

YOUNG MAN: Come on, Blood. I did everything you told me.

BLOOD: But nothing worked! Nothing worked! You fucked up! Now we're right back where we started.

YOUNG MAN: I can find Mickey. I'll go look for him and find out what happened.

BLOOD: There's bigger stakes now.

YOUNG MAN: What do you mean?

BLOOD: The Sidewinder Computer. That snake you heard that guy screaming about?

YOUNG MAN: What about it?

BLOOD: We want that snake. We want it bad. You dig?

(A FOREST RANGER *enters from right. The Blacks are very cool.* HONEY *desperately tries to gesture to the* RANGER.)

RANGER: You folks having trouble?

BLOOD: Yeah. As a matter of fact we are. We've been trying to get to Ubehebe Crater for the past hour and a half now and we haven't been able to find it.

RANGER: Well you folks should have stopped in at the Ranger station before venturing off on your own. This desert's no place to play around in.

BLOOD: Yeah, we realized that but we just got so excited about seeing the sights that we couldn't wait.

RANGER: Things are especially dangerous now since there were two men killed not too far from here just last week. We still haven't found the killer.

BLOOD: Is that right. Well if we see anything we'll . . .

RANGER: Is the young lady all right?

BLOOD: Sure, she just got a little sunstroke.

RANGER: What's she got in her mouth?

BLOOD: A wet cloth. They say that's the best thing for a sunstroke.

RANGER: Well not stuffed in her mouth like that. She's liable to suffocate.

BLOOD: She'll be all right in a little while.

RANGER: Say, how come she's tied up like that? Now wait a minute. I'm no fool.

(BLOOD *pulls out a gun and levels it at the* RANGER.)

BLOOD: You're the biggest fool around, baby. Now drop your gun. Go on!

(There is a long pause as the RANGER *considers what to do next. Suddenly he tries to draw his gun and* BLOOD *fires three shots into him. He falls dead.* HONEY *sobs through her gag.* BLOOD *points the gun at the* YOUNG MAN's *head.)*

BLOOD: Now you got one last chance to redeem yourself, Charlie. That extra-sized snake that Mickey Free's got is something we need. We need it bad. Now I want you to find it and bring it back to us. The head and all. You dig? Now if you goof once more I suggest that you and your foxy lady here head for south of the border and start yourself a pot farm or something 'cause we're gonna' be after your ass.

(BLOOD turns the YOUNG MAN *around and cuts his arms loose with a knife.)*

YOUNG MAN: I can travel better on my own. Can't you take her back with you?

BLOOD: She's gonna' lead you to that snake, boy. Now you cut her loose.

(BLOOD hands the knife to the YOUNG MAN.)*

BLACKOUT

("Bad Karma" is played.)

BAD KARMA

    I got that bad karma baby
    Gonna lay it on you
    Got that bad karma baby
    Nothing better to do
    And when that bad karma hits you
    Gonna holler and moan
    Got that bad karma baby
    Gonna bring it all home
    I try so hard
    I try to behave
    But that bad karma baby gonna lead me to my grave.

    I'm as down as a wart hog on a summer day
    I'm as down as a depth charge in my own sweet way
    I'm a down bringing back biting evil thing doer

I was born in an outhouse and I live in a sewer
I try so hard
I try to behave
But that bad karma baby gonna lead me to my grave.

When I'm reincarnated I get meaner yet
You may think I'm the lowest it's a damn good bet
But if I ain't the lowest I'll find out who is
And if his karma's badder I will rip off his
I try so hard
I try to behave
But that bad karma baby gonna lead me to my grave.

by STAMPFEL & ANTONIA
Music by HOLY MODAL ROUNDERS

SCENE TWO

The song fades out. Candles are lit onstage. Soft yellow light comes up revealing a small cave in the mountains. The home of the SPIDER LADY. *She is a wizened old Indian shaman with long white hair, Mexican blankets hung around her shoulders and across her lap, long tooth and bone necklaces, turquoise rings, etc. She is seated cross-legged in the cave to stage left with several candles around her. Seated directly across from her is* MICKEY FREE *with the sidewinder's head held in his cupped hands and the red eyes blinking on and off and the tongue spitting out. Behind them, upstage in the cave are the two* INDIANS *seen with* MICKEY FREE *in Act One. They are also seated cross-legged and pass a small bowl of steaming liquid back and forth between them from which they drink. Around them are their rifles, ammunition and more candles. Hanging from the roof of the cave are several long ribbons, red fox tails and religious artifacts. Bowls of incense are lit and placed in niches in the wall of the cave with smoke gently rising out of them.*

MICKEY FREE: I am afraid, Spider Lady. I find myself holding a great power. I have not the wisdom to use it. Speak to me of its secret.

SPIDER LADY: A great war is about to begin. It will mark the end of the Fourth World and the preparation for the Emergence to the Fifth. Do not be afraid, Mickey Free. You have a part to play in this Emergence. Do not seek shelter. It is only materialistic people who seek to make shelters. Those who are at peace in their own hearts already are in the great shelter of life. There is no shelter for evil. Those who take no part in the making of world division are ready to resume life in another world. They are all one, brothers. The war will be a spiritual conflict with material things. Material matters will be destroyed by spiritual beings who will remain to create one world and one nation under one power, that of the Creator. The time is not far off. The head of this serpent spirit has come to you as a sign. You must see it through to its rightful end.

MICKEY FREE: What does it mean? This spirit head.

SPIDER LADY: In the beginning there were the Star Gods. They descended to earth in flaming discs and created two great clans of man. One, the Snake Clan, the other the Lizard. To each were given tasks. The Lizard Clan was to harvest the crops and raise the children and the Snake Clan was to see to the spiritual needs of the people. For this purpose the Snake Clan was given a giant spirit snake to communicate with the Gods and keep peace in the hearts of the people. The Lizard Clan soon grew jealous and wanted the giant snake for its own. There came a day of the great tug of war between the two clans. The Lizard Clan pulling the head, the Snake Clan pulling the tail. Suddenly the serpent spirit split in two parts, the head going with the Lizard Clan, the tail going with the Snake. At that moment, it is said, the people lost all knowledge of their origin. The Gods vanished from the earth. The people were lost. The two tribes went separate ways and wandered endlessly and with no purpose. More and more people left the clans and wandered their separate ways, taking up homes and founding separate communities, until all over the earth there was mistrust and hatred. Then a vision occurred to a small group of chosen ones who today live on the high mesas of this desert. A blue star descended to earth in the form of a spirit from the Star Gods and told the people that their Emergence was at hand. It spoke of the severed halves of the ancient spirit snake and that they soon would be joined together again on a night of the great dance. That once the two halves were joined the people would be swept from the earth by a star, for they were to be saved from the destruction at hand. That soon after the spirit snake would again be pulled in half by the evil ones and the Fourth World would come to an end.

MICKEY FREE: What must I do?

SPIDER LADY: You must be strong. For too long now you have been used by the white man's cavalry, Mickey Free. You have cheated your red brothers to the south. You have tracked and hunted down your own kind for the white man's money. . . .

MICKEY FREE: And for my freedom! Better to hunt and kill than to be trapped behind bars in their camp! How could I choose! Geronimo was ready to surrender! I had no choice!

SPIDER LADY: You must let this head speak to your heart, Mickey Free. You must see the truth of this myth I have told you. You can read it in the earth itself. In the stars. Within your own conscience. Take this powerful spirit and deliver it to those who await it. To the Chosen Ones atop the high mesa.

MICKEY FREE: But what of the body? I have lost the body.

SPIDER LADY: It will come. It is written. All things have a plan, Mickey Free.

(MICKEY FREE *bows his head slowly to the* SPIDER LADY *as the lights dim out.*)

(*"I Disremember Quite Well" is played.*)

I DISREMEMBER QUITE WELL

You'll pardon me if I act strange
but we've been out of touch
I know that time is on your side
but time can do so much.
Are you still making it with time?
I disremember quite well

Yes I can see as I come close
time has been good to you
Just for a moment's truth you almost
had the face I knew.
But now, of course, it's not for real
I disremember quite well

I used to know you when you turned
your water into wine
You played the shell game with yourself
and won it every time.

But where are you going to keep your prize?
I disremember quite well

I used to walk on water too
and float above the sand.
And hang the stars like diamonds on my
outstretched greedy hands.
But I've forgotten how that game goes
I disremember quite well

And did you ever do whatever thing
it is you're for?
Or does an old idea like that have meaning
anymore?
The maybe that I loved has gone, but where?
I disremember quite well

by ANTONIA
Music by HOLY MODAL ROUNDERS

SCENE THREE

The song fades out. A woman STENOGRAPHER'S VOICE *is heard in the dark.*

STENOGRAPHER'S VOICE: Ready, Captain Bovine!
CAPTAIN BOVINE'S VOICE: All right. Let's see 'em.

(A large color slide is shown on the upstage wall in the darkness. All the slides are of outlaws from the 1800s. CAPTAIN BOVINE *speaks in the dark. The slides keep changing.)*

CAPTAIN BOVINE'S VOICE: Now these faces that you're gonna' see here, Billy, are all known criminals that, as yet, we haven't been able to pin down. Besides the young man in question here, if you happen to run across any other faces that you might have seen on the desert, it would be more than helpful if you pointed them out.
BILLY'S VOICE: Nope. Not a one.

BOVINE'S VOICE: Well, take your time now. We got a whole stack to go through.

(The faces keep flashing on the wall upstage. They get faster and faster as they go on, creating a strobe effect.)

Any identifying marks that you can remember? I mean besides the long hair and bare feet. That's pretty common amongst your outlaws anyhow. Any scars or things like that?

BILLY'S VOICE: Nope. Nary a one.

BOVINE'S VOICE: Did he have an accent? A limp? Anything at all would be helpful, Billy.

BILLY'S VOICE: Nope. Healthy as a yearling colt, that one.

BOVINE'S VOICE: What about the others? Any of the others ring a bell?

BILLY'S VOICE: Nope. Nary a one.

(The last slide is a full head shot of the YOUNG MAN *with a mustache. It stops still.)*

BOVINE'S VOICE: Shall we go through 'em once more for you, Billy? You might have missed a couple and it's very important for our records.

BILLY'S VOICE: I think not. I mean—I think—

BOVINE'S VOICE: Yes?

BILLY'S VOICE: You folks wouldn't have a hot cup a' java layin' around the back room here, would ya'? Jest a little somethin' to wet the old whistle.

DR. VECTOR'S VOICE: Java? Java?

GENERAL'S VOICE: Lights please, Edith!

(The lights pop up revealing BILLY *with his pots and pans sitting in a chair downstage with his back to the audience and his pack on the floor beside him. Next to him is the* STENOGRAPHER, *Edith, who is shutting off the projector and turning the lights on, etc.* GENERAL BROWSER *and* COLONEL WARNER *are sitting behind a table upstage, facing* BILLY. CAPTAIN BOVINE, *Chief Inspector for the CIA, paces around the middle of the stage, chain-smoking cigarettes and dressed in a gray suit.* DOCTOR VECTOR *is also seated at the table with the* COLONEL *and* GENERAL BROWSER.*)*

GENERAL: Edith, would you get Billy a cup of coffee, please. Do you take cream and sugar, Billy?

BILLY: Nope. Black like midnight.

(The STENOGRAPHER goes out and closes the door. The room is plastered with Air Force insignia, the flag, photographs of planes, the desert, slogans, etc., including: "To protect and to serve" in large letters. The three pistols that the YOUNG MAN gave to BILLY are sitting on the desk in front of the GENERAL. CAPTAIN BOVINE walks up to them.)

CAPTAIN BOVINE: Now, Billy, you're gonna' have to understand something here right off the bat. Unless we come up with some evidence leading us to this kid you say you got these guns off of, then we got no other choice than to assume that these weapons belong to you.

BILLY: Oh now don't go handin' me that malarkey, Captain Bovine. What the hell's a prospector out in the middle a' no-man's-land gonna' do with three newfangled irons like them.

CAPTAIN BOVINE: Exactly. What is he going to do?

BILLY: Nothin'! He's gonna' hand 'em over to Mickey Free like he said he was 'cause Danny paid him to. That's what. Nothin' else. Shucks, the way you fellas carry on here anyone'd think there's a plot goin' on to overturn the damn government.

CAPTAIN BOVINE: Danny? Did you say Danny? Was that the kid's name? Answer me, Billy! There's no point covering up for him. If we don't get him someone else will.

BILLY: Danny, Johnny, Jimmy! I don't know what his handle was. I never paid it no never mind. We just got to know each other so well we didn't need no names.

BOVINE: Now listen, Billy. You may not realize it, since you've been out of touch with society for some time, but this country's in trouble. Big trouble. Over the past few years there's been a breakdown of law and order and a complete disrespect for the things we've held sacred since our ancestors founded this country. This country needs you, Billy. It needs your help to help root out these subversive, underground creeps and wipe the slate clean once and for all. You don't realize the trouble they've been giving us. Every time there's a holiday or a bunch of people want to have a good time and just peacefully celebrate some national hero or something, there's always a bunch of these creeps hanging around making faces and giving the finger and shouting obscene things around and carrying cards and doing wild dances and what not. It's become worse than a disgrace, Billy. It's not even funny anymore. There was a time when the whole thing was a joke. But not anymore. Now they've got sympathizers, inside agitators and con men in the White House. All over the country it's going on. I saw it all coming a long time ago. Ever since those bushy-haired creeps started infiltrating from England in 1964. Before that even. Playing Negro music and gyrating their bodies and stuff like that. I'm telling you, Billy, it's about time we brought this whole thing to an end. If we don't do something soon we'll be overrun with these creepy faggots and leather-jacket types. Things have stayed the same for too long now. It's time for a change!

(The STENOGRAPHER enters with the coffee and gives it to BILLY. Then she sits down behind a steno machine and starts taking down the proceedings as though it were a court trial.)

STENOGRAPHER: Here you are, Billy. A nice hot cup of java.

DR. VECTOR: Java?

BILLY: Well now. That's fine. Thank ya', peaches.

STENOGRAPHER: You're welcome.

GENERAL: Captain Bovine, perhaps we could find out something more about this Mickey Free.

CAPTAIN BOVINE: Later. First I want to nail this kid. He's the source. Mickey Free was obviously a go-between, just like Billy here. How does that make you feel, Billy? To know that you were used by this punk.

BILLY: No different. I knew it all along. Me and him was pals. I coulda' cared less about what his real aims were. We just struck it off real fine and let me tell ya', that's a rarity on the desert. Yessir. Why I could tell you stories—

CAPTAIN BOVINE: Good. Tell us a story right now, Billy. The story of how you met this kid and everything you can remember about him. We'll listen.

BILLY: Well I was out near the Harmony Borax Works out there trying to tap a vein that I'd had me an eye on for quite a spell. Seems like forever. Well, with me ya' know, it's more of a way a' life than anything else. I mean not like them weekenders what come out fer a taste a' yeller fever, all hog tied with them electric Geiger counters and metallic metal finders and what all. Us old-timers, a lot of us, don't really hanker for no heavy payloads. Naw. Just a little chicken scratch to keep the vittles comin' is cause enough to keep us on.

CAPTAIN BOVINE: What about this kid?

BILLY: I'm a-gettin' there, mister. And don't get yer hackles up on this old buzzard, sonny, 'cause I'm as likely to clam up on ya' as spew on about somethin' close to my heart when I ain't got no willin' ears to catch it.

CAPTAIN BOVINE: All right. I'm sorry.

BILLY: I come down off the shale part a' the slope and headed toward my burro when I look and see this here kid what appears to be takin' a sunbath. Yeah. Right out in the middle of the blazin' sun he's a-lyin' on his backside and gazin' right into thet big yeller ball. So I walks up and right off I offer him some rashers and a hot cup a' java. Figured he could use somethin' in that belly. Looked like it ain't done nothin' but gurgle for the last fifty miles. So we set ourselves down and get right into talkin' and spinnin' yarns. And let me tell ya' he had some doozers.

CAPTAIN BOVINE: What did you talk about?

BILLY: Well, he told me some a' the galldarnedest tales I ever did hear. Dope peddlers, prostitutes, pretty girls and I don't know what all. Told me one about some street up in Frisco where he stayed and had his-self a different woman every darn night for over a week. Now don't that beat all? Enough to make an old man skiddadle off the desert like a water bug.

CAPTAIN BOVINE: Did he ask you any questions?

BILLY: Danny? Never seen nobody with so many questions. Day in and day out he'd be askin' me stuff about the desert, the Indians, the sky, the night, the sun, the stars, any damn thing he could lay his brain on.

CAPTAIN BOVINE: How much time did he spend with you then?

BILLY: Must a' been well over a fortnight.

CAPTAIN BOVINE: How long is that? Let me see. A fortnight?

BILLY: Better part of a couple weeks. I thought you coppers was supposed to know everything.

CAPTAIN BOVINE: All right. It slipped my mind. You say he asked you about the Indians. What did he ask?

BILLY: Everything. Their magic, how they cooked corn. Where the reservations were. How to get to them. The different drugs and medicine. How to tell the tribes. The symbols, the legends, the religion. How to make water out of sand. Stuff like that. So after a while I figured if he was so all het up about the red man I might as well introduce him to a real live one. Let him learn from the horse's mouth. So I took him up to meet Mickey Free. He ain't a full-blood but a half-breed has all the wits of a Indian plus the gumption of a white man. Mickey's one a' the few real wild ones left. I believe you boys might a' even heard tell of him. Seems like he helped ya' find yerselves some a' this Indian land yer settin' on right now.

GENERAL: Yes. The name rings a bell.

BILLY: Yup. Old Mick's been doin' dirty work for white men ever since he was knee high to a scorpion. Most Injuns hate his guts. Say he's cold-blooded, turns in his own kind. Yup. He's the one supposed to have outfoxed Geronimo. Boxed him into a canyon or somethin'.

COLONEL: Captain Bovine, do we have to sit here all day listening to this? There's important business at hand!

GENERAL: Please, Warner.

CAPTAIN BOVINE: Let me handle this, gentlemen. Now listen, Billy. You'll have to understand that what we're primarily interested in here is the young man who gave you these guns and how it's tied up with these Indian affairs. You can skip all the local color.

BILLY: Well I'll try to scrape it right down to the bone for you fellas, but there's an awful lot bouncin' around this old head a' mine. Can't rightly figure where one thing leaves off and the other begins.

CAPTAIN BOVINE: We understand. It would help if you could clear up the connection between Mickey Free and this punk for us.

BILLY: Well, like I say. I left Johnny off up there at Mickey's wikiup. They hit it off like grease hits the skillet, them two. Just a-cracklin' back and forth between 'em. They stuck it out together for quite a spell, then that blond boy up and left. He come back to me and started talkin' all different from what he done before. Talkin' about a plan with a bunch a' poor folk back in the city. How I was to figure in this play by deliverin' guns to Mickey. Then one night I'm sittin' out there in a lonely spot, moonlit and all, waitin' for Danny when I hears these low kind a' moanin' sounds and I looks down and layin' right in front a' me there is—

CAPTAIN BOVINE: Just the pertinent facts, Billy!

BILLY: Boy, I do believe you fellas wouldn't let the light a' day shine on a sidewinder in the zoo, 'less you had the keeper there beside ya'.

(DR. VECTOR stands abruptly.)

DR. VECTOR: Sidewinder! Did what you say was sidewinder?

GENERAL: Take it easy, Doc. Sit down.

COLONEL: He did say "sidewinder" though. I heard him say it.

CAPTAIN BOVINE: Why did you mention the word "sidewinder," Billy?

BILLY: Just came off the top of the head, gents. The Hopis say the top of the head has a door and if you keep that door open all kind a' wonders come to ya'.

CAPTAIN BOVINE: Have you ever heard that word used on the desert before?

BILLY: You must be pullin' my long johns, sonny. That's a snake. A tiny poisonous rattler what likes the shade and—

CAPTAIN BOVINE: Did you ever hear the kid use that word? Answer me!

BILLY: I think if it's all the same to you, boys, I'll just mosey on.

(BILLY starts to get up. CAPTAIN BOVINE shoves him back down in his seat. DR. VECTOR sits back down.)

CAPTAIN BOVINE: You'll stay right here until you're released. Withholding information from a government official is punishable by law, in case you're not aware of it.

BILLY: Well slap my daddy. Thought I was too old to get myself into more trouble.

CAPTAIN BOVINE: Whether you like it or not, Billy, you've gotten yourself mixed up in a pretty messy situation. A very confidential government-authorized computer has escaped from this Air Force base. This computer goes under the code name of "Sidewinder." Your mention of the name has only further confirmed our suspicions that you are in some way connected with its disappearance. Unless you reveal to us more useful information in this regard then I will have no other recourse than to arrest you for possession of arms without a license.

BILLY: The only reason I was—It was just a figure o' speech. I mean—I was a-gettin' set to tell ya' about this other snake that I seen.

(DR. VECTOR *rises again. The* GENERAL *coaxes him back in his wheelchair.*)

DR. VECTOR: Snake! What snake?

BILLY: Like I say, I was waitin' for my rendezvous with Danny when I hears these groanin' sounds comin' outa' the night. I looks down and there in front of me I sees this pretty young thing all tangled up in the biggest and most gigantic galldanged sidewinder I ever did see. I mean I think it was a sidewinder. It had them telltale horns over the eye sockets. But she was so damn big!

(DR. VECTOR *lets out a jubilant shout. He starts buzzing around in his wheelchair.*)

DR. VECTOR: That's it! My sidewinder! It's alive! My sidewinder is alive! It lives! It lives! My beautiful sidewinder lives! Beautiful, beautiful sidewinder!

GENERAL: Doctor, please! Dr. Vector! Calm yourself!

BILLY: Nope. It's dead.

(DR. VECTOR's *wheelchair comes to a screeching halt.*)

DR. VECTOR: Dead!

BILLY: I mean I think so. It has to be.

DR. VECTOR: What does this mean! You just said it lived! It was alive!

COLONEL: What's this all about?

CAPTAIN BOVINE: Explain yourself, Billy.

BILLY: Well I seen the head up on top of the high mesa with Mickey. They were worshipping the damn thing. Minus the body. I went lookin' for Mickey up at his wikiup but he'd flew the coop. Couple a' his sidekicks says he went off to the high mesa to take part in some ritual of the tribes. So I followed his trail and sure enough there he was right in the middle a' the most highfalutin ceremony I ever did see. And I seen plenty. Lots a' tribes were there. All gathered together peaceable like and gathered around the snake head like it were some kind a' god or somethin'. And there was Mickey, old "one eye" himself, just a-sittin' there pretty as ya' please, beamin' from ear to ear and holdin' that head right in his lap. So I sallies over to him and show him the guns. Figured he'd be pleased as punch. But nothin' doin'. All of a sudden the whole shootin' match comes to a dead stop and they all just stand there a-starin' right at me like I brought the devil hisself. Well right off the bat I could tell I done somethin' outa' step. Then I look in Mickey's face and see that toothy grin a' his disappear fast as a swaller and he stands up and looks real serious and sad and mad all at once and tells me he don't want nothin' never more to do with guns or killin'. I mean I like to drop my silver fillin's right on the spot. Words like that comin' from the most feared Injun-killin' bronco the West ever knowed. Then he reaches in his pouch and pulls out these here little plastic bags and tells me to take the guns and these bags back to the white devil what he got 'em from.

CAPTAIN BOVINE: What bags? What do you mean?

BILLY: Right here. I got 'em right in my pack.

(BILLY *reaches into his pack and pulls out the plastic bags of dope that the* YOUNG MAN *had given* MICKEY FREE *in Act One.* BOVINE *snatches them away. Rips them open, wets his finger and sticks it in the bag, then tastes the powder. He marches to the telephone and picks it up.*)

CAPTAIN BOVINE: Hello. Get me the special detail of Desert Tactical Troops over here immediately. It's an emergency!

(BOVINE *hangs up the phone.* BILLY *stands.*)

DR. VECTOR: But what of my sidewinder!

BILLY: You can't send no soldiers out there, Captain Bovine. They'll interfere with the ceremony. The Indians won't hanker to it one bit. You better pick up that phone and call off them troops. I ain't kiddin', Captain. That's serious business them redskins are up to. I wouldn't mess with it to save my soul.

CAPTAIN BOVINE: Pipe down, old-timer. It's just a routine checkup.

BLACKOUT

("*C.I.A. Man*" *comes on in the dark.*)

C.I.A. MAN

Who can tell if Egypt's got the bomb
Even if the atmosphere is calm

Fuckin A Man C.I.A. Man

Who can train guerrillas by the dozen
Train 'em all to kill their untrained cousins

Fuckin A Man C.I.A. Man

Who can plant the bug on anyone
Who would never eavesdrop just for fun

Fuckin A Man C.I.A. Man

Who will do just what he has to do
All the way from Dallas to Peru

Fuckin A Man C.I.A. Man

Why is Mao scared to start a hassle
Mao isn't mean enough to rassle

Fuckin A Man C.I.A. Man

Who is diplomatically immune
Who else but the hero of this tune

Fuckin A Man C.I.A. Man

by PETER STAMPFEL, TULI KUPFERBURG & ANTONIA
Music by HOLY MODAL ROUNDERS
Copyright — United International 1966

SCENE FOUR

The song fades out. Total silence. Black stage. Thundering sound of many feet pounding on the floor. Silence. Low moaning sound of many voices chanting in unison.

HOPI CHANTS

The lights come up slowly as the chanting goes on. Center stage is MICKEY FREE's *wikiup, a small oval-shaped structure made out of bent twigs, old sheets of metal, mud, strips of cloth and a dark blanket covering the door. A thin column of smoke comes from the top. Stage left of the wikiup is a group of eight* INDIANS *seated in a semicircle around an open pit. These are the* SNAKE PRIESTS. *They are chanting and preparing themselves for a ceremony. In front of them are three large pottery jars, the tops covered with antelope skins. Behind them is the snake altar: a large screen of an-*

telope skin stretched on four long sticks. Three large Hopi kachina dolls are painted on the skin with other symbols, semicircles and figures. Large snake bodies and heads protrude from the skin in bright colors; these operate like hand puppets from behind the screen, so at a certain point in the ceremony they will come alive and wriggle to the dance.

In front of the screen are several stalks of corn and tall poles with feather and ribbon streamers dangling from their tops. Encircling the entire group and the altar is a line of sacred yellow cornmeal. All the INDIANS *are very dark-skinned, have long black hair with eagle feathers at the back of the neck, are naked except for loin cloths and moccasins. A large white oval is painted over each of their breasts and shoulder blades, their foreheads and the fronts of their throats are painted white, the rest of their faces are painted black, the forearms and legs below the knees are painted white. They each wear turquoise and shell necklaces; their loin cloths are blue with a black snake design in front and back. They wear belts with long fringe around the waist, and a fox skin and tail fastened to the belt in the rear. Tied to each right knee is a tortoise-shell rattle. Their moccasins are reddish brown buckskin with fringe and shell designs. They wear white armlets around the bicep and anklets just above the moccasins. The* CHIEF SNAKE PRIEST, *who sits more or less in the center, holds a bow standard decorated with feathers and horsehair.*

They chant in a low moaning unison for a while and sway from side to side. The CHIEF SNAKE PRIEST *slowly places both his hands on one of the jars, the others follow and place their hands on the other two jars. The* CHIEF *removes the skin from the top of the jar and tips the jar toward the pit. The other priests do the same with their jars. The chanting mounts in volume and intensity.*

Suddenly, on cue from the CHIEF, *they all dip the jars down into the pit. Dozens of snakes of all sizes and colors slither from the jars into the pit. The chanting keeps up until all the snakes have disappeared into the pit.*

HONEY *and the* YOUNG MAN *pop onto the stage from left; the sidewinder's body is in the* YOUNG MAN'S *hand. The* INDIANS *are jolted into silence. The* YOUNG MAN *and* HONEY *stare at them. The* INDIANS *rise in unison and walk off left.*

HONEY: Maybe we oughta' come back tomorrow.

YOUNG MAN: Shut up.

HONEY: Look, I've done my bit already. I found you your dumb snake so why don't you let me go. You said before that I just slowed you down.

YOUNG MAN: I need you around.

HONEY: 'Cause you're scared. You've been scared right along and you thought I didn't know it. Right? You're scared shitless.

YOUNG MAN: Will you cool it!

HONEY: No, I won't cool it! I'm not one of your hippie sluts you can drag through the streets and any damn place you feel like going! Giving her clap and hepatitis and everything else.

YOUNG MAN: Look—

HONEY: No, you look! You killed my Dukie! I'll never forgive you for that. Just 'cause I go to bed with you doesn't mean I forgot.

YOUNG MAN: Just hang loose a little bit longer, all right? Please? I promise as soon as we're through getting this snake put back together we'll go into town and have a really neat time. OK?

HONEY: Can we go to the movies?

YOUNG MAN: Sure. Anything you want. We'll get us some hot apple pie and coffee at the truck stop and then we'll go to the movies.

HONEY: There's a new Elvis Presley movie on. Did you see it?

(The low sound of chanting comes from the wikiup. The YOUNG MAN *sneaks toward it with* HONEY *behind him.)*

YOUNG MAN: I saw *Jailhouse Rock*.

HONEY: No. This is a new one. He plays the part of this stock-car driver who always wins, so he gets real rich. But he's such a good guy that he gives all his money away to his friends and people who are poor. You know, he buys them cars and refrigerators and stoves and TVs and all that kind of stuff. But then he gets in trouble—I mean all his friends like him and everything and he's real popular but he gets in trouble with the Internal Revenue Service because they say he didn't pay a lot of his taxes. So he tells them he wrote off all those gifts as tax-deductible charities. But the Internal Revenue doesn't go for that and they say he has to go and take back all those things that he bought for all those people and give them to the government. So he goes and takes back a few things but what happens is that all his friends start hating him because they think he's an Indian giver and everything. So—

(Suddenly the two INDIANS *who were with* MICKEY FREE *in Act One jump out of the wikiup with knives and pin the* YOUNG MAN *and* HONEY *to the ground.* HONEY *screams.)*

YOUNG MAN: Wait a minute! Wait a minute! Paza! Paza! Tanta muy bien amigo! Amigo! Tosa entra por Mickey Free! Nada mas! Nada mas! Para Mickey Free. Entiende? Sabe?

*(*MICKEY FREE *comes out of the wikiup slowly. His face is painted with white zigzags. He is stripped to the waist and wears an embroidered loin cloth and high buckskin moccasins and an Apache headband around his head. The huge knife still dangles from his crotch. He crosses slowly to the* YOUNG MAN *who is still pinned to the ground. He smiles and releases the* INDIANS. *They back off.)*

YOUNG MAN: Mickey.
MICKEY: Kachada. Why have you come back?
YOUNG MAN: I have to talk to you.
MICKEY: I talk no more of guns and drugs. Of plans to conquer worlds. If you come to get back your guns I have already give them to Billy.
YOUNG MAN: No. The guns don't matter. It's the snake. The snake you found on Honey. What did you do with the head?
HONEY: Remember? You saved my life. You cut off its head.
YOUNG MAN: This is the body. You have the head.

(The YOUNG MAN *holds up the sidewinder's body to* MICKEY, *who stares at it, then smiles broadly and lets out a shrill scream. He hugs the* YOUNG MAN *and picks him up, dancing with him and laughing. The other* INDIANS *smile.)*

MICKEY: You are the Pahana! You have come! You have brought us our salvation!

(MICKEY grabs the sidewinder's body and holds it over his head, dancing with it wildly. The other two INDIANS join in. The YOUNG MAN tries to grab the snake back. HONEY lies dazed on the floor.)

YOUNG MAN: Wait a minute! Wait a minute! That's mine! That belongs to somebody else! Mickey! Cut it out! You can't have that snake! They'll kill me if I don't bring it back! Mickey! You've got to give it back! Give it back!

MICKEY: The Spider Lady has told me the truth. She said you would come. The body would join the head of its own will. And now it is here. The ceremony can begin!

YOUNG MAN: What ceremony? That's a machine, you creep! It's not real. The Air Force cooked it up to trace flying saucers! The spades want it to trace the Air Force. I want it because it means my life if I don't get it back to them.

MICKEY: My brothers and I have followed many separate ways, sometimes killing each other. Tonight we shall all see the kingdom. Tonight the spirit snake shall become one again and with it shall join all its people. You and your bride might also come on this journey, Pahana.

HONEY: He's not my husband. He killed my husband.

YOUNG MAN: That's a machine. Mickey. A computer. Not a god.

MICKEY: You are free, Pahana. You have brought us to our emergence. It will take us to a place we will never come back from. You are welcome to enter and follow us there or stay here on this earth and follow your will. The stars will watch you as you go.

(MICKEY turns and walks back into the wikiup with the sidewinder's body in his hand. The INDIANS follow him in.)

YOUNG MAN: Let's go. Come on.
HONEY: Wait. What did he mean?
YOUNG MAN: Never mind. Let's get out of here.

(The chanting comes again from the wikiup, low and then rising.)

AH WAY NEH YO-0-0-0   AH WAY HEN YO-0-0-0

HA-WAY HA-WAY   HUN NAH   WAY-AH-WAY   AH WAY EH CHOE-0-0-0

WAY YA-NEH YO-0 WAY-HA-WAY   WAY YA-NEH YUN-NAH WAY-AH-WAY

HONEY: What's that?

YOUNG MAN: Never mind! Are you coming or not?

HONEY: I never heard that before.

YOUNG MAN: They're sacred songs. It'd take you a year to understand the first word.

HONEY: It's so soothing. Like hearing the wind.

YOUNG MAN: I know. I know. If you get hooked on it we'll never get out of here. Now come on! Look, we gotta' head for Mexico right now! Blood is going to be after my ass before too long. It was you who wanted to go see the movie before! Remember? Honey! Get up, and let's go.

(She is in a kind of trance state. She rises slowly and moves toward the wikiup. The YOUNG MAN runs to her and grabs her shoulders. He shakes her. She stares at him blankly.)

YOUNG MAN: Goddammit! I'm not walking back down into that desert alone! Do you hear me! It's the middle of the night! I might get shot for having long hair or smelling bad or something! Honey! Snap out of it! It's not for white people's ears! It's secret stuff! It'll make you crazy! If we go in there they'll never see us again! Never! We'll be scooped up! Taken away! Can't you understand me! I need you! I need you with me! I can't come back here again! Why don't you listen! Honey!

(He shakes her, then lets her go. She walks like a sleepwalker straight into the wikiup. The chanting reaches a kind of chord as she enters.)

Honey! You'll never see daylight again!

(A blue flash in the sky. The sound of a jet as the YOUNG MAN *looks up at the sky. The chanting grows louder. The* YOUNG MAN *clenches his hands together and starts to say the Lord's Prayer as he walks slowly toward the wikiup.)*

Our Father who art in Heaven. Hallowed be thy name. Thy kingdom come, thy will be done, on earth as it is in heaven. Give us this day our daily bread and forgive us our trespasses as we forgive those who trespass against us. Lead us not into temptation but deliver us from evil. For thine is the kingdom, the power and the glory. Forever and ever. Amen.

(The chanting grows to an incredible pitch as he enters the wikiup on the word "Amen." A pause as just the wikiup is seen with the chanting coming from it. Another flash of blue in the sky. Then the beam of light going across from stage left to stage right as in Act One. Then one at a time eight ANTELOPE PRIESTS *come out of the wikiup in single file. They are dressed similarly to the* SNAKE PRIESTS *except they have painted themselves ash gray with white zigzag lines running up from their breasts to their shoulders, and down the arms to the fingers and down the front of the legs to their big toes. They each carry a large steady rhythm. Their chins are outlined by a white line drawn from ear to ear. Their loin cloths are white with black snake designs and embroidered sashes. They are followed closely by the eight* SNAKE PRIESTS. *They all continue the chant in a low murmur and walk single file to the snake altar where they face*

*each other in a double line, eight on either side of the snake pit. Simultane-
ously they stomp with their right feet on the floor. A loud boom like thunder
comes forth. They all begin to sway from left to right in unison and shake the
rattles in time. They form a circle, then fan out into single file again and circle
the entire stage four times chanting over and over again in rhythmic pattern
and stomping their right feet in unison on the beginning accent of the word.
Each time they stomp, the sound should come like thunder. The rhythm is slow,
deliberate and powerful. Everything about the dance is spiritual and sincere
and should not be cartooned or choreographed beyond the unison of the rhythmic patterns. After they have circled the stage four times they again go to the
snake pit and line up across from each other, but closer to each other this time
and forming a circle of bodies. They link arms and bend over the pit. They make
a chord with their voices, rising from a low pitch to extremely high and shrieking. As they do this, the* CHIEF PRIEST *of the snake group kneels down and puts
his head into the pit. He comes up with a snake in his mouth. The others fan
back and the* CHIEF SNAKE PRIEST *dances with the writhing snake in his
mouth. The* ANTELOPE PRIESTS *fan off and dance to the right side of the stage
and stand in a line, swaying from side to side and chanting as they stomp their
right feet. The* SNAKE PRIESTS *line up stage left and do the same. One of the*
SNAKE PRIESTS *dances out from the line toward the* CHIEF *and waves two long
eagle feathers over the snake's head as the* CHIEF *dances with it. The snake goes
limp and the* CHIEF *lets it drop to the floor. A third* SNAKE PRIEST *dances out
with a stick and waves it over the snake, then bends down, picks it up with both
hands, holds it aloft and dances over to the* ANTELOPE PRIESTS. *He hands it to
one of the* ANTELOPE PRIESTS *at the end of the line. He takes and holds it, coaxing it with one hand as he continues to chant. The* CHIEF *walks back to behind
the snake altar where he starts to operate one of the snake puppets in short jerky
movements. Another* SNAKE PRIEST *puts his head into the pit and comes up
with another snake between his teeth. The same process goes on as with the*
CHIEF *until each* ANTELOPE PRIEST *in the line has a snake in his hand and
each* SNAKE PRIEST *has danced with a snake and returned to behind the snake
altar to operate one of the puppets. Once this is finished the* ANTELOPE PRIESTS
are all visible, dancing and chanting with the snakes. The SNAKE PRIESTS *are
all unseen behind the snake altar, and the snake puppets are moving vigor-
ously around.* MICKEY FREE *comes out of the wikiup. He is dressed the same
way, stripped to the waist, but he wears a blue kachina mask on his head. He
holds the head of the sidewinder in his left hand, the body in the right. He
holds them aloft. Behind him are* HONEY, *the* YOUNG MAN, *and the two* INDI-
ANS *from before.* HONEY's *face is painted like the* SNAKE PRIESTS' *and the* YOUNG

MAN's *like the* ANTELOPES'. HONEY *wears a long black dress, a blue loin cloth over it and a white and red cape. Her hair is loose, with eagle feathers attached at the back. Around her neck is a necklace of turquoise and shell. She holds an earthen jar out in front of her containing sacred oil. The* YOUNG MAN *has an eagle feather tied to the front of his hair, his body is painted ash gray with white zigzag lines like the* ANTELOPE PRIESTS' *on his body, arms and legs. He also holds a jar filled with oil. The* SNAKE PRIESTS *come out from behind the altar single file and line up downstage. The* ANTELOPES *follow suit on the stage-right side. One of* MICKEY's INDIAN *friends leads* HONEY *by the arm to the line of* SNAKE PRIESTS *where she kneels in front of the* CHIEF. *The* YOUNG MAN *is led to the* ANTELOPES *by the other* INDIAN *and he kneels to their* CHIEF PRIEST. *Both* HONEY *and the* YOUNG MAN *seem to be in a totally different frame of mind now. Calm, spiritual, totally accepting of the whole ritual.* MICKEY *stands downstage center, changing and holding the segmented sidewinder aloft, moving the two parts toward each other, then away. The* SNAKE CHIEF *and the* ANTELOPE CHIEF *exchange places and walk to opposite sides of the stage. The* ANTELOPE CHIEF *faces* HONEY *and the* SNAKE CHIEF *faces the* YOUNG MAN. *They each simultaneously place their hands on* HONEY's *and the* YOUNG MAN's *heads, then slowly push their heads down into the jars of oil they hold in front of them, so that their hair becomes saturated. They raise their heads up.* HONEY *and the* YOUNG MAN *stand. They are led by the respective* CHIEFS *downstage in front of* MICKEY FREE. *The* CHIEF PRIESTS *exchange positions again and then wash* HONEY's *and the* YOUNG MAN's *hair in the oil. They touch their heads together and then twist their hair together so that it becomes tied. The chanting continues the whole time.* MICKEY, *at the moment* HONEY's *and the* YOUNG MAN's *hair has been tied together, joins the sidewinder's body to its head. A tremendous bolt of blue light issues from the sidewinder, matched by one in the sky. Thunder booms. The sky lights up blue again. The combination of the voices chanting reaches an incredible shrieking, like lightning. The whole scene crackles like high-voltage wires. Then suddenly everything stops abruptly as three* "DESERT TACTICAL TROOPS" *with machine guns, pistols, helmets, uniforms, etc., enter briskly from right. The* INDIANS *freeze.)*

1ST DESERT TACTICAL TROOP: All right! Everybody put up your hands! Everyone! Put 'em up!

2ND DESERT TACTICAL TROOP: Let's see some identification! That goes for everybody! Get it out!

3RD DESERT TACTICAL TROOP: You people are in big trouble! You got any idea what you got in your hand there, buddy? That's government property! United States Government property, buster! Now let's have it!

(*The* 3RD DESERT TACTICAL TROOP *grabs for the sidewinder which* MICKEY *still holds over his head. A bright blue light comes from the sidewinder, then from the sky. The* D.T.T.s *jump back. All the* INDIANS *and* HONEY *and the* YOUNG MAN *stay frozen.*)

3RD DESERT TACTICAL TROOP: Now look, buddy! I don't know what's going on here but that snake belongs to us! Now hand it over!

(*The* 3RD DESERT TACTICAL TROOP *makes another move toward the sidewinder and again it lights up, answered by a light in the sky.*)

You wanna' get run in for resisting arrest too? We're not playing games here with you punks!

(*Suddenly* MICKEY *begins the chant "Wunti Hayano Diwitia" and all the* IN-DIANS *plus the* YOUNG MAN *and* HONEY *join in. They start to move slowly toward the three* DESERT TACTICAL TROOPS *with* MICKEY *leading them, still holding the sidewinder over his head. They begin to form a large circle around the* D.T.T.s *as they try to get away from them.*)

2ND DESERT TACTICAL TROOP: All right! Hold it right there! Hold it!
1ST DESERT TACTICAL TROOP: Stop that singing! Stop where you are!

3RD DESERT TACTICAL TROOP: ·We're going to open fire in about three seconds if you don't stop and hand over that snake! One! We're not kidding around! Two! This is no joke! We mean business! This is your last chance! Stop in the name of the law! Three!

(The DESERT TACTICAL TROOPS *open fire on the* INDIANS *with their machine guns. The* INDIANS *keep coming. They form a circle with* MICKEY *at the head of it and the* DESERT TACTICAL TROOPS *in the center firing again and again. The* INDIANS *just sway back and forth to the rhythm of the chant. The sidewinder lights up, the sky lights up. The* 3RD DESERT TACTICAL TROOP *rushes straight toward* MICKEY FREE, *firing his machine gun into him.* MICKEY *just chants and sways. The* 3RD DESERT TACTICAL TROOP *reaches up and grabs the sidewinder and yanks it from* MICKEY's *hands. The body separates from the head again. Bright bolt of blue light from the sky. The* D.T.T.s *scream as though being blinded. The lights go to black after the blue light, then back to bright blue. Each interval of light and dark lasts about five or six seconds. From pitch black to bright blue. Huge gusts of wind blow from upstage directly out into the audience, changing from hot to cold. Wind also blows across stage. Streams of smoke come from all around the proscenium arch and upstage. The chanting increases. A high frequency volume. The chanting becomes amplified. The bright blue light flashes on, the* INDIANS *are in ecstasy as they chant. The* D.T.T.s *are cringing on their knees center stage. The lights go to black. The blue light again and this time all the* INDIANS *plus the* YOUNG MAN *and* HONEY *are gone. Just the* DESERT TACTICAL TROOPS *holding their ears and shielding their eyes. The lights stay up and become brighter. The whine and the chanting get louder, then everything goes black.)*

The Mad Dog Blues

A TWO-ACT ADVENTURE SHOW

The Mad Dog Blues was first presented by Theatre Genesis at St. Mark's Church-in-the-Bowery on March 4, 1971, with the following cast:

KOSMO:	Morris Lafon
YAHOODI:	Jim Storm
WACO TEXAS:	John Bottoms
MARLENE DIETRICH:	Kathleen Cramer
MAE WEST:	O-Lan Johnson-Shepard
CAPTAIN KIDD:	Leroy Logan
PAUL BUNYAN:	Robert Glaudini (later replaced by Beeson Carroll)
GHOST GIRL:	Nina Glaudini
JESSE JAMES:	Ralph Lee
MUSICIANS:	Sam Shepard, Lamar Alford, Robin Remaily, Michael Winsett

It was directed by Robert Glaudini and designed by Ralph Lee.

CHARACTERS

KOSMO: A rock-and-roll star. Dressed in a green velvet satin cape with tight blue velvet pants, teased hair and no shirt. He carries a conga drum.

YAHOODI: His sidekick. Dressed slick like a big-city dope dealer. Shades, short-brimmed black hat, and black suit with black patent-leather shoes. He carries an Indian flute.

WACO: A drifter from Texas. Dressed in raggedy pants and shirt, a long overcoat, and a cowboy hat and boots. Carries around a broken guitar.

MARLENE DIETRICH: Dressed in short shorts with teased hair, lots of makeup, high heels, and a whip.

MAE WEST: Dressed in a long sequined evening gown with a feather boa.

CAPTAIN KIDD: Dressed like a swashbuckler with saber, boots, and the whole bit.

PAUL BUNYAN: Dressed in giant proportions, with an ax.

GHOST GIRL: Dressed like a South Sea island girl. Carries a spear.

JESSE JAMES: Dressed like Jesse James, with a long raincoat.

SCENE

An open, bare stage. All the places the characters move through are imagined and mimed. Some minor props can be used, but the production should stay away from heavy scenery. The lighting should designate where the characters are in time and space, following the rhythm of the action. The characters, costumes, and lights should be the main focus. All the offstage sound effects should be performed live, like those on old-time radio shows (a large sheet of metal being shaken for thunder, and so on). The music should also be live, with the band in a pit below the stage as for a vaudeville show. Maybe the piano player could follow some of the action like they did with the old silent movies.

The play opens with the theme music which KOSMO *keeps hearing throughout the play. This music is heard at different times, but not necessarily when* KOSMO *says he hears it in the script. After the music, lights come up on* KOSMO *and* YAHOODI *on opposite sides of the stage. They speak directly to the audience.*

Prologue

KOSMO: Kosmo. Tall, lean, angular, wolflike. Leads with his cock. Intuitive decisions based on a leaking-roof brain. Lots of dashing images. Taken with himself as a man with the ladies. Has a sadomasochist hid in his closet. Fights him off in favor of a more heroic pose. Has no control over his primeval violence. Hates politics, philosophy, and religion. Asks for God's help. Gropes in the dark without a game. Invents one without no meaning. Gives the impression from the outside that he's winning. Moves from spot to spot across the planet hoping to find a home.

YAHOODI: Yahoodi. Short, dark, strikes like a serpent. Perfected a walk that cuts through the pavement. Loves how the brain works. Sucks in the printed word. Prefers isolation. Hates to be lonely. Has a weakness for soft things but hates to have them seen. Walks around the block five times preparing to cop. Passes himself off as a nigger. Watches for men in trenchcoats. Trades his mojo for a bag of coke and disappears in the night.

(Blackout. Theme music, fading as the lights come up.)

ACT ONE

Lights up. KOSMO *and* YAHOODI *still at opposite sides of the stage. Music fades.*

KOSMO: *(Calling across a vast expanse)* Yahoodi! Hey, Yahoodi!

YAHOODI: Yeah!

KOSMO: I've had a vision!

YAHOODI: Here I come! *(Traveling through different terrain.)* Here I is.

KOSMO: I've had a vision.

YAHOODI: Yeah?

KOSMO: It came to me in music. It was like old rhythm-and-blues and gospel, a cappella, sort of like The Persuasions but with this bitchin' lead line. Like a Hendrix lead line. Like a living Hendrix lead line right through the middle of it.

YAHOODI: What about the visuals? Did ya' see any pictures?

KOSMO: A tall golden woman like Marlene Dietrich or something. In short shorts and teased blond hair. Carrying a whip.

(She appears and cracks her whip.)

YAHOODI: Sing it.

KOSMO: I can't. I can't get my head straight. I have to take a trip. I have to go somewhere else.

YAHOODI: Me too.

KOSMO: The city's gettin' me down. Too many tangents. It's no place to collaborate.

YAHOODI: Maybe we could do it by mail. I'll go to the jungle and write you.

KOSMO: Good idea. I'll go to San Francisco and do the same.

YAHOODI: Good luck, brother.

KOSMO: Same here.

(They travel in different directions. YAHOODI *winds up in the jungle and* KOSMO *in Frisco.* MARLENE *comes down to the audience. She sings "Jungen Mensch.")*

MARLENE:
Silly boys just young men
Go away and then they come again
They don't yet know who they are
Silly boys just young men following a star

They hurry here and they hurry there
Eager with their empty hands
Their heads are full their hearts are too
Oh hurry how hurried my lovely fools

End and then begin and end again
Like reflections in a pool
And loneliness comes like a dart
There's nothing to find till you find your heart

KOSMO: *(Calling across a great expanse)* Yahoodi!

YAHOODI: *(Calling back)* Yeah!

KOSMO: I've had another vision!

YAHOODI: Already!

KOSMO: Yeah! It's Mae West singing the blues like Janis Joplin!

YAHOODI: No shit! Should I come back?

KOSMO: Not yet. I haven't been able to give it any form. She's just sort of strutting around. There's so much cigarette smoke you can barely see her.

YAHOODI: What's it like there?

KOSMO: Full of inspiration! Jack Kerouac country! The Grateful Dead, The Airplane, Quicksilver. The air is full of grist for the mill. The Pacific is blue as hell. How 'bout you?

YAHOODI: Steaming jungle! Coconut girls! Giant pythons! Swinging in my hammock all day long.

KOSMO: Are you off the needle?

YAHOODI: Don't put me down.

KOSMO: I can't help it. I get concerned.

YAHOODI: How about you! How's your depressions?

KOSMO: They come and go like the wind. Here today, gone tomorrow. If I could just put something together. I keep feeling like I'm getting closer and closer to the truth.

(MAE WEST enters and saunters around KOSMO.)

YAHOODI: That's good. It's nighttime here and all the stars are out. The jungle makes the weirdest sounds. Jaguars are running wild. The little kids are sucking on mangoes. Suck, suck, suck, all night long.

KOSMO: *(To MAE WEST)* Could you take me for a trolley ride?

MAE WEST: I'll take ya' for everything ya' got.

KOSMO: Outa' sight.

(They go for a trolley ride.)

YAHOODI: Ever since I was a little boy I used to watch the subway come up out of the ground and wonder about all those people. How all those people were just living their lives and couldn't care less about me. About how separate we were. Them on the train and me watching them. Them in their life and me in mine. I could see them and hear them and smell them but they didn't even know I existed. Good for them I'd say. Good for me. Hurray for life.

KOSMO: *(To MAE, still riding the trolley)* You're much smaller than the image I have in my head of you. You seemed so big in the movies.

MAE WEST: Big surprises come in small packages.

KOSMO: I could really fall for someone like you.

MAE WEST: You're not exactly a dog yourself.

KOSMO: I had this vision of you, and you were singing like Janis Joplin.

MAE WEST: Never heard of her.

KOSMO: She's dead.

MAE WEST: Maybe that's why.

KOSMO: She was a lot like you. Lots of balls. She could really belt it out.

MAE WEST: Yeah, well, beltin's not exactly my specialty.

KOSMO: She was lying facedown between two double beds with her right hand holding the phone so hard that the veins were standing out on her thumb. She had a squirrel fur wrapped around her neck with little black eyes that stared out at me. There were ostrich feathers lying around on the rug and blowing into the air-conditioning. The air-conditioner made this high, whining sort of sound. The sound went right through me as though it were her voice talking to me, even though she was dead. Then it started to sing. Not like she sang when she was alive, but another kind of voice. A crystal voice. It passed right through me and then the window broke behind me. Like her voice went right through the window. I ran outside into the parking lot of the hotel. I could see her voice sailing over the parked cars. Sailing out over Sunset Boulevard. I ran after the voice. I tried to catch up, but each time I got nearer it took off again, like trying to catch a runaway kite. It sailed higher and higher, and then I saw you.

MAE WEST: Me? What was I doing there?

KOSMO: You were dancing to the voice. You were all dressed in red and you swayed back and forth. You swallowed the voice with the most delicious gulp and then you started to sing. You sang "When a Man Loves a Woman." And right then everything stopped. I saw the whole world come to a dead stop and everyone was listening. Just listening. It was the most beautiful dream I've ever had.

MAE WEST: What do ya' say we get us a bottle of hooch and find us a nice cozy place?

KOSMO: Okay by me.

(They get a bottle and find a nice cozy place.)

YAHOODI: (*Calling across a great expanse, but* KOSMO *doesn't hear*) Kosmo! It's starting to hit me! Like a sledgehammer! Right in the chest! I need to get off! Kosmo! I need some Doliphine at least! Just a little something to tide me over! This jungle's tearing me apart! The bugs are driving me bats!

*(*MARLENE *enters and goes to* YAHOODI.)*

MARLENE: You put too much emphasis on the pain. Take your mind off the pain. Take your mind off the pain. Your friend is safe and sound in San Francisco.

YAHOODI: Fuck him! Fuck my friend! What good's he do me now? (*To* MARLENE) What are you doing here? You got any money? If only I was better known! If only I was famous! I could fly back to the city and put a needle in my arm! I could buy a farm in the country and raise a family and be a happily married man.

MARLENE: It's a good thing to dream.

YAHOODI: What do you know? What do you know about my suffering? What's your suffering compared to mine?

MARLENE: I could take it away. I could steal it from you.

YAHOODI: I don't need sex! I need some dope! Dope! I need some dope!

MARLENE: I need, you need, we all need some ice cream.

(*They go into a heavy clinch and slurp each other up. Then they fall asleep.* KOSMO *and* MAE WEST *are now riding in a limousine.*)

KOSMO: I keep hearing music. Where are we?

MAE WEST: I took the liberty of having my chauffeur pick us up. You were gettin' a little feisty back at the Blue Onion.

KOSMO: Blue Onion? Where are you taking me? I want to go home.

MAE WEST: Just a little cruise down to Big Sur. Thought we'd watch the waves crash against the rocks and all the seals makin' whoopee.

KOSMO: I gotta' get back. The revolution's on.

MAE WEST: What channel?

KOSMO: No, no. It's now or never. If I miss my moment in history it may never happen again. I've got to become involved.

MAE WEST: You were doin' all right by me.

KOSMO: I've gotta' make bombs and speeches and mobilize the people. I've gotta' work for the party. I've gotta' see to it that justice is done. It's now or never. Now is real!

MAE WEST: You said it, brother.

KOSMO: Lemme outa' the car! Lemme out! Lemme out!

(*He falls out of the car and rolls across the stage into* PAUL BUNYAN.)

PAUL BUNYAN: You seen Babe? I been lookin' all over.

KOSMO: I don't know what you're talking about.

PAUL BUNYAN: My ox. Babe. He's blue. You see him?

KOSMO: I don't know. Look, do you know how to get back to New York City? I do believe I've had enough. What highway is this?

PAUL BUNYAN: This is the North Woods. Ain't no highway for miles. Just lumber camps and diners and trucks and chain saws. Sell ya' a good ax if ya' need one. That's all I use. These new fellas they use the chain saws, but not me. I can outchop the fastest chain saw around.

KOSMO: I believe it. Just point me in the direction of home, okay?

PAUL BUNYAN: I need to find my ox or I'm up shit creek without a paddle. There's nothin' like a good ox. Worth their weight in gold. Especially old Babe.

KOSMO: My mind's going a mile a minute! I've got to slow down.

PAUL BUNYAN: This is the best place for it. Nothing like the North Woods for a little peace and quiet. Just chew on some acorns. Hum a little tune. Whittle your fingernails.

KOSMO: But I'm a musician! I've got to create! I've got to get back to the city. Back to my band. Back to my roots. I've lost touch with my roots.

PAUL BUNYAN: You city folks are all alike. Always tryin' to make a buck.

KOSMO: No. I'm not in it for the money. I'm an artist.

PAUL BUNYAN: Me, I'm a lumberjack. See ya' around.

(He exits. YAHOODI wakes up. MARLENE stays asleep.)

YAHOODI: (*Calling across a great expanse*) Kosmo! I had a dream! I dreamed I was Crazy Horse! I was leading a raiding party against the Crows. I wore a small yellow stone under my left ear, and a hawk circled over me as I rode into battle. I felt what it was like to have no fear. To be completely free from fear. Nothing could touch me. The arrows flew all around me but none of them touched me. It was like I had an understanding of space in another dimension. I knew where the arrows would land. I knew—(*He notices* MARLENE.) Hey! Hey, Marlene! Hey. Wake up. Stupid broad. What are ya' gonna' do, sleep the day away? Hey, Kosmo, I think she's OD'd or something. Kosmo!

KOSMO: I was on a Greyhound bus out of Carlsbad heading for Loving, New Mexico. Back to see my dad. After ten years. All duded out in a double-breasted suit with my shoes all shined. The driver calls out "Loving" and I get off the bus. The bus takes off and leaves me in a cloud of dust. Nothing but dust. The dust clears and there I am. Standing right in the middle of a ghost town. Nothing. The stores all boarded up. The windows all busted out. I pick up my bags and start hoofin' it down the street. There's the old Bijou Theatre with Anita Ekberg's name still on it from 1959. And Rose's Cafe where I used to have enchiladas and tamales. And there, way down at the end of the road, rising up like a beautiful vision is my old man's bar. The Palace Saloon! I walk in and all the music comes blasting out at me. It's Pedro Enfantes on the juke box. And my old man behind the bar. His shoulder holster bulging out underneath his coat. I order a beer. And he says sure, son, have a beer. And I say don't call me son. And he says why not and I say because I *am* your son. And he says sure. And I say I am! And he says fuck off. So I say fuck off. Don't you recognize me? It's me, your son!

YAHOODI: (*Calling across a great expanse*) Kosmo!

KOSMO: Yeah!

YAHOODI: I've had a vision!

KOSMO: Here I come! (*He travels through different terrain and arrives at* YAHOODI.)

YAHOODI: I had a vision you were coming.

KOSMO: Here I am.

YAHOODI: How was your trip?

KOSMO: I lost my way. It's no fun being on the road.

YAHOODI: I know what ya' mean. Still, it's good to get away for a while. This city's a real drag. All I ever do is shoot doogie.

KOSMO: What about your vision?

YAHOODI: A giant American bald eagle flying through a smoke-filled sky with the world clutched in his talons. He flies higher and higher until he can't fly anymore and then he lets the world drop. The world falls faster and faster through the smoke-filled sky and plunges into the ocean and explodes sending a huge tidal wave up to the surface.

KOSMO: I'm getting fucking tired of apocalypses. All I ever hear anymore is apocalypse, apocalypse. What about something with some hope?

YAHOODI: It's up to you, boy.

(WACO *enters. An old cowboy in an overcoat, boots, hat, with a beat-up guitar. He sings:*)

WACO:
I been fightin' like a lion.
But I'm 'fraid I'm gonna lose.
I been fightin' like a lion.

But I'm 'fraid I'm gonna lose.
'Cause there ain't been nobody can whip these old TB blues.

Old Jimmie. Jimmie Rodgers. Good old Jimmie Rodgers. He had
heart. That's what he had. Heart. I'm gonna' put him back on the
street. 'Cause I love him. Gonna' put him right back on the street.
You boys know him?

KOSMO: Jimmie Rodgers? Sure.

WACO: Not the young one. The old one. Old Jimmie.

KOSMO: Yeah. I know Jimmie Rodgers.

WACO: You know old Jimmie? Good old boy. That was his last song. "The
TB Blues." TB's a motherfucker, boy. It'll tear you up. He knew he
was goin' out. He knew it. You got a cigarette?

KOSMO: Yeah, sure.

WACO: Thanks, boy.

YAHOODI: Well look, Kosmo. I'm gonna' take a trip.

KOSMO: Again? You just got back.

YAHOODI: I can't stand it anymore. I gotta' get out of here.

KOSMO: You're always running out on me. Every time something gets
rough you walk out.

YAHOODI: I got to, man.

KOSMO: Okay. Split.

YAHOODI: Well, don't get mad. It's got nothing to do with you.

KOSMO: Just split!

WACO: He knew he was goin' out and he was singing' just the same.
(*Sings*) "I been fightin' like a lion . . ."

YAHOODI: You're cracking up.

KOSMO: Me! It's not me, boy! You're the one that's fucked. You're the
junkie! You're the morbid little nihilistic junkie! Not me! I got my
whole life in front of me. And I'm not going down in your hole with
you just because you can't see the sun in the morning.

YAHOODI: Fuck you!

KOSMO: Fuck you!

WACO: He had heart. That's what he had. A man's gotta' have heart. Go
where the heart goes.

YAHOODI: Shut up!

KOSMO: Don't tell him to shut up. He's a friend of mine.

WACO: That's right. Name's Waco. Waco Texas. That's where I was born.

YAHOODI: Who gives a rat's ass?

KOSMO: You turn everything into shit.

YAHOODI: You're really cracking up. Look at you. Shaking all over. Your mind's blowing up. You got no patience. If you could just slow down. You're going to burn yourself up.

KOSMO: I gotta' play some music. I gotta' find my band, I gotta' find a guru or something. Go to the country and eat brown rice and hoe my own garden and plant my own seeds. Listen to the music. I keep hearing the music.

YAHOODI: It's all in your head.

KOSMO: Get away from me! Get out of here! Go on! Take your trip! Go as far away as you can! Get out of my sight!

(YAHOODI takes off and winds up by MARLENE. He doesn't hear KOSMO.)

KOSMO: No! Yahoodi! I'm sorry! Come back! I need you! We're brothers! Yahoodi! I love you.

WACO: Just follow your heart. That's what a man's supposed to do. The only thing a man can do. Just follow your heart.

KOSMO: Maybe you're right.

WACO: Sure.

KOSMO: But look where it got you. You're from Texas?

WACO: Born and raised.

KOSMO: How'd you wind up here?

WACO: I'm just here. That's all. I'm just here.

KOSMO: I know what you mean. It doesn't seem right to suffer. You know? I'm going to stop suffering right now. I'm going to have some bacon and eggs and stop suffering. The air tastes really good. Come on, Waco Texas. We're gonna' live!

(WACO and KOSMO move to another part of the stage to have some bacon and eggs.)

WACO: *(Sings)*
I been fightin' like a lion.
And I do believe I'm gonna win.
I been fightin' like a lion—

(Song fades out.)

YAHOODI: Marlene? Marlene? You all right?

MARLENE: (*Waking up*) I feel, how do you say, "A-OK."

YAHOODI: What happened?

MARLENE: I lost another man. It's a long sad story. My heart is very heavy.

YAHOODI: How about a mango? Could ya' go for a mango?

MARLENE: Sure. A mango in the morning is sometimes better than a man.

YAHOODI: Sure feels good to be outa' the States. Ya' know? I was getting so uptight up there I couldn't see straight.

(*They take a stroll.*)

MARLENE: You're a very sensitive man. You're an artist.

YAHOODI: Maybe I could get a job as a short-order cook or something. Maybe working in the oil fields. Or gold! How about gold! Did you ever think of that?

MARLENE: No. You did.

YAHOODI: Yeah. Sure. Gold! Why not. If I could just find Humphrey Bogart we'd be in business.

MARLENE: But he's so crude. You need a man with finesse.

YAHOODI: To hunt for gold?

MARLENE: You need a man who knows the ropes.

YAHOODI: We could buy the mules in Nogales. Plenty a' cheap mules in Nogales.

(*They run into* PAUL BUNYAN.)

PAUL BUNYAN: You see Babe? He's my ox. A blue ox.

YAHOODI: That's it! We'll use oxen instead. Hey, where could I buy some cheap oxen? You got any for sale?

PAUL BUNYAN: You city slickers are always looking to buy and sell things. I've lost my Babe. That's all I know.

MARLENE: It's hard to lose a loved one.

PAUL BUNYAN: It's even harder to find one.

YAHOODI: Listen, I'm gonna' wire Kosmo for some money. We could really strike it rich out here. I'll be right back. You two get acquainted while I'm gone. I won't be long. (*He goes to the telephone and calls* KOSMO.)

MARLENE: You've got such mysterious eyes.

PAUL BUNYAN: Listen, ma'am, I've lost my ox and I can't do a thing without him.

MARLENE: Your eyes. Such mysterious eyes.

(They go into a long clinch.)

YAHOODI: *(On the phone)* Kosmo! That you?

KOSMO: *(On the phone)* Yahoodi? Where you been?

YAHOODI: Listen, I've run into a hot deal down here in the jungle and I need some fast money. Say a couple G's.

KOSMO: A couple G's? I'll check out my royalties. I think I can swing it. What is it, dope?

YAHOODI: No, gold! Lots and lots of gold!

KOSMO: Out of sight! I'll send it right away!

YAHOODI: Thanks, pal. *(He hangs up.)*

KOSMO: *(To WAÇO)* That was Yahoodi. He's struck gold.

WACO: Gold? In the Yukon?

KOSMO: Nope. Somewhere in the jungle.

WACO: Hot diggity.

KOSMO: We gotta' get down there, Waco.

WACO: Not me, boy. I'm allergic to mosquitoes.

KOSMO: Come on, it's now or never.

(They travel south. YAHOODI goes to MARLENE and PAUL BUNYAN.)

YAHOODI: Listen, I just contacted my man. He's sending us a couple of G's. So we're all set. All we need now is the mules.

(CAPTAIN KIDD enters.)

CAPT. KIDD: What do ya' wanna' play around with mules for, limey? I got a treasure all hid away to make the likes a' gold seem like dog shit.

YAHOODI: Who're you?

CAPT. KIDD: The name's Kidd, Captain Kidd.

YAHOODI: How do. This is Marlene Dietrich and Paul Bunyan. My name's Yahoodi. That's what they call me anyway. What's this about a treasure?

CAPT. KIDD: Spanish bullion tucked away in a neat little island protected by the prettiest cove ye' ever laid eyes on.

YAHOODI: Must be gone by now. Somebody musta' run across it.

CAPT. KIDD: No sir. It's protected by a ghost. An Indian girl who hides deep in the cave where it's buried.

MARLENE: Sounds pretty risky, darling.

PAUL BUNYAN: Yeah, you can count me out. All I want is my Babe. I'll see you around. (*He exits.*)

YAHOODI: Wait a minute! That always happens. Just as things are beginning to look up everybody cops out.

MARLENE: Listen, darling, it does sound a little farfetched. It could be, how do you say, a "wild goose chase."

YAHOODI: You too? Everybody's turning against me. Go then! Go!

MARLENE: Now don't be so hasty, darling.

YAHOODI: Ya' got a map of this island, Kidd? I guess we'll have to take a boat, right?

CAPT. KIDD: Right. Here is the map.

(*He pulls out a huge map.* YAHOODI, MARLENE *and* CAPTAIN KIDD *examine it. We go to* WACO *and* KOSMO. *As they travel along, they sing "Travelin' Shoes."*)

WACO AND KOSMO:
   I'm just travelin' along in my shoes
   Payin' my dues, travelin' along

   When I get that hold down blues
   I get on the move with my travelin' shoes

   La da la da la da da la da la da la

(*They sing this through twice.*)

WACO: Say listen, ain't we gone quite a fer piece? This is gettin' a little tiring.

KOSMO: Let's just sit down here by the side of the stream and take a little breather.

(*They sit and drink from the stream.* MAE WEST *sneaks up behind* WACO. *He sees her reflection in the water.*)

WACO: Sure is a long trip. I never woulda' come if I'd a' knowed it was gonna' take so long.

KOSMO: It'll be worth it once we're .here. All that gold! Just think of it! We'll be able to go anywhere and do anything and be anyone we want to.

WACO: Could I be Jimmie Rodgers?

KOSMO: Sure, why not?

WACO: Who're you gonna' be?

KOSMO: I don't know. A different me.

WACO: Why don't you be somebody else. Somebody different from you. You could be Gene Autry or somebody like that. That's great! You be Gene Autry and I'll be Jimmie Rodgers and we'll form a singing team. How 'bout it?

KOSMO: No thanks. I got my own music to sing.

WACO: Boy, your feet sure do smell. Don't you ever take yer boots off?

KOSMO: *My* feet? I was gonna' say the same about your feet.

WACO: Well, I know my feet smell but that ain't no excuse for lettin' yer feet go to pot. You gotta' take care a' yer feet, boy. That's what gets ya' around.

KOSMO: I got other things to worry about besides my feet.

WACO: Maybe that's yer whole problem. If ya' worried more about yer feet smellin' so bad and less about things that don't exist you'd be a happier fella. Take me as a case in point. I've spent my whole life worrying about things that might happen that never did happen.

KOSMO: Sure is nice country out here. Too bad we have to move on.

WACO: Yeah, well that's the thing about travelin'. Ya' never get to see the things in between where yer comin' from and where yer going to. Say, you been noticin' any change in my appearance lately?

KOSMO: No. Why?

WACO: Well, my reflection sure does remind me of this beautiful broad I used to know back in Omaha.

MAE WEST: Coulda' been Pensacola for all the attention ya' gave me.

(He turns around and grabs MAE *by the waist and dances around with her.)*

WACO: Mae! Well, I'll be a snaggle-toothed hog-whomper! If it ain't old Mae!

MAE WEST: Easy on the merchandise, big boy.

(He puts her down.)

WACO: Last time I seen you, you was holdin' four kings to my four queens.

MAE WEST: You never was much with the ladies.

KOSMO: What made you show up at such an opportune moment?

MAE WEST: I can smell a gold mine a mile off. Same as a man, only sweeter.

KOSMO: I suppose you figure we're going to cut you in on this deal.

MAE WEST: Listen, I know how to wrap that Yahoodi character around my little finger. I'll have him eatin' outa' the palm a' my hand. All you fellas have to do is step in and take things over.

WACO: Sounds good to me.

KOSMO: I don't know. He's a friend of mine.

MAE WEST: Listen, big boy, what do ya' think he's doin' down there in that Mexican jungle with Marlene? Sellin' lottery tickets? He's gonna' rip you off for your two G's, grab the gold, and head West.

KOSMO: Yahoodi? He wouldn't do that.

MAE WEST: I've seen suckers, but you take the bananas.

WACO: What're you gettin' at, Mae?

MAE WEST: We play it cool. We go down in disguises and infiltrate into the village where they're camped out. One of us finds out the low-down. Then we give them the money.

KOSMO: But he doesn't even know I'm coming.

MAE WEST: That's why the disguise. Soon as we find out what the plan is we step in and take the whole thing over.

WACO: Just like that?

MAE WEST: Just like that.

KOSMO: Wouldn't it be better to follow them to the mines to make sure we can find them?

MAE WEST: We'll play it by ear.

KOSMO: Let's go.

(They travel south, singing a snatch of "Travelin' Shoes." Meanwhile, back to MARLENE *and the* BOYS.*)*

YAHOODI: This is a hard map to follow, Captain.

CAPT. KIDD: Leave it to me, me lad. It's clear sailin' all the way.

YAHOODI: We still gotta' wait for the money. Kosmo promised he'd send it. I've been thinkin' we oughta' divvy up the loot with him, too.

CAPT. KIDD: What's this! Another party! I hadn't bargained for another party, laddie.

YAHOODI: Now wait a minute. He's my friend. I can't just cut him out of the deal.

MARLENE: But darling, he's so rich. He's a famous pop star.

YAHOODI: That don't cut no ice. A friend is a friend. We took the oath. We drank each other's blood.

MARLENE: That's disgusting.

YAHOODI: Besides, what do we need his money for, anyway? We've got a boat.

CAPT. KIDD: We have to travel. We have to eat.

YAHOODI: I'm beginning to have my doubts about this whole thing. How come you need us to go and get your treasure? I mean, you have the map and everything. You know where it is. Why are you so all fired up to cut us in on the deal?

CAPT. KIDD: You have no idea how much there is. Chest after chest piled so high you can barely see the top. A treasure so vast it would take one man a lifetime to bring it up to the surface. Besides, I'm getting old. I'm not long for this earth, and it would do my heart joy to see two young people such as yerselves partake of such riches.

YAHOODI: I don't know. I don't like doin' my friend dirty like that. I mean just taking his money and running away.

MARLENE: But think of our life together, Yahoodi. We could go to San Francisco, Paris, Rome, Berlin. Ah, Berlin!

YAHOODI: What do I wanna' go to Berlin for? I'm an American.

CAPT. KIDD: Then forget the whole thing. I'll go find some peasants.

(He rolls up the map in a huff.)

YAHOODI: No! Wait. I'll do it. I'll do it.

MARLENE: That's more like it, darling.

CAPT. KIDD: Now the first thing we gotta' do is wait for the money.

YAHOODI: Right.

MARLENE: I'll handle your friend when he comes. Just leave him to me.

(Back to MAE WEST and the BOYS. They have on ridiculous disguises—beards and masks and stuff. False noses would be good.)

MAE WEST: Now listen, Kosmo, what you gotta' do is pretend you're a peasant that's working for Western Union. You got a special cablegram to deliver this money to Mr. Yahoodi. You got that?

KOSMO: Got it.

WACO: What do we do?

MAE WEST: Just sit tight. We'll think a' something. Okay, now go to it.

(KOSMO sneaks over to MARLENE and the BOYS in his special disguise with a black satchel full of money.)

KOSMO: Cablegram for Meester Yahoodi!

YAHOODI: That's me.

KOSMO: Oh. Well I got thees money for Mr. Yahoodi. Special delivery from Meester Kosmo.

YAHOODI: Good. Hand it over.

(He hands over the stachel. YAHOODI looks inside.)

Thank you very much.

MARLENE: Darling, tip the boy.

YAHOODI: Oh, yeah. (*He pulls out a bill and hands it to* KOSMO.) This is for you.

KOSMO: Thank you, señor.

YAHOODI: Oh, and send a cable back to Mr. Kosmo telling him thank you very much we got your money.

KOSMO: I don't got a pencil.

YAHOODI: Okay, forget it.

KOSMO: Okay, gracias, señor.

YAHOODI: Yeah. Gracias.

CAPT. KIDD: Adios.

(KOSMO goes back to MAE and WACO. YAHOODI and the OTHERS break into cheers.)

YAHOODI: We got it! We got it! We're gonna' be rich!

KOSMO: (*To* MAE) I think the dirty rat was plannin' on cutting me out of the deal all along.

MAE WEST: It's all right. We got him where we want him. It's only a matter of time now.

WACO: Well, let's build us a fire and have some hot fritters.

MAE WEST: No. We let them build the fires. We let them make the moves. We just follow along in their footsteps. We're gonna' shadow them right to that treasure, boys.

(MARLENE *and the* BOYS *build a fire and sit around eating and talking.*)

YAHOODI: What about this boat, Captain? Don't we need a crew or something?

CAPT. KIDD: Naw. As worthy a vessel you've never seen. The three of us can handle her easy.

MARLENE: Darling, where exactly is the treasure located?

CAPT. KIDD: A little island near the Aleutian group. It shouldn't be hard to recognize. I'll remember once we get there.

YAHOODI: What's the treasure like, Captain Kidd? I mean what is it, jewels and stuff?

CAPT. KIDD: Aaah, laddie. 'Tis a treasure to make a man's eyes dance out of his head. There's a ruby ring as big as your fist plucked from the hand of a young maiden who boldly resisted. I was forced to sever her finger from her hand with my saber while her lover stood helplessly by. Those were the days before my conversion, before I saw the light. The cruel days.

YAHOODI: What made you become a pirate in the first place?

CAPT. KIDD: Everyone was doing it. I was sent by the king to put a stop to all this swashbuckling nonsense. But after several days at sea I realized I was working for the wrong side. No one was a bigger pirate than the king himself. So I decided to beat him at his own game. I would become as ruthless, as fearsome and as cruel as all the fancy-dressed snuff-sniffers riding their gilded carriages to and from the palace.

MARLENE: What other treasures are there, darling?

CAPT. KIDD: Sapphires, topaz, diamonds, and pearls. A gold watch with emerald hands on inlaid ivory and ebony, snatched from a poor lad as he was walking the plank. Pouches of gold and silver. Coins of every description. Shimmering platters and vases. Crystal chandeliers. Gold fillings from those who disobeyed. Deeds to land in faraway places. Hand-carved muskets with mother-of-pearl handles.

YAHOODI: It's amazing! All that just waiting for us. Just waiting for the taking. All of my dreams are going to come true. Sure wish Kosmo was here.

MARLENE: Just listen to those nightingales.

CAPT. KIDD: Them is katydids, ma'am. Katydids.

YAHOODI: In the jungle? Katydids in the jungle?

CAPT. KIDD: Or maybe crocodiles.

YAHOODI: That's more like it.

MARLENE: Darling, I think I'll turn in. The night chill is creeping into my bones.

CAPT. KIDD: Same here, lady. Tomorrow's a big day.

(They turn in. Back to MAE *and the* BOYS, *trying to get to sleep.)*

KOSMO: Can't we build a fire, Mae? We're gonna' freeze our buns off out here.

WACO: Yeah, besides there's big cats out there. Tigres. They liable to eat us alive.

MAE WEST: You ain't in the Boy Scouts. This is real life.

KOSMO: I was thinking. Maybe we oughta' give up on this whole thing. I mean I'm rich and famous. What do I need a bunch of gold for?

MAE WEST: Gettin' butterflies already, huh?

WACO: I could sure go for a little nest egg myself. Get me a little cattle ranch out in Arizona. Raise a family.

MAE WEST: Go to sleep.

(They fall asleep. Both camps are sleeping. The night sounds of crickets and small jungle creatures. YAHOODI *and* KOSMO *talk to each other in their sleep. The* OTHERS *stay asleep.* YAHOODI *tosses about as though having a nightmare.)*

YAHOODI: Kosmo! It isn't really me. Not my voice. It's you. No. That doesn't make sense. We'll meet up sooner or later. You've taken my place. That's an awful thing to lay on someone. I'm so many different people at once. I keep running away from unseen executioners. You dig where I'm coming from? My feet are caught in the quicksand.

KOSMO: I don't want to die in my sleep. I just want to know I was here. I have an awful memory of places I never was. I was never there. Yahoodi! It's me. It's me again in a different place.

YAHOODI: I can hear you. We've developed a telepathy. You don't have to explain.

KOSMO: I'm following you. I'm dogging your trail. You'll never get away. This is the end of the trail, buckaroo.

YAHOODI: And how long is this night supposed to last? Not nearly as long as the one coming up. The big night in the sky.

KOSMO: Don't get poetic. You'll wake up with a shock. Don't worry. The sun is coming for you, boy.

(A loud roar offstage. They jump up.)

What was that?

WACO: One a' them tigres. I knew it. We're gonna' die. We're all gonna' die.

MAE WEST: Don't get your panties in a bunch. It's just the call a' the wild.

(Back to MARLENE and the BOYS.)

YAHOODI: Marlene?

MARLENE: Yes, darling?

YAHOODI: Did you hear something?

MARLENE: No, my pet. Go to sleep. You need your rest.

YAHOODI: You know, ever since we started this treasure thing I've had the strangest feeling we're being followed.

MARLENE: It's just your imagination. The jungle does that to you.

YAHOODI: I'm going to wake up Captain Kidd.

MARLENE: But darling—

YAHOODI: Hey! Captain! Captain Kidd!

(CAPTAIN KIDD snores loudly and turns over. YAHOODI kicks him.)

Wake up!

MARLENE: Darling, let him sleep. We have a big day ahead of us.

YAHOODI: Hey, Captain! Wake up!

(CAPTAIN KIDD jumps to his feet, saber at the ready.)

CAPT. KIDD: Scuttle the mainsail! Swab the port bow! Every man for himself!

YAHOODI: Hold on. Wait a minute.

CAPT. KIDD: Oh, it's you. What do you mean waking me out of a sound sleep?

YAHOODI: Listen, I think we oughta' take off tonight. I think we're being followed.

CAPT. KIDD: Followed?

YAHOODI: Yeah. I've been hearing all these weird noises.

CAPT. KIDD: Followed! We're being followed!

MARLENE: It's just his imagination.

CAPT. KIDD: Well, if it's true then you're right. By all means. We leave tonight! We leave this instant! Pack up your gear.

(Music. They take off on a march and wind up at the boat. They climb in the boat and set sail. Meanwhile back to MAE and the BOYS.)

KOSMO: Listen, Mae. I think I'm going to go check their camp out. Just to make sure they're not pulling any funny stuff.

WACO: I think we oughta' stick together. Them tigres can be mighty fierce.

MAE WEST: You think they're up to something, huh? All right, but be quick about it. Me and Waco here'll hold down the camp.

KOSMO: I'll be right back.

(KOSMO sneaks off through the jungle to where MARLENE and the BOYS were camped.)

WACO: Listen, Mae, to tell you the truth I'm scared shitless. I mean I ain't used to the jungle. The open prairie's my stompin' grounds.

MAE WEST: Yeah, well just cool yourself out. The worst is yet to come. I wonder what's keeping Kosmo.

WACO: The tigres probably got him. I knew it! I knew it! We're all gonna' die!

(KOSMO discovers that MARLENE and the BOYS have split. He goes running back to MAE and WACO with the news.)

MAE WEST: Just take it easy. SHHH! I think I hear someone comin'.

(KOSMO comes running up to them out of breath.)

KOSMO: They've left! They're gone!

MAE WEST: Are ya' sure?

KOSMO: Positive.

MAE WEST: Why the dirty double-crossers. So they flew the coop on us. Well, let's get a move on.

WACO: Right now? We're leaving right now? In the dark? We're goin' out there in the dark?

MAE WEST: We gotta' catch up to 'em before they get too much of a head start.

KOSMO: Right. Let's go.

(They move out into the jungle. Back to MARLENE *and the* BOYS *riding the high seas on their boat.* CAPTAIN KIDD *sings "Fadin'.")*

CAPT. KIDD:

I once was the master of the torrid high seas
I pillaged the king's ships, I stole what I pleased
My heart was full sail tattooed with sin
You could rest my good deeds on the head of a pin

I raged and men feared me, they called me black heart
Gold tooth and black patch and tongue like a dart
The women all wanted me and called me a louse
Though tempted by treasure and my black pirate mouth

With visions of white ships I crawled through the night
A victim of penitence and clean-living light
I traded my dark deeds for an angel's good word
My soul fled the devil like a trembling bird

My masthead throws a shadow black as a spade
On the torrid high seas where Captain Kidd fades
On the torrid high seas where Captain Kidd fades

I deceive all that's evil, offer gifts from the sea
The navigator saints all smile on me
And the Book I once branded a book black as hell
Floats broken and damaged in the earth's briny cell

Yet I once was the master of the torrid high seas
A skull and crossbones draped around me

I wear my past proudly tight like a glove
My terrible deeds twist me like love

My masthead throws a shadow black as a spade
On the torrid high seas where Captain Kidd fades
On the torrid high seas where Captain Kidd fades

YAHOODI: This is the life. What a life. How 'bout it, Marlene? Ain't this the life!

MARLENE: (*Hanging over the side of the boat*) I think I'm going to be sick.

YAHOODI: What a life. Say, Captain, I wouldn't mind taking that treasure and sailing around the world. Just taking a nice long cruise. What do ya' say?

CAPT. KIDD: No, laddie, I think I'll be settling down somewhere off the coast of Spain. Me and the high seas have seen too much of each other.

YAHOODI: Sharks! Look! There's sharks!

CAPT. KIDD: No, me lad. Them's dolphins. Hard to tell the difference at first. But they're a friend of man. If ya' listen real close they sing a certain song. Us old sea dogs can hear it a mile off.

YAHOODI: I think I hear it.

CAPT. KIDD: No, you can't hear it. Only us old sea dogs can hear it.

YAHOODI: But I hear it. I swear I can hear it.

CAPT. KIDD: Well, I can't hear it, so how could you be hearin' it?

(MARLENE *keeps puking over the side.*)

YAHOODI: Then it is my imagination. Like last night. I was hearing something last night too. I am hearing something. We *are* being followed. Faster, Captain Kidd! Faster!

CAPT. KIDD: Just settle down, me lad. There's nothin' around for miles. Take a look for yerself. Nothin' but the deep blue sea.

YAHOODI: Gimme your telescope. I'm going to take a look.

CAPTAIN KIDD *hands him a telescope.* YAHOODI *looks behind him.*)

CAPT. KIDD: Well, what do ya' see?

YAHOODI: I see a bunch of Mexicans waving a flag and dancing around a fire.

CAPT. KIDD: What else do ya' see?

YAHOODI: I see two men on a raft eating Tootsie Rolls.

CAPT. KIDD: What else do ya' see?

YAHOODI: I see the whole world going up in smoke and everybody's asleep. There's one old man with a long gray beard trying to wake everybody up but nobody can hear him. They just keep sleeping and sleeping.

CAPT. KIDD: Give me back the telescope. You've gone mad, me lad. It happens to the best of us. But this old ocean does funny things to the mind of man.

YAHOODI: You really think I'm crazy?

CAPT. KIDD: No crazier than the likes of me.

YAHOODI: I wish she'd stop throwing up. It makes me sick.

(Back to MAE *and the* BOYS *caught in a storm on the high seas. They're in a row-boat.)*

WACO: I knew it! We're gonna' die! We're all gonna' die!

KOSMO: Will you shut up. It's just a storm. It'll pass.

MAE WEST: Watch the port bow, boys. There's a real crusher wave coming up.

WACO: I think I'm gonna' be sick.

*(*WACO *throws up over the side.)*

MAE WEST: I've seen useless men in my day, but he takes the cake.

KOSMO: He's all right, Mae. He's just used to dry land. He's a cowboy. Cowboys don't go to sea.

MAE: Cowboy, my eyeball. He's a useless twerp. We shoulda' canned him right from the start.

KOSMO: Now don't start that. Just because we're in a crisis doesn't mean we can't get along.

MAE: Man the starboard keel! Bring her about! Bring her about!

KOSMO: Where'd you learn all that lingo?

MAE: I've been around, sonny.

KOSMO: Looks like it's gonna' clear up.

MAE: Just like that?

KOSMO: Looks like it. Looks like it's going to be a beautiful day.

MAE: All right, you can stop being sick, mister. The storm's over.

KOSMO: Yeah, it looks like it's going to be clear as a bell.

MAE: Here, take a look through this thing and see if you can spot their boat.

(She hands him a telescope. KOSMO looks through it.)

MAE: You see anything?

KOSMO: Wild dogs.

MAE: What do you mean?

KOSMO: Wild dogs. Circling around. Tracking something down.

MAE: You must be going crazy. Gimme that thing.

(He hands it to her. She looks through it.)

MAE: It's them. I can see them.

KOSMO: Really?

(WACO pukes over the side.)

MAE: Looks like they're having trouble. Marlene's sick. She's puking over the side. Looks like one of their sails is broken. There's sharks circling all around the boat. They're in real trouble. Looks like we're gonna' catch up to 'em after all.

KOSMO: Lemme see.

(He takes the telescope and looks.)

MAE: Can you see them?

KOSMO: Nope. I keep hearing music. Jimi Hendrix.

MAE: You can't see them? You must have cotton in your eyeballs.

KOSMO: Oh, yeah. Now I see them. Paul Bunyan's pulling them ashore with his ox.

MAE: Are you kidding?

KOSMO: No. Look.

(She takes the telescope and looks.)

MAE: I can't see them anymore. Where'd they go? Full steam ahead. Come on! Let's get a move on! Row! Row! Row! Faster! Faster! We're losing them!

(They all start rowing like crazy. Back to CAPTAIN KIDD.*)*

YAHOODI: Hey, Captain, how many months have we been out here?

MARLENE: Oh, don't say it. It makes me sick to think of it. What a waste of a good life. I could be in Berlin having a good time. Or Copenhagen. Anywhere but here in this awful ocean.

CAPT. KIDD: I'd say maybe six or seven months as the crow flies.

YAHOODI: That long, huh?

MARLENE: It's awful. My makeup has faded. My furs are all wilted. My stockings are torn. And I'm starving to death.

YAHOODI: Shut up, will you? All you ever do is bitch, bitch, bitch. Just be thankful we're still alive.

*(*CAPTAIN KIDD *spots land.)*

CAPT. KIDD: Land ho! Land ho!

YAHOODI: Really! Land! It is! It's land, Marlene! We're safe! Look!

MARLENE: Oh, thank God. Land. At last.

YAHOODI: Well, what are we waiting for? Let's go ashore.

CAPT. KIDD: Not so fast. The natives could be dangerous.

YAHOODI: Fuck the natives. I'm going ashore.

(They all pile out of the boat and go ashore. CAPTAIN KIDD *gets out his map.)*

CAPT. KIDD: Now if me memory serves me right it should be right in this vicinity.

YAHOODI: Let's go, let's go. Stop fucking around with the map.

MARLENE: Don't be so impatient, darling.

YAHOODI: I wanna' get the treasure. Let's go.

(They march off into the boondocks. Back to MAE *in the boat, looking through the telescope.)*

MAE: I think I see them. They've landed or something.

KOSMO: Landed! They've found land!

WACO: Water! I need some water.

KOSMO: Lemme take a look.

(She hands him the telescope.)

KOSMO: They have! They've landed. They're heading right for the treasure.

WACO: Water, water.

KOSMO: I keep hearing music. Like distant drums.

MAE: It must be the natives.

KOSMO: No, like Janis Joplin. Like Big Brother.

MAE: You're just getting paranoid.

KOSMO: Thousands of people screaming. More! More! More!

MAE: Gimme the telescope.

(She grabs it away from him and looks through it.)

WACO: Water, water.

MAE: Looks like the natives have spotted them. They're circling around them. They're killing off the natives.

KOSMO: Well, let's get ashore. What are we waiting for?

MAE: We can't let them see the boat. We'll have to swim.

KOSMO: Swim ashore?

MAE: That's right. You think you're up to it?

KOSMO: *I* am. I don't know about him, though.

WACO: Water, water.

MAE: We'll just dump him overboard. He'll have to sink or swim.

KOSMO: All right. Let's go.

(They dump WACO over the side and they all start swimming ashore.)

WACO: I can't swim! I'm going to drown!

MAE: Grab ahold of him. Get him by the neck. Swim, you fool! Swim!

WACO: I can't! I'm going to drown!

KOSMO: What's that! It looks like sharks! Heading this way! It is! It's sharks!

MAE: Swim! Swim for your lives!

(Back to CAPTAIN KIDD. He unfolds his map. The OTHERS sit down exhausted.)

CAPT. KIDD: I think this is the spot. Right about in here.

YAHOODI: That's what you said before.

MARLENE: These mosquitoes are eating me alive.

CAPT. KIDD: Come on. The cave should be right behind these bushes.

MARLENE: Oh, can't we just rest for a while darling? I can't take another step.

YAHOODI: Come on. We're being followed, I tell ya'. We can't waste any more time.

CAPT. KIDD: Here it is. The cave. I've found it. I knew it was here.

YAHOODI: We found it! We found it!

MARLENE: Thank God!

(An Indian GHOST GIRL appears with a spear.)

GHOST GIRL: That's far enough.

CAPT. KIDD: It's the Indian ghost girl I told you about. (*He speaks to her in an ancient tongue.*) Santo lala gronto. Muchamo no le santiamo.

GHOST GIRL: Buzz off, buster. This is Captain Kidd's treasure. He told me to watch it for him while he was gone.

CAPT. KIDD: But I am Captain Kidd. Don't you recognize me?

GHOST GIRL: He warned me of impostors. And you're about as phony as they come.

CAPT. KIDD: Wait a minute. I'm real. I'm the real Captain Kidd.

YAHOODI: He is. He's the real one.

GHOST GIRL: Oh yeah? And I suppose she's supposed to be Marlene Dietrich or something?

MARLENE: I don't have to stand here and be insulted.

GHOST GIRL: That's right, sister. If you don't like it you know what you can do about it.

MARLENE: Are you challenging me, darling?

GHOST GIRL: Choose your weapons.

MARLENE: Fingernails and teeth.

GHOST GIRL: Okay by me.

(The GHOST GIRL and MARLENE square off for a fight. MARLENE takes off her boa and her furs.)

MARLENE: Here, darling, hold these for me.

(She hands them to YAHOODI. MARLENE *and the* GHOST GIRL *tear into each other and fight all over the stage.)*

YAHOODI: Hold her off, Marlene! We'll be right back with the treasure.

*(*CAPTAIN KIDD *and* YAHOODI *go offstage for the treasure while* MARLENE *and* GHOST GIRL *fight.* MAE *and the* BOYS *make it up onto the shore.* WACO *is water-logged.* KOSMO *gives him artificial respiration as* MAE *watches the fight.)*

MAE: Musta' been a real hunk a' man to get them two so all fired up. Probably one a' the natives.

KOSMO: Mae, I don't think he's gonna' make it.

MAE: Okay, we'll leave him for the buzzards. He's been a real drag right from the start.

KOSMO: We can't just leave him here.

MAE: We'll come back and pick him up later. After we get that treasure.

KOSMO: I don't know. He's been a real friend.

MAE: This ain't the time to be gettin' sentimental. Let's get a move on.

KOSMO: Okay. So long, Waco, old buddy. Hope you find Jimmie Rodgers in heaven.

MAE: He ain't dead yet.

KOSMO: All right. Let's go.

(They follow CAPTAIN KIDD *and* YAHOODI *offstage. At this point the fight has reached its climax, and* MARLENE *is winning. She has* GHOST GIRL *by the throat.* GHOST GIRL *collapses in a heap.* MARLENE *pulls herself together. She looks around the stage.)*

MARLENE: It's always been this way. Right from the start. Always left behind. Always left in the lurch. I guess I'm just a born loser.

*(*PAUL BUNYAN *enters.)*

Oh, it's you again. You with the mysterious eyes. Have you found your Babe?

PAUL BUNYAN: Nope. I've just about given up hope.

MARLENE: Oh, no. Never give up. Never say no to life. Come with me. We'll find your Babe. I promise you.

PAUL: You think we can?

MARLENE: I'm sure of it.

PAUL: Boy, lady, you sure are one hunk a' woman. I could almost forget my ox for you.

MARLENE: Let's go away together.

(They exit. WACO starts to come to. He shakes his head and sits up, feeling drunk. He looks out over the audience.)

WACO: *(Sings)*
I been fightin' like a lion.
But I'm 'fraid I'm gonna lose.

What happened to my hat? I had me a hat. Given to me special. Can't see nothin' but ocean. Nothin' but the deep blue sea. Can't figure out this life. Here one minute, gone the next. Just a space traveler. Just a driftin' fool. Wake up in the mornin' and find yerself in the ocean. Now ain't that the damn truth. *(He notices the GHOST GIRL and goes to her.)* Well now, lookit that. A fair young maiden. Lookit that. Hey! This here's Waco talkin'. Listen to me. I'm so lonely and hungry for love that my stomach is stranglin' my backbone. And that's the truth. Feel like a mule driver eatin' nothin' but borax for a mile. Listen to me, honey. *(He sits down next to her and strokes her hair.)* Oh, my heart's just about ripped wide open just from the sight of somethin' like you. Yessir. Good thing yer unconscious to this babble. You wouldn't believe the journeys I've made. You wouldn't believe. Say, if I told ya' a secret you wouldn't tell nobody, would ya'? It's somethin' I've been savin' up fer a long, long time. I never told it to nobody before. I'm the real Jimmie Rodgers. That's right. It's me. He lives in me, that's how I figure I'm him. Same thing as though he'd never died at all. I can feel him breathin' down deep inside me. You know how that is. A man gets into yer soul. Same as a woman or a piece a' land. He's alive in me. And that's how I'm gonna' put him back on the street. He died too fast. A man like that just doesn't come and go. He lives on. He lives in yer heart. He's alive right now. Can ya' hear him? Listen: "I been fightin' like a lion. / But I'm 'fraid I'm gonna lose." Ya' hear that? He's in there. I know it's him. It's gotta' be him. It ain't me, that's for sure. It sure ain't me. *(He takes off his boots.)* My mind's as raggedy and tore up as this old pair a' boots. Nothin' holdin' it together no more. Not even the desire left. Just follow yer heart. That's what I say. Follow the heart. It'll lead ya' right outa' this world right into the next. I got no expectations. The world's a motherfucker, boy. I got nowheres to go and nothin' to see. Nowheres. And that's the truth.

(The lights dim out.)

ACT TWO

The lights come up on YAHOODI *and* CAPTAIN KIDD *sitting by a campfire with two big bags full of gold.*

CAPT. KIDD: I can't understand it. How they coulda' found it in the first place. How they coulda' got past the ghost girl. And how come they left two bags behind. I just can't understand it.

YAHOODI: You sure you ain't holding out on me now?

CAPT. KIDD: Now laddie, why would I even have asked ye' to come along with me in the first place if I was plannin' on double-crossin' ye?

YAHOODI: Yeah. Well, I'm thankful that we got out of there with our skins. Those natives were getting pretty fierce. These two bags should last us quite a while if we play our cards right.

CAPT. KIDD: I'm not a greedy man by nature. There's enough in this bag to see out the rest of my days.

YAHOODI: Yeah, well, you're an old man. Me, I got my whole life in front of me. I wanna' live high. I wanna' live real high.

CAPT. KIDD: Sure puzzles me what coulda' happened to Miss Marlene. Unless that ghost girl dragged her off into the woods.

YAHOODI: Maybe the natives got her.

CAPT. KIDD: She was such a fine woman.

YAHOODI: She was all right.

CAPT. KIDD: But I thought you loved her.

YAHOODI: We had an understanding. That's all. Just an understanding.

CAPT. KIDD: Boy, if I had a woman like that I'd tie her to my waist and never let her out of my sight.

YAHOODI: Shhh! What's that!

(He stands and listens to the space. Silence.)

CAPT. KIDD: You hearin' things again? There ain't nothin' out there but the wilds.

YAHOODI: There's something out there, I tell ya'. There's something been following us ever since we left the jungle. I can feel it. A presence. Something real. Maybe it's Kosmo. Maybe he's been dogging my trail all this time. (*He calls across a vast expanse.*) Kosmo!

CAPT. KIDD: Listen, son. I got an idea. How 'bout if the two of us broke up and went our separate ways? We got nothin' more to do with each other. It's time we followed our own paths.

YAHOODI: Broke up? Oh, no. I get it. You wanna' get me out there alone in the jungle. You know the jungle and I don't. That's it, isn't it? You wanna' come sneaking up on me and bump me off and take my half of the treasure. Isn't that the truth?

CAPT. KIDD: After all we been through? After all that, you can say something like that to me?

YAHOODI: Maybe you got a deal worked out with Kosmo. The two of you. You sneak off and meet him, and then the two of ya' do me in. Maybe that's it. Maybe he's out there right now. Just waiting for your signal. Just waiting for me to fall asleep.

CAPT. KIDD: Now slow down, kid. You've got the fever. Yer mind's been twisted up.

(YAHOODI *pulls a gun on* CAPTAIN KIDD.)

YAHOODI: Oh no! Not this time. This time the tables are turned. It's me who's gonna' take over. It's me who's gonna' take your half and leave you in the lurch. Now hand it over! Come on! Hand it over!

(CAPTAIN KIDD *hands over his bag of the treasure.*)

CAPT. KIDD: You're makin' a big mistake, laddie. I have no evil in my heart for you.

YAHOODI: You think I'm falling for that goodness and kindness routine, you're crazy. This is my show and I'm running it my way. Now turn around! Turn around!

CAPT. KIDD: You can't just shoot me in the back and leave me here to die.

YAHOODI: I can't, huh? Just watch me. You haven't got the guts to do it. You're so moral and self-righteous you couldn't pull the trigger. Isn't that right? Well, not me, Captain Kidd. I'm gonna' blow your brains out.

(KOSMO's *voice comes from offstage as if from many miles away.* YAHOODI *turns toward the sound.*)

KOSMO'S VOICE: Yahoodi?
YAHOODI: Kosmo? That you? You're out there. I know you're out there. You're trying to drive me crazy. But I'm too smart for that. I got the upper hand. You're not going to get away with it. I'm going to win!

(CAPTAIN KIDD *springs on* YAHOODI. *They struggle with the gun.* CAPTAIN KIDD *finally grabs it away from him and points it in his face.*)

CAPT. KIDD: Now get up!

(YAHOODI *stands.* CAPTAIN KIDD *covers him with the gun.*)

YAHOODI: Looks like the tables are turned again, eh, Captain Kidd?
CAPT. KIDD: Looks that way, doesn't it?
YAHOODI: What're ya' gonna' do now? You can't shoot me 'cause you haven't got the guts. You can't leave me here to die in the jungle because your conscience wouldn't let you. So it looks like you'll have to take me with you.
CAPT. KIDD: It looks that way.
YAHOODI: And sooner or later you're gonna' have to sleep. Sooner or later the tables will turn again.
CAPT. KIDD: Time will tell that tale. Now come on, we're movin' out into the desert.

(*They travel to the desert.* KOSMO *and* MAE *enter from the opposite side.* KOSMO *yells across a great expanse.*)

KOSMO: Yahoodi!
MAE: Pipe down. What do you wanna' do, let the whole jungle know we're here?
KOSMO: I don't care anymore. I don't care about the treasure or the natives or anything. I just wanna' find my roots.
MAE: Well, ya' ain't gonna' find 'em by screaming your head off.

KOSMO: (*Calling*) Waco! Hey, Waco!

MAE: Will you shut up? That old buzzard's long gone by now.

KOSMO: But where'd he go? Where's my friend? Where's Yahoodi? Where's all the people I love? I can't hear the music anymore. I can't hear the band.

MAE: Stop blubbering. Once we get that treasure I'll buy you a dozen bands.

KOSMO: I want *my* band. I don't want a dozen bands. I just wanna' play my music. My own special music.

MAE: Oh, if I just had me a man. A real man. We could rip off this treasure and have us a ball. But now I get strapped with a kid. A rock-and-roll punk.

KOSMO: (*Calling across a great expanse*) Yahoodi! I had a vision! Jimi Hendrix and Janis Joplin and Buddy Holly and Sam Cooke and Big Bopper and Otis Redding and Brian Jones and Jimmie Rodgers and Blind Lemon Jefferson! They're all in heaven and they've started a band! Yahoodi! Can you hear me?

MAE: You've flipped your cake, buster. You've really gone bananas.

KOSMO: I wanna' go home. I wanna' see my wife and kids again.

MAE: So, now you're a married man.

KOSMO: Sure, what's so strange about that?

MAE: What about all them groupies? All them group gropes? The string of broken hearts from here to Tupelo?

KOSMO: You're making that up. You're trying to drive me crazy. Once I thought I loved you.

MAE: You ain't the first man to spit out them words. Listen, honey, I wanna' live high. I mean really high. You think I wanna' spend the rest of my life in the jungle?

KOSMO: Look at me. I was living high. I was living in wall-to-wall carpets with color TVs and all the dope I could want and girls climbing all over me and my name in all the papers. Look where I am now. The same place as you. So what's the difference? You want what I have and I want what you have and we both have each other.

MAE: You're confusin' my mind. I'm a simple gal. I don't like talkin' in riddles.

KOSMO: What's gonna' happen when we do find Yahoodi? We steal his treasure and then what?

MAE: We hit all the big ones. Saint Louis, New Orleans, San Francisco, Baton Rouge. We wine and dine with the best of 'em. We knock 'em dead with our glitter. Folks'll say, "Who's that couple? They sure do know how to live."

KOSMO: But I'm a country boy.

MAE: Then go back to the country. Quit draggin' my time. I'll take that treasure myself. I've done it before without no help from a man, and I'll do it again.

KOSMO: But which way is home? I don't know where to start. We don't even have a compass. I'm lost. We're both lost.

MAE: I know exactly where I'm going, honey. And it ain't to the poorhouse. If ya' wanna' tag along you're welcome to. Just stop confusin' my ambitions. (*She sings "Back Street Boy."*)

There's a back street boy that comes around
I know he'd like to take me out on the town
But I'd lay odds he doesn't have a cent
And after all I'm a doll who's lookin' for a gent

He sure do have a mournful air
We sure would make a handsome pair
But fate ain't plannin' on takin' that route
'Cause what the hell, I'm a gal who's looking for some loot

I'm a gal who goes for high high livin'
Breakfast served in the afternoon
I'm the type can take whatever's given
And though I'm partial to honey, I ain't askin' for the moon

There'll always be room in my memory
For that back street boy and how he looked at me
But I ain't dwellin' on what never could be
'Cause it's for sure scrubbin' floors ain't my fantasy

(*Cut to* PAUL BUNYAN *and* MARLENE *under the shade of an apple tree, munching on apples and snuggling in each other's arms.*)

MARLENE: You know something, Paul?

PAUL: What, honey bunch?

MARLENE: It sure is too bad about your ox.

PAUL: Yeah, old Babe was the only thing I had in life until I met you.

MARLENE: You're such a gentle man. So strong and gentle.

PAUL: I try to be just like I am, ma'am. That's the best way I've found.

MARLENE: Those poor darlings back in the jungle. Searching for treasure. What a silly thing.

PAUL: Yeah, I figure what's the use in striving for things when all ya' gotta' do is sit back and have 'em come to ya'. Except old Babe. I don't know if he'll ever come back.

MARLENE: What made him leave in the first place?

PAUL: I guess I was just workin' him too hard. You know how it is with an ox. Same as a woman. You can't drive 'em too hard or they start yearnin' for a way out.

MARLENE: I know what you mean.

PAUL: That's what I like about you.

MARLENE: What?

PAUL: You know what I mean. I don't have to go through a whole lot of explainin'.

MARLENE: What wonderful music.

PAUL: Music?

MARLENE: In the air. Spring music. Mountain music. Music that sounds like golden leaves.

PAUL: I'm sorry, ma'am, but I don't hear nothin' but the breeze.

MARLENE: You can call me Marlene if you want.

PAUL: All right, Marlene. You sure are swell.

MARLENE: You're pretty swell too, darling.

PAUL: (*Sings "Marlene"*)

Marlene Dietrich, you took my breath away
If I was born in another day
The dogs couldn't keep me away from your door

Marlene you're so fine
Marlene you're so fine

Some say the stars up in the skies
Are there just because we got eyes
But I could see your star up on the screen
If I was blind as a bean

Marlene you're so fine
Marlene you're so fine

I'd bury my nose in your furs
I'd swallow you whole with your pearls
I'd fight off the dukes and the earls
I'd even give up on all of my girls for you

Marlene you're so fine
Marlene you're so fine

(They go into a clinch. Cut to WACO *and* GHOST GIRL *on another part of the stage.)*

GHOST GIRL: *(Waking up)* What happened to that bitch? I'm gonna' kick her ass.

WACO: Now hold on there, tootsie roll. The war's over. Why don't ya' just sit down here beside me and give me a little squeeze?

GHOST GIRL: Who're you anyway? Where'd you come from?

WACO: I'm just here. That's all. Name's Waco. Waco Texas. Born and raised.

GHOST GIRL: Were you hooked up with that broad?

WACO: Not me. I'm my own man. Or God's man. Whatever way ya' wanna' look at it.

GHOST GIRL: Looks like they got what was left of the treasure. Dirty pigs. I knew they were phonies. Right from the start. A bunch a' phonies. Boy, is Captain Kidd gonna' be pissed.

WACO: You shouldn't worry about him. You got your own life.

GHOST GIRL: Yeah, I guess you're right. I don't know what I'm doing anymore. Hangin' around this dumb island. Pickin' coconuts. Kickin' sand all day long.

WACO: What a life.

GHOST GIRL: What do you do for a living?

WACO: Me, I'm a drifter. Just follow the breeze. One place is just as good as another for me.

GHOST GIRL: Sounds kinda' lonely.

WACO: You get used to it.

GHOST GIRL: What do you say we get outa' here? We could go to the States.

WACO: I just came from there. Besides, I just took my travelin' shoes off.

GHOST GIRL: I wanna see all those famous people up there. That must be really something, to see a famous person. You know what I mean?

WACO: Like who, for instance?

GHOST GIRL: Like Elvis Presley. I'd really like to see him. He really turns me on.

WACO: Never heard of him. I like Jimmie Rodgers myself.

GHOST GIRL: I never heard of him either.

WACO: How come a native island girl like you knows about famous people in the States?

GHOST GIRL: He's not from the States, he's from Memphis. And I'm not a native island girl. I was dropped off here by Captain Kidd. He was on his way to Bimini and he just dropped me off and told me to take care of his treasure.

WACO: Where'd he pick you up in the first place?

GHOST GIRL: Some bar in Frisco. That was back in the seventeen hundreds.

WACO: What're you tryin' to do, drive me crazy or something?

GHOST GIRL: I'm a ghost, stupid.

WACO: Yeah, well, I know just how ya' feel. I feel that way myself sometimes. Just a ghost. Stuck somewheres between livin' and dyin'.

GHOST GIRL: But I'm really a ghost.

WACO: Okay, okay. How's about some lovin'?

GHOST GIRL: No thanks. I'm saving myself up for Elvis. I'm going to meet him someday. Someday soon. We'll be walking down the street and we'll run into each other. It'll be an accident. A real accident.

WACO: Guess I'm too old fer ya', huh?

GHOST GIRL: No, it's not that. It's just that you want something special to happen the first time around, you know what I mean?

WACO: You mean to tell me you're a virgin?

GHOST GIRL: Are you kidding? I'm just dreaming. A girl can dream, can't she?

WACO: Sure. Sure.

(Cut back to CAPTAIN KIDD and YAHOODI. CAPTAIN KIDD is trying to sleep sitting up, his gun trained on YAHOODI, who sits across from him with his hands tied behind his back.)

YAHOODI: It's hard, ain't it, Captain Kidd? Hard to sleep and keep your eyes peeled at the same time. How long do you think you can keep it up? How much longer? Sooner or later you're gonna' have to fall asleep. Then it's gonna' be my turn. Then the tables are gonna' turn again.

CAPT. KIDD: Just keep yer trap shut, limey.

YAHOODI: Not much longer. Not too much longer. You're a real fool, Captain Kidd. A real fool. Why don't you kill me? You know I'm gonna' do it to you once I get the chance. Why don't you kill me now and get it over with? You could just leave my body for the buzzards. They'd pick me clean. Nobody'd know the difference.

(CAPTAIN KIDD falls fast asleep. YAHOODI slips out of his ropes, sneaks over to him, and takes the gun out of his hand. He kicks CAPTAIN KIDD in the ribs.)

YAHOODI: All right! On your feet! I warned you the whole time. You can't say I wasn't fair. On your feet!

(CAPTAIN KIDD struggles to his feet, dead tired from exhaustion.)

Now turn around! Turn around!

(CAPTAIN KIDD turns around. YAHOODI kicks him viciously.)

Now march!

(They march all over the stage, with CAPTAIN KIDD falling down from exhaustion and YAHOODI kicking him up on his feet. Finally they get to a lonely spot.)

All right, here. Right here is good.

CAPT. KIDD: I'm so tired. Can't you let me sleep for a while? Just a little while?

YAHOODI: You're gonna' sleep forever, Captain Kidd.

CAPT. KIDD: Thank God.

(YAHOODI fires and hits CAPTAIN KIDD in the back. He falls to the ground, dead. YAHOODI rushes back and picks up the bags of treasure. As he's doing this CAPTAIN KIDD, who turns out to be only wounded, starts pulling himself across the stage until finally he's completely off. YAHOODI talks to himself.)

YAHOODI: Thought they could fool me. Ha! Now look who's on top. Thought they could outfox the Yahoodi. Ha! Now I have it all. It's all mine. Guess I'll head for Nogales and cash it in for dollar bills. No, maybe I'll cash half and keep the other half hid away someplace. No, then they'd find it. They're still out there. I can feel them out there. (*Calling*) Kosmo! That you? I know you're out there somewhere. Kosmo! (*To himself*) Maybe it's not him. Maybe it's Captain Kidd. Maybe I didn't really get him good. Maybe I only wounded him. Maybe I'm going crazy. Maybe it's just me. It could be me. My imagination. My imagination running wild. No. There's someone out there. (*Calling*) Marlene! Marlene! Is that you? (*To himself*) Couldn't be. She's long gone by now. Maybe she's dead. Maybe they're all dead. That's it. They're all dead. It's just me. It could be their ghosts. Maybe they're haunting me or something. (*Calling out*) Is that it? You're all dead and you've come back to haunt me! (*To himself*) No. It must be Captain Kidd. I'm going to go check. Just to make sure. I'll put a few more shells in him just to make sure. No harm in that.

(*He travels back thorough all the space they marched through before and arrives at the spot where he shot* CAPTAIN KIDD. *He discovers that* CAPTAIN KIDD'S *gone.*)

Couldn't be. It just couldn't be. I drilled him good. No man could walk away from that. (*Calling out*) Captain Kidd! Captain Kidd! It's me! Yahoodi! I've decided I was wrong! I'm willing to go fifty-fifty again! Can you hear me? (*To himself*) He's going to track me down like an animal. He knows the jungle and I don't. Why didn't I think of that before? How am I going to get out of here? I don't know the ropes (*Calling out*) Kosmo! Marlene! Is anybody out there? Help me! You can't let me die! Not now! Now that I'm rich! You can't! (*To himself*) There's nobody out there, you fool. Stop wasting your energy. It's what they want you to do. Can't you see they're trying to drive you crazy. They want to drive you to suicide. That's it. (*Calling out*) That's it, isn't it? You're trying to make me kill myself! Well, I won't do it! I'm too smart for that! I have my pride! I'm going to fight this jungle! I'm going to fight it! And I'm going to win! Do you hear me? I'm going to win!

(*He collapses in a ball. Cut to* MAE *and* KOSMO *sneaking through the jungle toward* YAHOODI.)

MAE: It's this direction. I heard it. I distinctly heard it. We're gettin' warm now, brother.

KOSMO: You sure it was him? It could be a tiger or one of those wild parrots. They scream sometimes.

MAE: It wasn't no parrot.

KOSMO: You sure you wanna' go through with this? I'm getting kind of nervous.

MAE: Shut up. It was right around here someplace.

(YAHOODI sits up and puts the gun to his head and pulls the trigger. A loud gunshot. He topples over on the treasure.)

KOSMO: What was that!

MAE: It must be him. Come on!

(They arrive at YAHOODI.)

KOSMO: Yahoodi! Yahoodi. You went and did it. I knew it. I knew he was gonna' do it. I knew this was gonna' end up like this. Yahoodi, why'd you have to do it?

MAE: Quit blubbering. We got the treasure now. Help me get him off of it.

(They pull YAHOODI off the treasure.)

KOSMO: He didn't have to do it. There was other ways. He didn't have to off himself. Why'd he do it?

MAE: We're rich! We're rich!

KOSMO: All you care about is the money. I've lost a friend.

MAE: Come on, let's get out of here before the Federales come. Grab one of these sacks and let's get out of here.

(JESSE JAMES enters, with a black bandanna over his face and both his guns drawn.)

JESSE: Not so fast, lady.

MAE: Oh, brother. I suppose you're supposed to be Jesse James or something.

JESSE: That's right, lady. Now hand it over.

MAE: Looks like you got the upper hand, don't it?

JESSE: Sure looks that way.

MAE: Maybe we could make a deal, big boy.

JESSE: No deals. Just hand over the treasure.

KOSMO: Just like that you'd run out on me. After all we been through.

MAE: I go where the action is. What do ya' say, Jesse? We split the dough fifty-fifty, and I'll let ya' come up and see me sometime. How's that sound?

JESSE: What're ya' gonna' do with him?

MAE: Who, Kosmo? He'll find something. He's a very enterprisin' young man. Back in the States he packs 'em in. Don't ya', Kosmo?

KOSMO: Sure, sure. You two go ahead and have yourselves a ball. I'm going to stay and bury my friend.

JESSE: I don't know. I been ridin' alone recently, and a woman might slow me down.

MAE: Not this woman, doll. I got the fastest action this side a' the Delaware Water Gap.

JESSE: That just might come in handy. All right. Let's get outa' here then.

MAE: (*To Kosmo*) So long, honey. I'll drop you a line, let ya' know how things are cookin'.

(She kisses KOSMO and grabs the treasure. MAE and JESSE exit.)

KOSMO: Yeah, take it easy. Don't buy any wooden nickels. (*He takes a moment and looks around the stage. Then, to* YAHOODI) All right, all right. You can get up now. Come on. Look, it's not going to work out if you go and off yourself right when everything gets going so good. You just bring the whole fucking thing to a dead end. We got all these characters strung out all over the place in all these different lives and you just go and rub yourself out. What a fucking drag. Is that responsible? Now I ask you, is it? Yahoodi! If you don't want to go through with this thing then just tell me. Just come right out and tell me. But don't kill yourself off in the middle of the plot.

(YAHOODI comes to and slowly sits up.)

YAHOODI: Well, it seemed like the right moment.

KOSMO: What do you mean? If you die, then everything comes to an end.

YAHOODI: No, it doesn't. There's other parts to the story.

KOSMO: Like what? The love life of Marlene Dietrich and Paul Bunyan? What's so interesting about that?

YAHOODI: It's a beautiful relationship. I thought it was going good.

KOSMO: Until you decided to commit suicide it was great.

YAHOODI: It was driving me crazy. I was driven to it. I can't help it. It was an intuitive decision. I needed to get off. I can't see doing something unless you're going to get off.

KOSMO: I know, but there's other ways besides suicide.

YAHOODI: I'm a dark person. I do it my way, you do it yours. What's the big deal?

KOSMO: Then, there's no way to continue.

YAHOODI: I wouldn't say that. You could do it yourself.

KOSMO: Where would you go?

YAHOODI: I'll take a trip. I need to get away anyway. This city's driving me crazy.

KOSMO: And just leave me with all the loose ends.

YAHOODI: All right, then you take a trip and I'll stay.

KOSMO: But I've got no place to go.

YAHOODI: Go to Mexico. Go to San Francisco. There's plenty of places.

KOSMO: Oh no. I get it. You just want to get me out there alone somewhere. Out on the open highway so you can run me down in your Mustang and take all the treasure. Well, I'm not falling for it.

YAHOODI: You're crazy. I don't give a shit about your treasure. There is no treasure. What is all this pot of gold shit at the end of the rainbow? You're ripped in the head, boy.

KOSMO: You wanna' come sneaking up on me in the Badlands somewhere and knife me in the back.

YAHOODI: I'm splitting. I can't even talk to you anymore.

KOSMO: Okay, go! Go then! Take the treasure with you!

YAHOODI: I don't want the fucking treasure!

KOSMO: But you invented it! It was your idea!

YAHOODI: It was not! It doesn't exist!

KOSMO: You called me on the phone! You asked me for money!

YAHOODI: That was a long time ago!

KOSMO: I don't care! When are you going to pay me back?

YAHOODI: You can have all the treasure!

KOSMO: I don't want the treasure! Mae West took it, anyway!

YAHOODI: That's your problem! I'm leaving!

KOSMO: No, wait a minute. It's gone too far. We're both infected with the same disease. If you leave now, it's all over. I can't keep chasing around with an open wound.

YAHOODI: Well, what'll we do then?

KOSMO: I don't know.

YAHOODI: Look. Look at me!

KOSMO: I am.

YAHOODI: Can you recognize my demon?

KOSMO: Sometimes.

YAHOODI: Do you believe I can recognize yours?

KOSMO: Sometimes.

YAHOODI: Do you believe it's the same demon?

KOSMO: No.

YAHOODI: Then there's nothing to do but—split up. Right?

KOSMO: How did we come together in the first place?

YAHOODI: We have something in common.

KOSMO: We support each other's inability to function. That's no friend-ship.

YAHOODI: You can't see my demon and you think you're alone. That's the truth, isn't it! You think you're all alone.

KOSMO: Fuck your demon! What about your angel?

YAHOODI: I don't get along with angels.

KOSMO: What about *my* angel then? If you see my demon you must be able to see my angel.

YAHOODI: I don't look for angels. I don't like angels! I'm struggling with something in me that wants to die!

KOSMO: And I'm struggling with something that wants to live.

YAHOODI: I guess that sums it up.

KOSMO: I guess so.

(A long pause.)

YAHOODI: Goodbye, Kosmo. I'll see you sometime.

KOSMO: Goodbye.

(YAHOODI splits. KOSMO looks around the stage, then calls out to WACO across a vast expanse.)

Waco! Waco!

(Cut to WACO *and* GHOST GIRL.*)*

WACO: Shhh! You hear something?

GHOST GIRL: Nothin'. What're you talkin' about?

WACO: Sounded like my old friend.

GHOST GIRL: You're nuts. This is a desert island. Nobody but you and me.

WACO: What about the natives?

GHOST GIRL: Killed off by treasure hunters.

KOSMO: *(Calling)* Waco! Waco!

WACO: There! You hear it? It's him, I tell ya'.

GHOST GIRL: Listen, mister, don't try and scare me. I don't scare easy. I been through a lot of tough scrapes and it takes a lot to get me freaked.

WACO: I've gotta' go and find him. Maybe he's in trouble.

GHOST GIRL: What am I supposed to do?

WACO: I don't know. It's every man for himself.

*(*WACO *splits and starts searching for* KOSMO. KOSMO *is searching for* WACO, *but they never meet. Meanwhile* YAHOODI'S *at another part of the stage calling out to* MARLENE.*)*

YAHOODI: Marlene! Marlene! It's me! Yahoodi! It's me! I want you back, Marlene! I'm sorry for running out on you and everything! Marlene! Can you hear me?

(Cut to MARLENE *and* PAUL BUNYAN.*)*

PAUL BUNYAN: What's the matter? You've been acting awful edgy lately, Marlene.

MARLENE: I keep hearing a voice. Something far away. Like an old friend. Listen, can you hear it?

YAHOODI: Marlene! Marlene!

PAUL BUNYAN: It ain't nothing but the wind. Come on, let's neck some more.

MARLENE: Can't you hear it? So lonely. So distant.

PAUL BUNYAN: Who cares? We're together. What difference does it make?

MARLENE: But it's like my own voice. My own voice calling me back. Back to where I belong.

PAUL BUNYAN: Don't be silly. You belong right here with me.

MARLENE: No. It never would have worked. We're from different worlds. I belong somewhere else.

PAUL BUNYAN: Well, so do I, but that don't mean we can't love each other. I thought we were having a good time together.

MARLENE: We were, but it's useless to go on.

PAUL BUNYAN: What're you talkin' about? First it's my Babe and now you. You can't leave me, Marlene. You're the only thing I've got.

(MARLENE *wanders off in search of* YAHOODI, YAHOODI *in search of* MARLENE, *but they never meet.* PAUL *tries to follow her but he gets lost.*)

PAUL BUNYAN: Marlene! Come back! You can't leave me now! Marlene!

MARLENE: Yahoodi! Is that you? Can you hear me?

PAUL BUNYAN: Marlene!

KOSMO: Waco! It's me! Kosmo! Are you out there?

GHOST GIRL: Waco! Waco!

WACO: I hear ya', boy! Just keep yellin'! I'll find ya'!

KOSMO: Waco!

YAHOODI: Marlene!

(Cut to MAE WEST *and* JESSE JAMES. *They enter another part of the stage with the treasure. The* OTHERS *keep searching for each other but never meet, even though at times they may pass right by each other. They keep calling out each other's names.* MAE WEST *stops and sits down, exhausted.*)

JESSE: Now listen, you promised when we started out that you wouldn't hold me up.

MAE: I know, I know. I just gotta' take a little breather. What happened to your horses, anyway?

JESSE: They drowned in the damn river. Piranhas got 'em. It was awful. You ever seen a piranha devour a horse before?

MAE: Can't say as I've had the pleasure.

JESSE: It was awful.

MAE: What's that sound?

JESSE: What? I don't hear nothin'.

MAE: Sounds like voices.

JESSE: You're crazy.

MAE: Listen, mister, a woman don't have to be insulted just 'cause she's of the opposite sex. I hear voices, I tell ya'.

JESSE: It might be the Federales. Maybe they've picked up our trail.

MAE: It ain't likely. Sounds like all the people I used to know. Back in the States.

JESSE: Come on. We're wastin' time. We gotta' get this stuff back across the border.

MAE: Such a mournful sound.

JESSE: Are you comin' or not?

MAE: Just hold your horses.

JESSE: Let's go.

(They move out. They travel right through all the other characters, who keep on calling and searching.)

KOSMO: Yahoodi! It's gotten worse! It's like a nightmare! I can't keep it up much longer!

YAHOODI: *(Calling out to KOSMO)* Just let go! Let everything go! It'll take care of itself! I'll meet you in L.A.!

KOSMO: But what about the smog and the cops and the earthquakes and the tidal waves and all that stuff! It's too dangerous! There must be a safer place!

YAHOODI: You worry too much! Everything'll work out for the best!

KOSMO: I can't hear the music anymore! I'm going deaf!

YAHOODI: It'll come back! Everything takes time!

KOSMO: No! Yahoodi!

GHOST GIRL: Waco! I'm sorry for what I said! Waco! You're not too old for me! You're just right! You've got heart! Fuck Elvis! I want you! Waco! You're real! You're a real man! I love you, Waco!

PAUL: Marlene! Forget about Babe! She never meant that much to me anyway. All I want is you! Marlene! Answer me! I've got a cozy little cabin all tucked away in the woods. We could hide out there. We could have coffee and toast in the morning. I'd chop wood all day long. We could make it, Marlene! Marlene!

WACO: Hold on, son! Just a little bit longer! Kosmo boy! Take it easy now! You saved me from drownin'! I'll never forget that! I'll save you, boy! Just keep yellin'! I'll find ya', boy! Just keep callin' out! Don't ever give up!

KOSMO: Yahoodi! It's out of control! The whole thing's crashing in on me! Yahoodi!

MARLENE: Yahoodi! Is that you, darling! I can't see! The trees are so dark. So close together! The moss keeps the sun out! We have to get away from here! We have to go someplace warm. Someplace where the sun always shines and the people dance. Someplace where there's music in the air. We could be so happy! Yahoodi! I know we could be happy!

(They all keep up their search, calling out to each other across a vast expanse. The lights go to another part of the stage where CAPTAIN KIDD *is pulling himself across the floor in agony, clutching his wounds.)*

CAPT. KIDD: If only I was on the Ivory Coast. I know that area. This is strange to me. I feel like a dead man. Dead for a million years. Dying forever. I can't call out or he'll hear me and come back and finish off the job. I've got to keep low to the ground. Be part of the jungle. A low animal. Part of the swamps. The swamps will take me. The snakes will take me. They'll crawl through my bones. Only I will know how I died. Only me. There'll be lies. There'll be legends. But only I will know. Why can't I stop? I keep crawling. What am I crawling for? I could stop. Right here. It could end right here. The motion keeps me alive. Life keeps me moving. The blood keeps on pumping. The brain keeps on working. And where does the mind go? All the visions in space. All the things dreamed and seen in the air. Where do they go? Something flies away. I can see it flying. Taking off like a flamingo. Soaring higher and higher. A beautiful pink bird flying alone. Out over the everglades. Out over the swamps. Higher and higher, straight into the sun. If only I could sing.

(Cut to MAE *and* JESSE. *The* OTHERS *keep calling and searching.)*

JESSE: Faster, woman! Faster! I can almost see the border.
MAE: You can? The good old US of A? We're really going to make it.
JESSE: If you get your ass in gear.
MAE: I'm trying, I'm trying. I keep hearing the voices. They keep calling me back.
JESSE: Forget about the voices. The Federales are closin' in.

(Sound of horses' hooves approaching.)

MAE: What about the Customs? What if they check in the bags?

JESSE: Never thought about that. Maybe we should just take what we can carry in our pockets and leave the rest hid. Then we can come back and pick it up some other time.

MAE: Are you crazy? After lugging these things for miles.

JESSE: Well, they're bound to catch us if we try to take the bags across.

MAE: If we only had us a horse. Just a good horse.

(BABE THE BLUE OX *enters and wanders over to* MAE *and* JESSE.)

JESSE: Wait a minute. What the hell.

MAE: Looks like an ox to me.

JESSE: Maybe we could just ride this critter right across the border. Crash right through the damn Customs. What do ya' think?

MAE: Looks pretty slow to me. Think we could get up enough steam to do it?

JESSE: We could sure as hell try. If we backed him up for maybe a quarter mile and whipped him real good, he just might make it.

MAE: Let's give it a whirl.

(*They climb up on* BABE's *back with the bags of treasure.*)

JESSE: Steady now. Steady.

MAE: Gimme a hand.

JESSE: Come on, come on. The Federales should be here any minute.

MAE: All right, I'm on.

JESSE: Good. Now kick the shit out of him and let's see what he can do.

(*They start kicking* BABE *in the ribs. He takes off at a gallop.* MAE *and* JESSE *let out the rebel yell. They crash though Customs and get safely to the other side. They dismount, and kiss and hug each other.*)

We made it! We done it, girl!

MAE: Yeah! We made it! We made it!

JESSE: Did you see the look on that Custom guy's face? He never saw nothin' like that before.

MAE: That was a custom he wasn't accustomed to.

(*They have a good laugh.*)

Look, I think it's about time we divvied up the loot. What do ya' say?

JESSE: Fine by me. I thought we'd just split it fifty-fifty like you said. You take one bag and I'll take the other.

MAE: Yeah, but there might be more in one than there is in the other.

JESSE: Well, let's take a look.

MAE: Okay by me.

(They dump the contents of the bags out on the floor. Tons of bottle caps come crashing out. MAE and JESSE stare at the bottle caps for a minute, then at each other.)

JESSE: Bottle caps. Millions of bottle caps.

MAE: Well, like they say. Don't carry all your eggs in one basket. What're ya' gonna' do now, Jesse?

JESSE: Guess I'll head back to Missouri and see my family. Ain't been back there for quite a spell.

MAE: Ain't that kinda' dangerous. I mean, ain't they lookin' for ya'?

JESSE: Sure, they're lookin' for me. Everybody's lookin' for me.

MAE: Wish someone was lookin' for me.

JESSE: Well, look, seein' as how you got no place to go, why don't you come on back with me? We'd treat ya' just like family.

MAE: Gee, that'd be swell, Jesse, but I ain't much of a family gal. Never was.

JESSE: No time to start like the present.

MAE: What about all the others? Maybe we could round them up, too. Maybe we could all go back home together.

JESSE: Sure, why not?

MAE: Wouldn't that be something though? All of us comin' into town. All of us together. All of us singin' and dancin' and carryin' on. What a party we could have. What an extravaganza! Just like the old days. Just like the new days! Just like any old day! Let's do it, Jesse! Let's go on home! Back where we belong!

(JESSE and MAE start singing "Home." One by one the OTHERS join in until they're all singing.)

HOME

Hitchin' on the Rio Bravo
Pick me up, won'tcha driver
'Cause ya know that I'm a true believer

In
Home
Home

I'll chance every hand that you deal
Ride behind your drivin' wheel
'Cause home is any place you feel
Like
Home
Home

Home is in the stranger's bones
Home is like a rolling stone
Home is holding something you own
Your own
Home

Crack up in the old ice age
Zoomin' in the super space age
Home got no rules, it's in the heart of a fool
Home is in the coach of a stage

Runnin' the length of a river
Slide me in your sailboat, sailor
My spinnin' brain is a failure
With no
Home
Home

Ride me in a silver airplane
Ride me in a passenger train
Move me against the grain
Move me
Home
Home

(They join hands and dance and march together around the stage, through the audience, and out into the street.)

CURTAIN

Back Bog Beast Bait

Back Bog Beast Bait was first produced at the American Place
Theatre on April 29, 1971 with the following cast:

SLIM:	Beeson Carroll
SHADOW:	James Hall
MARIA:	Antonia Rey
PREACHER:	Bob Glaudini
GRIS GRIS:	O-Lan Johnson-Shepard
GHOST GIRL:	Yolandé Pavan
BEAST:	Leroy

The production was directed by Tony Barsha.

SCENE ONE

The play opens with the song "Back Bog Blues" sung by GHOST GIRL:

BACK BOG BLUES

I got those boxed in back bog blues,
I know you heard them, they ain't nothin' new.
But if it's a crime to cry in your brew,
Somebody tell me what else I should do.

Crocodillies don't bother me,
I can't blame them for my misery,
It's just the climate of this swamp country,
I can't wait to get back home to Tennessee.

I need more than three squares and a bed,
I gots to take care of the state of my head,
If it weren't for snortin' an occasional red,
But I ain't sayin' that I wished I was dead.

I can't hitchhike on no bayou bog,
The best friend I got's a tiny green frog,
If I had me a Ford or a Cadillac,
I'd be out of here and I would never come back.

I still remember those Nashville nights,
The drive-in movies and the honky tonk lights,
But there's one thing that worries me,
If I go back, who's gonna recognize me?
(Repeat first verse)

Words and Music by SAM SHEPARD

A shack in bayou swamp country. A wall of bare boards upstage. A boarded-up door center with a large window on either side of the door. On the walls are pictures of Jesus and assorted saints and a crucifix. A table center stage with a Mexican-type silk tablecloth with fringe. An oil lamp in the middle, hanging from the ceiling. Two chairs either side of the table and two mattresses, one against each wall, covered with Indian blankets. The stage is dark. Soft swamp noises; frogs, birds, bugs—then the shriek of a wildcat. A baby cries. The lights fade up softly. A pause as the baby continues to cry. A loud knocking at the door. Pause. The baby stops crying. Another series of knocks. MARIA, *a dark-skinned woman with long straight black hair, a white cotton blouse, a long purple dress with red roses and a blue shawl with long fringe, comes on. She is very pregnant, has bare feet and carries a rifle. She squats down so she can't be seen through the windows from outside. More knocking.* MARIA *moves fast underneath the windows to the door and stands up, flattening her back against the door. A face appears in the stage-left window, peering in. Then one appears in the stage-right window. Both faces disappear. More knocking.*

MARIA: Who is there!

SLIM'S VOICE: It's the men you hired, ma'am!

MARIA: What men!

SLIM'S VOICE: The men from the high country!

MARIA: What is my name?

SLIM'S VOICE: Miss Maria, ma'am!

MARIA: How much I pay you to come!

SLIM'S VOICE: You ain't paid us nothin' so far, ma'am!

> (MARIA *unbolts the door and lets the two hired gunmen in:* SLIM *and* SHADOW. SLIM *is tall, he wears cowboy boots with spurs, jeans, a black satin shirt, a black leather jacket, a black cowboy hat with an Indian band, black leather gloves, and two pearl-handled handguns tied down to his hips.* SHADOW *is younger, shorter, and darker skinned. He wears moccasins, brown leather pants, a flannel lumberjack shirt, a beaded vest, and a Sioux headband. He has one handgun. They each carry rifles and packs over their shoulders.* SLIM'S *rifle is a Winchester and* SHADOW'S *is a sawed-off shotgun.*)

> (MARIA *quickly bolts the door behind them, then points her rifle at their heads. They raise their arms politely*)

SLIM: Now, ma'am, there's no need to be so uppity. Don't you recognize us?

MARIA: Come by light.

(She motions them over to the table and looks closely at their faces. She lowers the rifle.)

SLIM: Now that's better. Nothin' to make a man feel less sure of himself than a woman pointin' a rifle at his head. Eh, Shadow?

(He jabs SHADOW *with his elbow.)*

SHADOW: That's right, ma'am. Nothin'!
MARIA: You like coffee?
SLIM: Now that would sure hit the spot, ma'am.
SHADOW: Yeah, boy. And some fatback and biscuits if ya' got some.

*(*MARIA *nods and exits.)*

*(*SLIM *and* SHADOW *look around the shack, then set their gear down on the floor and sit in the chairs,* SLIM *stage left and* SHADOW *stage right.* SHADOW *pulls out some chewing tobacco from his vest and offers it to* SLIM.*)*

Care fer a little Red Man, Slim?
SLIM: No thanks.

*(*SHADOW *bites off a hunk and chews as* SLIM *cases the joint with his eyes.)*

Might as well've set ourselves up in a cracker box as try to defend this shack.
SHADOW: How ya' mean? Seems simple enough. One of us each on a window and the woman coverin' the rear. Ain't no one gonna' try comin' 'cross that back bog anyhow. And the front's clear.
SLIM: Like I tried explainin' to ya' before, Shadow, it ain't no "one," no person, it's a "thing," a beast.
SHADOW: Said yerself it was once a person, a man.

(He spits a big gob of tobacco on the floor.)

SLIM: It was. Maybe. Least that's what the woman said.
SHADOW: Well, ain't there no way to tell?

SLIM: We'll know soon enough.

SHADOW: If it was a person once then chances are it'll still act like one.

SLIM: We can't be countin' on that. We gotta' get ourselves ready fer anything.

(MARIA *enters with a tray of coffee and biscuits.* SLIM *leaps to his feet and draws both pistols lightning fast.*)

Oh. 'Scuse me, ma'am. Just keepin' on my toes. Gotta' make sure we earn our wages.

(MARIA *puts the tray down on the table.* SLIM *sits back down.*)

SHADOW: Speakin' a' wages, what is it you plan to pay us anyhow? Just outa' curiosity. My partner and I sorta' took the job outa' good faith, if ya' know what I mean.

MARIA: I cannot pay you nothing.

SHADOW: Now wait just a darn minute!

SLIM: Hold on, Shadow.

MARIA: But my man leaves me something.

(*She reaches in her blouse and pulls out a small gold wasp.*)

SLIM: Yer man? Well, where is he? How come he ain't here helpin' ya'?

MARIA: He is killed by the Tarpin.

SLIM: Oh. Well, I'm sorry to hear that.

SHADOW: What's the Tarpin?

(*He spits again.*)

MARIA: The pig beast. The beast kill my daughter. She about to be a woman and the Tarpin kill her. My man go after pig beast and not come back. He leave me this. You take.

(SHADOW *takes the wasp from* MARIA *and holds it in his hand.*)

SHADOW: What's this here? Looks like a hornet or somethin'.

(*He bites it.*)

Hm. Real gold, maybe. Can't be worth much though. This ain't even gonna' pay fer horse fodder, Slim.

(He spits on the floor.)

SLIM: Shut up. Look, Maria, did you ever see the Tarpin?
MARIA: Yes. I see.
SLIM: Could ya' tell us what it looks like?
MARIA: It is as big as man. Two heads.
SHADOW: Two heads?

(He spits again.)

SLIM: Shut up, Shadow. And quit spittin' on the woman's floor.
MARIA: Tusks like the wild boar.
SLIM: Does it make any sound?
MARIA: Snorts like a pig.
SLIM: That's all?
MARIA: Yes.
SHADOW: Two heads. Sure.
MARIA: It sometimes breathe fire. It have lights.
SLIM: Lights? What kinda' lights?
MARIA: Blue. Red. And gold.
SLIM: Where do the lights come from?
MARIA: The eyes. The head.
SLIM: What's the body look like?
MARIA: Thick brown skin. Like the pig. It is coming to kill my son.
SLIM: How do you know that?
MARIA: It has castrated all the sons in the lowland. My son is the last. It will kill my son. Then kill me.
SLIM: Why you?
MARIA: I am with child. It wants all children to die. All humans. It wants to stop our race.
SLIM: How do you know that?
MARIA: It tell me.
SLIM: It spoke to you?
SHADOW: She ain't playing with a full deck.
SLIM: Maria, it spoke to you, the beast?
MARIA: Yes.

SLIM: How? Did it use words?

MARIA: It speak through my brain.

SLIM: In English?

MARIA: In Cajun.

SLIM: Are you Cajun?

MARIA: No.

SLIM: Then how do you know it was Cajun?

MARIA: You are from high country. You do not know the ways of the low-
     land. It speak in Cajun.

(MARIA *exits*.)

SHADOW: Well, what do ya' make a' that?

(*He spits again.*)

SLIM: She's telling the truth.

SHADOW: So you really think there's a beast out there?

SLIM: Listen, I never been in this part a' the country before but I can tell
     ya' one thing. It weren't no human being that burned off that land
     that we come across. Not even a stick a' shrub pine left. It's gotta' be
     some kinda' beast that'd do a thing like that. All them antelope with
     their bellies ripped out. What hunger you ever seen leaves a carcass
     layin' like that?

SHADOW: Ya' got me, Slim. How come she says it talks though?

SLIM: Can't figure that out myself. Unless it's some kinda' mental telepa-
     thy like the Arapaho have.

SHADOW: Maybe it is an Arapaho in some kinda' crazy costume. A rene-
     gade gone loco.

SLIM: Not this far south. Nope, it's somethin' bigger and spookier than
     you or me can reckon to. Somethin's goin' on down here, Shadow.
     Somethin' horrible's goin' on.

SHADOW: Well, it ain't bad coffee the woman makes. I say we stick it out a
     couple days and rest up. Get some good grits in our gullets and move
     on. We can't be hangin' around just waitin' fer the damn thing to turn
     up.

SLIM: Didn't you hear what she said, Shadow? That Tarpin beast means
     to annihilate the human race. That's you and me, boy. It starts with

the kids. Kills them off one at a time. All the kids. The boys. You know what that means? No boys—no men. No men—no babies. No babies—no people. Do you remember seein' one living soul the whole time since we crossed over from the high country? Not a one. This woman and her baby boy and her unborn in her belly are the last living things in this neck of the woods. And once it finishes with its dirty work here it's gonna' move on. Move north. To the high country.

SHADOW: Well, you know me, Slim. I only took to this hired gun racket recently. Doggin' bulls was my specialty. The only reason I took up with ya' was 'cause I thought I'd make myself a tad more money. I never expected ya' to go in fer no heroism.

SLIM: It ain't heroism! Golldangit, Shadow! Come down to earth, boy. It's pure and simple survival. It's either us or him.

SHADOW: "It."

SLIM: "Him," "it," what's the difference. We're gonna' have to do somethin' about it sooner or later. It might as well be now. Better than goin' back home to the ranch and waitin' for it to come terrorizin' the wife and kids.

SHADOW: What wife and kids! What ranch! Come down to earth yer own self.

SLIM: I told ya' about my dreams, Shadow. Now don't begrudge me that. A man can dream, can't he?

SHADOW: Sure, but not all the goddamn time. Ya' can't always be walkin' around like a woman in love.

SLIM: And ya' can't be walkin' around like a mad dog kicked out in the cold, neither. I've had my fill a' lonely campfires and beans from a can. I want somethin' more. I'm gettin' on in years, Shadow. You, you're still young and wiry. You could always go back to bulldoggin' if ya' hankered to. Not me. There was a time when the speed a' these two six-guns was all the security I needed. Now, I've lost a good tenth of a second or more. Sometimes even the right draws faster than the left. There was a time last month when I even got my thumb stuck on the hammer. Things like that make a man start to wonder. I have nightmares a' bein' gunned down on the street by some a' these hotshot young dudes that a' been sproutin' up.

SHADOW: Shh! What's that?

(They both snap into action and duck down behind their chairs. They listen. Silence.)

SLIM: What? I don't hear nothin'.

SHADOW: Shh!

(They listen again. A scraping sound comes from outside, then a moan. They signal to each other, then quickly crawl over to underneath the windows. They listen. Again the scraping and the moan. SHADOW whips out a knife and signals to SLIM. SLIM slowly, carefully reaches over to the bolt on the door. A pause. SHADOW nods, then suddenly SLIM unbolts the door and yanks it open.)

(An old PREACHER with a long gray beard and a clerical collar staggers in. He is dressed like an Amish priest and covered with blood, his clothes ripped and slashed. SHADOW grabs him from behind and holds the knife to his throat. SLIM slams the door shut and bolts it. The PREACHER is dazed.)

State yer business, old-timer.

SLIM: Hold it, Shadow. Can't ya' see he's injured? What's the matter with you?

(SHADOW loosens his grip and puts the knife away. SLIM helps the PREACHER over to the table and lays him down on it.)

Come on now. It's all right. No one's gonna' hurt ya'. Jest lay yerself down there. Come on. That's it.

(SLIM lays the PREACHER on his back across the table with his arms and legs hanging over the edge.)

Shadow, get Maria. See if she's got any whiskey and some boiling water.

(SHADOW exits. SLIM starts ripping the PREACHER's shirt off.)

Just take her easy there, mister. We'll see to what ails ya'. That's right. Breathe deep. There ya' go.

(The PREACHER speaks as he struggles to sit up while SLIM pushes him back down.)

PREACHER: Take courage, my children, cry to God and He will deliver you from the power and hand of the enemy!

SLIM: Jest settle down, mister. No one's gonna' hurt ya'. Take it easy.

PREACHER: My children, endure with patience the wrath that has come upon you from God. Your enemies have overtaken you, but you will soon see their destruction and will tread upon their necks!

SLIM: Shadow! Hurry it up!

PREACHER: They shall be wasted with hunger and devoured with burning heat and poisonous pestilence, and I will send the teeth of beasts against them, with venom of crawling things of the dust!

SLIM: Shadow!

PREACHER: Then the earth reeled and rocked; the foundations of the heavens trembled and quaked, because he was angry! Smoke went up from his nostrils, and devouring fire from his mouth; glowing coals flamed forth from him! He bowed the heavens and came down; thick darkness was under his feet! He rode on a cherub and flew; he was seen upon the wings of the wind! He made darkness around him his canopy, thick clouds, a gathering of water! Out of the brightness before him coals of fire flamed forth! The Lord thundered from heaven and the Most High uttered his voice! And he sent out arrows and scattered them; lightning, and routed them! Then the channels of the sea were seen, the foundations of the world were laid bare, at the rebuke of the Lord, at the blast of the breath of his nostrils!

(The PREACHER falls back into a comatose state as SHADOW enters with MARIA carrying a bottle of whiskey and some hot water in a bowl.)

SLIM: Well, it's about goddamn time. Never cottoned too much to sermons ever since I was a kid.

MARIA: Who this man?

SLIM: Search me, ma'am. He's wounded pretty bad though. Looks like that beast done it. He'd probably be beholdin' to ya' if ya' fixed him up some.

MARIA: I no tell you to let strangers in.

SHADOW: We thought he was that pig beast, ma'am.

MARIA: Pig? He no pig.

SHADOW: I know, but we thought . . .

SLIM: Never mind, Shadow. Look, ma'am, if ya' don't mind, we're a little tuckered from the ride—could we just make use of yer mattresses?

MARIA: Yes. Sleep. I wake you up.

(MARIA *rips off the* PREACHER's *shirt and dresses his wound.* SLIM *goes to the stage-right mattress and gets ready for bed.*)

SHADOW: Well, that's a fine how-do-you-do. Here I'm all riled up about pig beasts and the annihilation a' the human race and you wants to sleep.

SLIM: Suit yerself, boy. Here's an old man talkin'.

SHADOW: Ya' want a bennie or a red or somethin', Slim?

SLIM: Sorry. Don't go in fer dope much. Straight whiskey's my nemesis.

SHADOW: Well, here.

(He *grabs the bottle from* MARIA *and offers it to* SLIM.)

Let's have us a little celebration on the successful crossing of the fearsome lowlands without one single tangle with the much heard about but seldom seen pig beast.

MARIA: That medicine. No for drink.

(She *grabs the bottle back and goes on with tending to the* PREACHER.)

SLIM: Listen, boy, we was hired to do a job. That job depends on us bein' fit and able. Now I ain't one to get in the way of a man's pleasures, but when it starts goin' contrary to the best interests of . . .

SHADOW: All right! I don't need no lecture. Go ahead and flake out. I'm takin' a walk in the moonlight. There any pretty young Cajun babes out there in the woods yearnin' fer the likes a' me, Maria?

MARIA: No Cajun.

SHADOW: Yeah, OK. Just thought I'd check. Well, see ya'all later on.

(He *picks up his rifle and goes out the door.*)

SLIM: Don't get ate up now!

(MARIA *crosses quickly to the door and bolts it.* SLIM *has his boots and guns off. He takes off his pants, revealing long john underwear underneath. He crawls under the covers.* MARIA *goes back to the* PREACHER.)

How's the old goat doin'?

MARIA: Goat?

SLIM: The preacher man. Think he'll pull through?

(MARIA doesn't answer.)

You don't savvy even half a' what I'm sayin', do ya'?

(Pause.)

How would ye' like a little roll in the old sack, baby?

(MARIA keeps dressing the PREACHER's wounds.)

How 'bout suckin' on my ding dong or somethin'? Talkin' that-away makes me feel almost as young as that Shadow boy. Almost. Bet you knocked 'em dead when you was nineteen, didn't ya', Maria?

MARIA: Yes?

SLIM: Nothin'. I'll just bet you had 'em lined up though. Yessir. A regular Mardi Gras Cajun queen. Funny you'd wind up way out here like this. On the lam. Runnin' scared. Too bad about yer old man. Musta' been a nice fella. Hell of a way to go. Gettin' ate alive like that. That is the way he does it, ain't it? Must be. Horrible death. Me, I always think about dyin' by the gun. You know, like in the Bible. He who lives by the sword and all that malarkey. Still, it's true. There's some young whippersnapper out there just waitin'. Just practicin' and practicin' on old soup cans and waitin' to put another notch on his six-gun. 'Course he don't know it's gonna' be me. We ain't never met personally. I don't really have no enemies 'cause I killed 'em all. Most of 'em wasn't even my own enemies. They was somebody else's. Still they're all dead and that's a good feelin', knowin' there ain't no one doggin' ya' night and day just to plug ya' in the backside. Ain't got no outstandin' debts neither. Guess I owe Shadow a nickel or two from poker and beer but that's about it. Don't owe no man nothin'. Guess you don't neither, do ya', Maria?

MARIA: Yes?

(The baby starts to cry softly in the next room. MARIA exits. The PREACHER lies unconscious on the table as SLIM keeps talking.)

SLIM: Guess not. Still it gets lonely just draggin' around from one two-bit town to the next. Lookin' fer people with enemies. Enemies and money is all I need to stay in business. Most of my clients are just plain cowards. Cowards or women or rich gentlemen from Boston that never learned to even holster a six-gun, let alone shoot the damn thing. Bankers and financiers and loan sharks. Men who make the country run. Not like me. Me, I'm out to make a few bucks. Save up a roll fer the ranch. The wife and kids. Keep the belly warm. It's no good bein' homeless, ya' know. It eats at a man from the inside out. Ya' wonder where all the people went. At night. They go away from ya'. They got fires and warmth inside. Outside the would swallows a man up. He gets lost in it. There's no end to it. He starts cravin' fer some warmth like a hungry dog. Fer a lover, a friend.

(The lamp and the lights start dimming softly.)

Just some conversation. That's sorta' why I hitched up with that Shadow boy. Just so's I could ramble on to some human being instead a' that damn pinto or the sage brush. I ain't alone though. I know that much. I ain't to be pitied no more than the rest of 'em out there. No more than this old preacher man. Hey, preacher man? I bet you got stories to tell. And the rest of 'em out there. That Shadow boy out there in the night with his heart poundin' just from bein' born. Just from the moon and the stars. I can still remember how that felt. To still feel part of the earth. Lost in all that space but not givin' a god-damn 'cause it meant you was free. Free to be alive. I can feel myself growin'. Not older, just growin'. Growin' outwards.

(The lights fade to black. Soft blue light comes up on the side of the stage. The GHOST of MARIA's dead daughter appears dressed in a long blue gypsy dress. She sings.)

LOWLANDS

Chorus:

Lowlands, lowlands, heave away, Joe.

I had a dream the other night.
'Bout a dollar and a dime a day.
Dreamed that the earth was sunk into the sea.
'Bout a dollar and a dime a day.

(Chorus)

Blue was the only color we could see
At a dollar and a dime a day.
Nothing but ship and star and sea
At a dollar and a dime a day.

(Chorus)

Hope that was just a dream I had
At a dollar and a dime a day,
If you don't drown the sea will drive you mad,
At a dollar and a dime a day.

(Chorus)

TRADITIONAL
New Words by STEVE WEBER and ANTONIA

(Cross fade to stage.)

SCENE TWO

The lights come back up to morning light. The PREACHER *is still on the table,* SLIM *is still in bed.* SHADOW'S VOICE *from outside.*

SHADOW'S VOICE: Rise and shine! Rise and shine!

(More banging. The sound of a girl giggling along with SHADOW.*)*

Every man to his post! The place is surrounded with pig beasts! Every man to his station!

(SLIM *suddenly rolls out of his bed across the floor with both pistols in his hands, at the ready. More banging.*)

Shake a leg in there! Slim! The sun's been up for hours!

(SLIM *gets up, goes to the door and opens it.* SHADOW *enters with* GRIS GRIS, *a young girl with long black hair and a long purple dress. She wears big gold earrings, rings on every finger, necklaces around her neck.* SHADOW *and* GRIS GRIS *have their arms full of large yellow mushrooms.* SLIM *locks the door behind them.*)

Good morning, old scout. This here is Gris Gris.

SLIM: Mornin'.

SHADOW: We picked ya' some breakfast. All we need is some hot boilin' water in a kettle and we're in business.

GRIS GRIS: Ya' *fry* mushrooms, ya' don't boil 'em. Ya' fry frog legs. Ya' fry fish eys. Ya' fry water moccasins. Ya' fry everything down here. Ya' fry men sometimes.

SLIM: Looks like you got yerself a live one there.

SHADOW: What's the old preacher man still doin' here? He's blockin' up our breakfast table.

SLIM: Where'd ya' expect him to spend the night?

SHADOW: Well, it ain't nighttime no longer. It's time he moseyed on. Come on, Gris Gris, set these over here.

(*They go to the other mattress stage left and dump the mushrooms on it.*)

Come on, Slim. Help me move this old dude off the breakfast table.

SLIM: Leave him be, Shadow. He had a rough day.

(SHADOW *hoists the* PREACHER *up on his shoulder and lifts him off the table. The* PREACHER *starts to babble again.* SHADOW *can't decide where to put him.*)

SHADOW: Come on now, Lazarus.

PREACHER: The Lord has set the sun in the heavens, but has said that he would dwell in thick darkness. I have built thee an exalted house, a place for thee to dwell in forever.

SHADOW: Well, it ain't this house, brother. It's crowded enough as it is. Gris Gris, move them mushrooms outa' the way there.

(GRIS GRIS *moves all the mushrooms from the bed over to the table.* SHADOW *flops the* PREACHER *down on the mattress.*)

PREACHER: He boasted that he would burn up my territory and kill my young men with the sword and dash my infants to the ground and seize my children as prey, and take my virgins as booty!

SHADOW: Aw, pipe down, ya' old stomper.

GRIS GRIS: Who's he?

SHADOW: Some old Bible thumper the wind blew in.

(GRIS GRIS *takes out a long knife from her boot and starts cutting up the mushrooms on the table.* SHADOW *kisses her on the cheek. She giggles.* SLIM *is getting dressed.*)

PREACHER: Then my oppressed people shouted for joy; for weak people shouted and the enemy trembled; they lifted up their voices and the enemy were turned back! The sons of maidservants have pierced them through; they were wounded like the children of fugitives, they perished before the army of my Lord!

SHADOW: Sure does know his Bible, don't he?

SLIM: Yer gonna' be old one day yerself, smart ass.

SHADOW: But I ain't gonna' be unconscious one minute and runnin' off at the mouth the next.

PREACHER: Woe to the nations that rise up against my people. The Lord almighty will take vengeance on them in the day of judgment . . . fire and worms He will give to their flesh! They shall weep in pain forever!

GRIS GRIS: Your ass. Who is this zombie, anyway?

SHADOW: I don't know.

GRIS GRIS: Why don't you kick him out? He's takin' up my oxygen.

SLIM: Look, girl, you just arrived here and ya' might have some respect for an older man.

GRIS GRIS: I might. I might get down on my knees and eat worms too but I ain't gonna'.

SLIM: Where'd you find this one, boy?

SHADOW: Ain't she somethin'?

SLIM: Y'all plannin' on eatin' this poison?

SHADOW: Sure. Gris Gris here knows how to tell the good ones from the bad. Don'tcha', girl?

GRIS GRIS: Sometimes. Sometimes I make mistakes and get the scuzzy ones. The dark ones. The ones with bloodstains marked on the rim.

SHADOW: Shoulda' seen it, Slim. A whole mountain of these yellow buttons. Looked like a poppy field from a distance, but Gris Gris knew right off they was magic mushrooms. . . . Didn't ya', girl?

SLIM: What mountain? There ain't no mountain. I wouldn't touch them things with a ten-foot pole.

(MARIA *enters.*)

MARIA: Who this girl?

SHADOW: This here's Gris Gris, ma'am.

MARIA: You eat, then go.

SHADOW: Now that ain't very neighborly.

SLIM: She's a swamp girl, Shadow. She belongs in the swamp.

SHADOW: You belong in the zoo, old man.

SLIM: You can't talk to me like that and get away with it.

SHADOW: Ya' wanna' go fer yer gun, old man.

MARIA: No fight! This is peaceful home. No fight. I fix breakfast, then these two go.

SLIM: I don't think the preacher's ready yet, ma'am. He's still babblin' on about God and such.

MARIA: You wake him up for to eat.

SHADOW: We picked ya' some nice fresh mushrooms, ma'am. How 'bout puttin' 'em in a skillet for us?

MARIA: Where you get these?

SLIM: Says they found 'em on top of a mountain. Now you tell me Maria, is there a mountain anywhere near here?

MARIA: No mountain.

SLIM: There. What'd I tell ya'.

SHADOW: Well, I guess it's our word against yours. And here's the evidence sittin' right here on the table.

SLIM: That don't mean nothin'. Ya' coulda' picked mushrooms anywheres. Maybe they belong to that pig beast. Maria, you ever seen mushrooms like these here?

MARIA: Not so big. So yellow. They bad poison. Black magic.

GRIS GRIS: Black as the inside of a dog's mouth. Black enough to burn holes through your skull. Black, black, black!

SLIM: I say they're beast bait, somethin' that beast put out there to trick us into eatin'.

MARIA: Then we all die.

GRIS GRIS: And our ghosts are taken by the voodoo man. And our souls are stripped down and licked clean by the sons of Osimandias.

(She plays her fiddle.)

SHADOW: Well, Gris Gris and I'll eat 'em then and you two can have ham and eggs. That way if we die there'll still be two of ya' left to fight off the beast.

SLIM: No dice, Shadow. We're gonna' need every gun we can muster up when that beast decides to come through the door.

SHADOW: Goddammit, we picked 'em and we're gonna' eat 'em!

SLIM: Shadow, fer once in yer young life listen to reason. Now I been around some and I learned how to smell out a trap or two in my time. This mushroom business smells mighty peculiar. Now first off ya' tell me ya' find these here toadstools on top of a mountain and there just ain't no mountains around here. Second of all—

SHADOW: Me and Gris Gris here is eatin' these mushrooms fer breakfast, Slim. And if you aim to stop us yer gonna' have to kill us.

MARIA: No fight here. Fight outside.

SHADOW: Anywhere ya' want it.

(A pause as SLIM and SHADOW face each other off. SLIM breaks the tension by going to the PREACHER.)

SLIM: Guess I'll try wakin' up the old geezer. Lord knows he could use somethin' in that belly after all he's been through.

SHADOW: Gris Gris, why don't you and Maria go in the kitchen and fetch us a skillet so we can get to fryin' these things. Go on.

GRIS GRIS: Come on, Mama Reux. Let's see what you got in your kitchen. Let's cook up a potion for these dudes.

(SHADOW picks up a piece of the mushroom and smells it. He pops it into his mouth and chews. He sits on the table and keeps popping pieces of mushroom into his mouth and watching SLIM, whose back is to him as he tries to wake up the PREACHER.)

SLIM: Come on, old-timer. Time to face a new day.

SHADOW: Never figured you to be one to back down, Slim. Least not from a bulldogger like me.

SLIM: (To the PREACHER) Come on, now. Get some hot breakfast in yer belly and you'll be a new man.

SHADOW: Me, I couldn't go on livin' with a fear like that. No sir. That kind of uncertainty about yerself. I'd rather die a fool than back down in front a' women folk like that.

SLIM: Jest open yer eyes and take a big yawn. Come on. Can't sleep the whole day away.

SHADOW: 'Course now, it just may be that you was takin' pity on me. Just may be that. Knew you was faster all along. Takes a lot a' courage to turn the other cheek. Don't it?

(SLIM *wheels around and knocks* SHADOW *off the table onto the floor. He gets on top of him and straddles his chest, pinning his arms to the ground.*)

SLIM: Now listen, you saddle tramp no 'count. The only reason I took you on was 'cause I was tired a' makin' it alone. If I needed a fast gun I could a' had my pick a' the best. Plus, I felt sorry for ya'. Sittin' around whittlin' on fence posts; carvin' yer initials in bar stools. Let me tell you somethin', boy. Now you listen good. Don't you ever push me again. You hear? Not never. 'Cause I'll blast you wide open like a bale a' sawdust.

(The PREACHER *suddenly sits up on the mattress and looks around as though waking up from a long sleep.* SLIM *and* SHADOW *relax and watch him. The* PREACHER *stands up and walks across the room. He stops and looks around. He sees the mushrooms on the table and walks over to them. He picks one up and eats it.* SLIM *stands.*)

Wait a minute. Don't eat them things. Them's beast bait.

(The PREACHER *smiles. He speaks as though talking to no one in particular.*)

PREACHER: And the Lord said to Moses and Aaron, "Say to the people of Israel, These are the living things which you may eat among all the beasts that are on the earth. Whatever parts the hoof and is cloven-footed and chews the cud, among the animals, you may eat. And the swine, because it parts the hoof and is cloven-footed but does not chew the cud, is unclean to you. Of their flesh you shall not eat, and their carcasses you shall not touch; they are unclean to you."

(The PREACHER crosses back to the mattress and lies down and goes back into a trance state.)

SLIM: Now if that don't beat all.

(SHADOW gets up off the floor.)

SHADOW: I say we turn him back out. He ain't right in the head, Slim.
SLIM: You wouldn't be neither if that beast had grabbed you out there.
SHADOW: There ain't no beast! Maria's made it all up. I'm tellin' ya', me and Gris Gris tramped all around out there last night and the worst thing we seen was a hoot owl with a water snake wrapped around its beak.

(GRIS GRIS enters playing her fiddle. As she enters the room, SHADOW doubles over in pain, clutching his stomach and moaning.)

SLIM: Shadow, boy!
GRIS GRIS: My fiddle plays a death song. I sing it through my ears. Frogs move in me. Crawdaddies play with my soul. Something moves my fingers over strings. Something strikes the bow like a torch.
SLIM: It's them damn toadstools! . . . Come on!

(GRIS GRIS makes no move to help but keeps playing her fiddle like a death chant. SLIM pulls SHADOW over to the stage-right mattress and flops him down.)

GRIS GRIS: You zombies rip me up. Your death walk. Death stance. Staring into what you can't see. Take me, not the night. Turn your back on the beast. But you can't. He's close now. His breath breathes your breath. You are him. He's in you.
SLIM: You put a spell on him! You're nothin' but a demon witch!
GRIS GRIS: Spells are meant to be broken. But you're locked in. You got no keys. You got no gris gris. You got no magic to use. Well, let me

give you some. I'll pass it around. There's stuff to spare in the air. Take it. Take some mojo root jam. Some John the Conqueroot jam. Some toad skin. Some fish tooth. Some cocoa leaf juice. Some swamp gas. Moss blood. Anything is useful. Use your dirty socks if you can find your feet.

SLIM: Maria!

GRIS GRIS: And don't think he ain't comin' 'cause I called him up. I talked to his teeth and he answers like the owl. He's hootin' out for this shack. This little pile of sticks. We're all gonna' burn at his stake. So get ready to see through fire. Get set to smell flesh. Signify on your knees if you got the balls. 'Cause snakes is gonna' slither on your zombie corpse!

(During this, SHADOW has been going through convulsions, with SLIM trying to hold him down. When GRIS GRIS finishes, SHADOW collapses. SLIM covers him with the blanket, then turns to GRIS GRIS.)

SLIM: You poisoned him.

GRIS GRIS: Poison's in the air, Jack. Some people take it, some leave it.

SLIM: You poisoned him with them toadstools. You knew they was poison. Shadow was my right-hand man. So now you gotta' look to your left. A left-handed gunman. Now that's something to strut your stuff about. None a' this candy cock sidekick shit. Use your left, baby. Look to your left. Watch out!

(SLIM wheels and draws to his left side as though about to fire at an unseen gunman.)

GRIS GRIS: There he is! Lurkin' in the Spanish moss. A dark black mustache man crouched in the leaves, crawling through the ferns with a knife gleaming 'tween his jagged teeth. He's out for you like a swamp dog smellin' coon blood. Your time is comin', cowboy.

SLIM: No! I done him in in Nogales. No! It was Santa Fe. No! Elko, Nevada. That was it. I finished him. I remember his face. His teeth were gushin' blood. He ain't comin'.

GRIS GRIS: There's another one! Watch it now!

(SLIM wheels again drawing his gun.)

He slinks, this one. He preys on wounded knees. He knows your hat size. He's followed your saloon trail. He knows your boot prints backwards.

SLIM: Not him! I got him good. Two chambers and he still kept comin'. But he died at my feet. At my feet! He kissed my boot! He kissed it and thanked me for it! I remember you! All month, trackin' through powder snow. Found him in a pine ridge. Not that one! He's gone! Gone, I tell ya'!

GRIS GRIS: There's more out there. More shadows.

SLIM: Nothin', I tell ya'! They all been done! No one's comin' but some beast we don't even know about! I'll tell ya' another thing. I dealt with witches before. You ain't the first. You ain't got no power over this fox, honey. I'm goin' out there. I'm goin' out there to find this here mysterious mountain you conjured up. And if I find it I'm gonna' tear it down. With my bare hands. I'm gonna' make a rumble that they won't stop hearin' till the lowlands falls into the sea! Then I'm comin' back for you and you best be ready. 'Cause no one puts a spell on this dude. No one! You hear?

GRIS GRIS: Good luck.

(SLIM *exits.* GRIS GRIS *crosses between the* PREACHER *and* SHADOW. *She looks them over and says a prayer.*)

She danced with a fish held high over her head. She breathed to the moon. The village killed her. Cut off her head and dropped it down a well. That spring all the people died from drinking the water.

(MARIA *enters.*)

MARIA: What happened to this man?

GRIS GRIS: He's drunk on air. Maybe you could pull some white charms out of your basket. Do him good.

MARIA: How he get sick?

GRIS GRIS: You must know some magic, Mama. Let's put the powers into play. Let's dance a dance. A spirit dance over this poor bull-doggin' fool. You take the right. I'll take the left. You take the white, I'll take the black. It's a little contest. You wanna' play?

MARIA: He very sick?

GRIS GRIS: Very sick. He needs a sycamore syringe up his ass.

MARIA: I help.

GRIS GRIS: Good. Then let the voodoo come!

(MARIA bends down over SHADOW and begins a ritual to exorcise his demons. GRIS GRIS goes to stage left and plays high wailing screeches on the fiddle and tries to possess SHADOW with the demons. MARIA hums softly.)

In the heat of a mongoose the lowlands prayed for rain. Rain in the tropics. The Cajuns clacked their teeth. The swamps dried up into cracked mud. Dead snapping turtles lay on their backs baking in the sun. Fish floated on the sand. The rocks turned green. The mystery was real and all the people felt the presence of the beast. Some say they saw him coming in their dreams. Dream language came out of their mouths. Symbols were seen in the shapes of clouds. Dust hung over their homes. A desert was growing. Coyotes took the place of the Blue Tipped Coon Hound. Howls broke branches in the night.

(During this, SHADOW begins to have tremors conflicting between the magic of MARIA and GRIS GRIS.)

Women covered their heads with black sacks with eyes cut like the slit eyes of a wolf. Men covered their mouths. Horses fell in the fields and went stiff with their hooves pointed toward the sun. The sky went black, then changed to white like a photograph of death. The crocodile dives to deeper water, touches bottom, crawls along the muddy bottom, hides his ears from the sound of the land. The stink moves from east to west, then changes wind and moves back again. Their noses are on fire. The eyes water and cause moss to grow on their cheeks. Everywhere the people move in bands of a dozen or less. Breaking up, coming together. Screaming crazy, throwing themselves on their own campfires. Eating the flames. The beast has come.

(The two heads of the pig beast appear in the stage left window. No sound. GRIS GRIS and MARIA have their backs to the window and don't notice. Just the audience sees it. It peers in, then disappears, then reappears in the stage-right window and disappears again. GRIS GRIS continues.)

He moves in their thoughts. Tracks them running. Tracks them walking. Tracks them sleeping. Blocks their escape. Tortures their minds with no hope. Drags them down in the bayou mud. Boils their eyes. Crosses their vision. Doubles their senses. Eats them raw and spits them back.

(SHADOW *begins to writhe and scream.* MARIA *keeps up her ritual.* GRIS GRIS *is relentless, wailing on her fiddle and screaming into the air.*)

Blood rains from the sky. The earth opens up and swallows them whole. The sky rips and tears like a paper bag. Carcasses turn into tumbleweeds. The wind blows them back to the sea. The sea bellows the voice of the beast. It rips up the trees and throws them down little broken ships. The sea evens out into a flat green glassy shine and smiles at its dirty work. The beast cackles like the jackal and broken things bob on the surface. The moon sinks behind the sun and the sun shines black. The beast has come. The beast has come. The beast has come.

(SHADOW *goes limp and lifeless.* MARIA *rises slowly. She takes a moment and looks at* GRIS GRIS, *then exits.* GRIS GRIS *stares out over the audience, then slowly opens her mouth and makes a silent scream.* MARIA, *at the very moment* GRIS GRIS *opens her mouth, screams from offstage.* MARIA *enters, hands dripping with blood.*)

MARIA: My son! My boy is dead!

BLACKOUT

(*during BLACKOUT* GHOST GIRL *is heard singing "Wrap Your Troubles in Dreams.")*

SCENE THREE

WRAP YOUR TROUBLES IN DREAMS

Wrap your troubles in dreams
Send them all away

Put them in a bottle and
Across the sea they'll stay

Speak not of misfortune
Speak not of your woes
Just steal yourself a holy death
Crouching by the door

Writhe and sway to music's pain
Searing with asides
Caress death with a lover's touch
And it shall be your bride

Purple is to yellow as
Sunlight is to rain
Happiness in death you'll find
Loveliness in pain

Slash the golden whip it snaps
Across the lover's sides
The earth trembles without remorse
Preparing for to die

Salty ocean waves and sprays
Come crashing to the shore
Bullies kick and kill young loves
Down on bar room floors

The gleaming knife cuts early
Through the midnight air
Cutting entrails in its path
Blood runs without care

Violence echoes through the land
And heart of every man
The knife it stabs existent wounds
Pus runs through matted hair

Excrement filters through the brain
Hatred bends the spine
Filth covers the body pores
To be cleansed by dying time

Words and Music by LOU REED

(As song is ended, the lights come up slowly on SHADOW and the PREACHER on different sides of the stage. They are both coming out of their respective spells, the rhythms of their language and action shifting from one side of the stage to the other. They are the only two onstage.)

SHADOW: Gimme a good bull! That's all I'm askin'! A good bull! All I need's a good ride! Just one good ride! That's all I'm askin'! Gimme the Twister or Buttermilk or the Monsoon! Any a' them! Gimme somethin' with some heart in him!

PREACHER: Now you kids be back before dusk and don't be bringin' back no slimy things. Empty your pockets out 'fore you come in the door. You hear? Stay away from the black folk. You cross the tracks and you'll get a whoopin' sure as I'm born. I seen you playin' with black Willie. I seen you. Now don't lie to me! Don't you lie or the Lord'll paddle yer blue jeans off.

SHADOW: Tucson. Couldn't make it in a day anyhow. Could hitchhike out to Omaha. Tuba city. The damn circuit. They don't make the circuit for a poorboy. Every cowpuncher come along thinks he's a star right off. Just off the range. Shoulda' stuck with stock cars. Get a damn Ford out there. Don't gotta' depend on no bull. Every Brahma's different. Stick to bulldoggin'. Never can tell. Not like a damn Ford. Just stomp it. 'At's it. 'Atta boy. Slipstream the mother.

PREACHER: The bobwhite says "Bob White." The whippoorwill says "Whip poor will." We could put a message in a White Lightning bottle and send it to a faraway place. Just toss it in the Gulf a' Mexico. No tellin' who'd find it. We could write a joke. Like "Who Killed Cock Robin."

(In another voice.)

You boys get on away from them skiffs. Get on, ya' hear! Go catch yerselves some catfish. Make yerself useful.

(Another voice.)

Let's play the jukebox down at Jango's place.

(Another voice.)

I don't like Jango. Last time he tried to whoop me fer stealin' sugar.

SHADOW: Least in football ya' got all that paddin'. All that cushion. More bones broke in a rodeo than ever was in football. Let me see the nurse. The head nurse. They got no right holdin' me here against my will. I gotta' earn me a livin'. I ain't gonna' go into traction neither. I don't care. I'll ride a damn Brahma with two legs broke and my collar bone flappin'. I don't give a damn. Lemme see the doctor. It's *my* leg, ain't it? Nobody else's. It's my neck.

PREACHER: Remember that Packard used to set out in front of Sukie's garage? That thing was so beautiful. I used to walk past there thinkin' about the shine on them fenders. I used to look at my teeth in that paint job and just grin and grin. Well, one day I stole it. That's right. I couldn't believe it. There it was just settin' there with the engine hummin' and the keys in it and everything. And I just hopped in the son of a bitch and took off. Drove and drove like a crazy man. Finally got it stuck in a bog. I just left it there. I just laughed and laughed and left it there.

SHADOW: They never tell ya' the worst. A man's got a right to know. It's my life, ain't it? Don't let 'em take my leg off no matter what. They'll have to shoot me first. They'll have to shoot me.

(Loud banging on the door. Outside SLIM is heard bellowing.)

SLIM'S VOICE: All right. Open up in there. What's going on?

(More loud banging. SHADOW and the PREACHER lie motionless.)

Open up, I tell ya'! It's me! Slim! What the hell's goin' on? Open up this door 'fore I bust it down!

(More banging as MARIA enters from the kitchen. She goes to the door and opens it slowly. SLIM enters. MARIA bolts the door behind him.)

SLIM: What's goin' on, Maria? Didn't ya' hear me out there?

MARIA: My son is dead.

SLIM: Dead? What do you mean?

MARIA: That beast kill my son.

SLIM: The beast? He was here? Now look, Maria, I been walkin' all over tarnation out there and I didn't see no sign a' no beast. Are you sure you're telling the truth about this whole thing?

MARIA: That beast come. My boy is dead.

SLIM: You know what I think? I think it's that damn swamp gypsy. I think she's at the root a' this beast thing. Where is she anyhow? Maria?

MARIA: My boy is dead.

SLIM: I know that. And I'm sorry. There ain't nothin' I can do about it now. We gotta' find that swamp girl and find out the truth about what's goin' on or we're all gonna' be dead. Now where is she?

MARIA: She gone.

SLIM: Well, where'd she go?

MARIA: She vanish.

SLIM: All right now, can the mumbo jumbo! I'm sick and tired a' all this fool magic stuff and visions flying around. Now where'd she go?

(GRIS GRIS *enters from the kitchen playing her fiddle gently. She saunters onto the stage.*)

GRIS GRIS: You lookin' fer me, cowboy?

MARIA: No! You go back. You hide.

GRIS GRIS: I'll hide when there's somethin' to fear, Maria. Right now I'm naked as a snake.

SLIM: Now you look here, girl. I don't know what yer game is, but you best come out with the truth or I'll be forced to take drastic measures.

GRIS GRIS: You gonna' stake me out in the sun and pour red ants down my ears?

MARIA: She knows nothing. She is Cajun girl. She is strange to you.

SLIM: She's strange all right. Strange enough to send me on a wild goose chase looking for a mountain full a' yellow mushrooms. Strange enough to put a spell on my partner here. Strange enough to conjure up some beast that don't exist. Now ain't that the truth? You been lying all along? Maria, is she the one who first told you about the beast?

MARIA: No.

SLIM: Well, who did then?

MARIA: We know. The lowlands know. There is a beast. There is something that comes in the night.

SLIM: Well, you're gonna' have to handle him alone then, 'cause me and Shadow is hightailin' it outa' here. Shadow! Shadow! Get up, boy!

(SLIM goes to SHADOW and shakes him. SHADOW jumps up as though wakened out of a sound sleep.)

SHADOW: I'm gonna' need some new tread on that left rear. Don't wanna' make no pit stops the first time around.

SLIM: Shadow! Listen to me! We been fooled! We been taken for a couple dumb ranch hands. There ain't no beast at all. You was right all along.

(SHADOW gets up and begins to move about the stage as though preparing for a stock-car race.)

MARIA: He very sick.

SHADOW: Just make sure the windows is busted out. I don't want to be stickin' my head through no glass. Where's my gloves? I need my gloves!

GRIS GRIS: Gloves coming up.

(GRIS GRIS goes to SHADOW and puts a pair of invisible gloves on his hands.)

SLIM: You stay away from him. You done enough damage already.

PREACHER: If you think I'm evil, evil is what I am. A poacher by trade. A preacher poacher. At night my skiff skims the surface of the bayou swamp. Slides noiseless down through lily pads. Bullfrogs jump out of my path.

(He sheds the skin of the PREACHER.)

SHADOW: I'll need my helmet too. Just in case. Don't wanna' get no whiplash.

GRIS GRIS: Helmet!

SLIM: Shadow!

PREACHER: We boys, we young ones ain't been schooled in the morals. A gator's a gator. Long scaly prehistoric, jagged-tooth fish beast. With a hide that brings money.

SHADOW: My dark glasses! My shades! My ankles need to be taped.

SLIM: What you done to him? What you done to my boy?

SHADOW: Check the crank case! Transmission! Four forward! On the floor! Radiator! Fan belt! Tachometer set! Rip off them mud flaps, we ain't gonna' be in no slush! This is asphalt country!

PREACHER: At night we go shinin'. Flashlights like little ember fires glazing along the surface. Catch the gleam of the gator's eyes. Like two big cigars burning in the night. A twenty-two short'll do the trick.

SLIM: You take that curse off him!

GRIS GRIS: He's not cursed. He's saved. Look at his eyes. He's in heaven driving flat out through the pearly gates!

SHADOW: Take the first bank at a hundred and twenty. Push the straightaway up to one eighty. Back it down! Down shift! Keep it outa' fourth! Slipstream the Corvettes! Watch out for the red Pontiac! Number seven! Number seven! Break him out of the chute! Now!

GRIS GRIS: Now! Go to it, cowboy!

(SHADOW *sits down on the floor and pretends he's behind the wheel of a stock car. He goes through the sounds and actions of shifting and driving in a full-tilt race to the death.*)

SLIM: Maria! Would you stop that mumbling! We gotta' get some order in this house! Maria!

PREACHER: Some boys like to rope and wrestle 'em. But not us. We like to be cruel. Shoot 'em right between the eyes. They die right on the soot and turn over on their backsides, and float right to the surface.

SLIM: All right! Cut out all this nonsense or I'm gonna' start whippin' some ass!

PREACHER: Then you drag 'em up on shore. Jamie Lee has his hatchet out and turns the gator over. He chops straight down into the neck. The legs jump out and twitch like a giant frog.

SLIM: Girl, you undo your black spell or I'm gonna' plug ya' right here and now. This has gone far enough. You got everybody off the deep end here.

GRIS GRIS: You gonna' plug me, gunman? You gonna' shoot me down with your six-gun? You gonna' make me believe you got power in your hands? You got no power. Look around ya'. Look where the power lies. You can't even pull a nickel outa' yer blue jeans, let alone a pistol.

SLIM: Now don't push me, gal. I'm about at the end of my tether.

GRIS GRIS: Oh, yeah, you a mean hombre. I can tell by your outfit.

MARIA: The saints bleed! And all around we are blind! We are blind to the sun! Blind to the moon and stars!

PREACHER: Then me, I use my knife. Got a clean line from the throat all the way down to the tail. We flop him back over on his belly and peel away that skin like a new suit a' clothes. It comes off clean with a little tugging.

SLIM: You don't know what it takes, girl. One twitch of the mind. One little snap of the head and I can turn you into a prairie dog, a varmint, a critter low enough to blast into dust. It don't take nothin' but a moment! All I gotta' do is decide. And if I make that choice, you bein' a female ain't gonna' save your hide.

GRIS GRIS: Well, come on then! What's holdin' you back? You can see the worst is comin'. You can see the worst is here knockin' at the door. What do you got to lose?

SLIM: I'm warnin' you!

PREACHER: Sometimes we gotta' use the pliers to get a good grip. And then we roll the skin up into a little package for the buyers and stick it deep down in a gunny sack. Nothin' left in the mud but a pink naked corpse with the blood oozing down into the earth.

GRIS GRIS: Now fight that corpse, boy! You gotta' fight that corpse! There's some life left in him yet.

(The PREACHER begins to wrestle an imaginary alligator. He writhes and moans all over the stage.)

SLIM: I'm warnin' you! A killer ain't a pretty sight. I done it before and I'll do it again! I've seen 'em with prayers in their eyes. I've seen 'em with wife and kids cowering in the corner. I've seen 'em bold and ready to die. All kinds. And they was all the same. At that moment they was all the same. Just like you standin' there, arms open, ready for the bullet. It's just a simple thing. Just a simple little thing.

GRIS GRIS: Come on, cowboy man! Come on!

(She plays her fiddle and dances, daring him to kill her.)

SLIM: But I ain't the same. Something's changed. It used to be like makin' love in the highest form. I felt clean and free after it was done. I felt cleansed by the hands of Jesus himself. I felt a flashing burn go up my spine and down the inside of my legs. They fell. They all fell. Oh, the power in that moment! If I could only have that power again! That incredible power to kill and not be afraid. If I could only get it back!

GRIS GRIS: It's here! Here it is! Here I am!

SLIM: To slaughter a lamb ain't the same.

GRIS GRIS: How 'bout a bird? An eagle or a crow! I can be what you make me. I can turn into a fawn. A white buffalo. An antelope! A wolf! Make me what you want!

SLIM: It's gone! It's gone, I tell ya'!

(MARIA rises and crosses downstage, a bright yellow spot on her.)

MARIA: And a great portent appeared in heaven, a woman clothed with the sun, with the moon under her feet and on her head a crown of twelve stars; she was with child and she cried out in her pangs of birth, in anguish for delivery.

SLIM: Everything's broken like glass. The time's gone. The past. The blood's gone from my hands. I'm frozen like a rock. Ancient. Nothing moves. I don't feel a thing.

(GRIS GRIS wails on her fiddle. SHADOW, the PREACHER and MARIA keep up their rituals. SLIM staggers around like a madman trying to find himself.)

I move outside myself. It must have been another time. That's it! Another time! This is wrong! I'm not here at all. It was honky tonks and bathtub gin! Railroad men and mule skinners! That was it! This is all wrong! I'm out of my depth. The hands reach for something else now! There's a different craving! A new hunger! I'm starving to death and fat on buffalo meat! What is it a man cries for when nothing fits? No sense to the music? A new kind of music! A new kind of dance!

MARIA: And another portent appeared in heaven; behold a great red dragon with seven heads and ten horns and seven diadems upon his head. His tail swept down a third of the stars of heaven and cast them to the earth. And the dragon stood before the woman who was about to bear a child, that he might devour her child when she brought it forth; she brought forth a male child, one who was to rule all the nations with a rod of iron, but her child was caught up to God and to His throne and the woman fled into the wilderness where she has a place prepared by God.

PREACHER: Ya' just tickle his belly. It's the simplest thing. He turns into a puppy dog before your very eyes.

(Suddenly the door crashes in and the beast enters. He is just as MARIA described. Two heads like a pig, he snorts and spits, lights come from his eyes. His skin is covered with slimy green moss. All the characters continue their rituals, oblivious of the beast's presence. The beast crosses downstage center and faces the audience. The action happens around him. Somehow the beast seems helpless and alone in the situation. He exits.)

SLIM: Something's taking me over! A scavenger! A coyote dog!

(GRIS GRIS starts hooting like an owl and playing her fiddle. She begins to take on the fluttering movements of the owl. The PREACHER becomes the alligator. He slithers across the floor and attacks SHADOW, chomping down on him. SHADOW becomes a bull, snorting and pawing at the ground, trying to gore the alligator with his horns. MARIA becomes a wildcat, screaming and prowling around the stage. They each have their own animal rhythms and play them out against each other. SLIM transforms into a coyote, howling at the moon. This happens slowly as he says his monologue. "Jilala" is heard softly in the background. It rises slowly through the scene and becomes deafening by the end of the play.)

You can't take me now! I ain't had my day! I mean I did! I did! But it ain't over! This can't be what I'm left with! Not now! I'll practice up! Just wait! Wait and see! I'll get it back! I'll get back the touch! I got some magic left! I'll take a little vacation! How's that sound? Go up in the hills and practice. Yeah. I could do that. No harm in a little rest. Won't take no jobs for a month. Maybe a year. Sure. A nice long rest. Get my nerves back.

(He howls.)

Just give me a chance! I got both my feet on the ground. I ain't a man a' God! I love the earth! I love the land! This is me talking! Just listen for a little bit longer. Just a little bit. Don't take me without a word. I

know you suffer. I can see your silhouette. I feel your pain. You don't
have to prove it. I'm your man. It's no mistake. But let me say my
piece. Just let me speak it out.

(He howls again.)

That's your voice. I've heard it in the West. I've heard it yapping
around my campfires. But you never listened to me! You never did!
Don't you think it's fair?

*(SLIM drops to his knees and begins to take on the soul of the coyote as he talks.
He starts to move around the stage on all fours.)*

I'm beyond prayers now! Can't you see that? I never chose my moves.
Something moved in me like a silent hand. Every action, every
thought. You can take me now! It's all right. Now you can have me!
Come on, you old desert dog! Come on! I howl!

(He howls.)

I yap!

(He yaps.)

I chew on the carcass of a skunk. I trot across highways where no cars
come for days. I devour my young. I am the beast. The beast is me.
I'm feeling your blood now. It's thinner. Your heart beats faster. You
look to the right and the left with quick jerks. Afraid to be eaten yourself. Small animals crawl through your skin. You're infected with
desert life. Your loneliness is beyond what humans know. You've
given yourself to the ground and I give myself to you. It's only fair. It's
only fair.

*(SLIM howls and turns into the coyote. The whole stage is animated with the an-
imal movements and sounds of the characters. The music rises to its highest
pitch, then everything goes to silence.)*

BLACKOUT

Killer's Head

A MONOLOGUE

Killer's Head was first performed at the American Place Theatre, New York, in 1975. It was directed by Nancy Meckler, with Richard Gere as Mazon.

SCENE

Bare stage. Center on slightly raised platform, MAZON *sits in electric chair facing audience. Hands, arms, legs, feet, chest, neck bound with bands of steel to the silver chair. He is barefoot, blindfolded, wears T-shirt and jeans, yellow spot on chair, rest of stage black. Lights rise slow on* MAZON *(speaks in clipped, southwestern rodeo accent).*

MAZON: Oh yeah, today's the day I buy the pickup. I've decided. Six-cylinder, three-quarter-ton bed, heavy-duty rear springs, three-speed column. Should pull the horses all right. 'Course with the three-fifty V-8 you'd get more power. Don't really need it though. Won't be goin' off the road much. Just up to Santa Rosa and back. Maybe sixty miles round trip. Just to take that mare up and get her bred. Jesus! You should see that stud, boy! Does the quarter mile in twenty-one seconds dead. Like to rip the silks right off that jockey. Said they never seen an Appaloosa like him. Should throw a blanket foal, that's for sure. Got a leopard on both sides of the pedigree. Could make a cuttin' horse too, what with that mare. She's almost one-third quarter horse herself. She can move, boy. I've seen her doubled in half over a cow. Anyway, that six-cylinder should do it. Save us some on gas. Don't plan on doin' much rodeo. That old Tommy Ferguson's got it wrapped up. Might try some halter shows up north. We got those yearling fillies we could show. They got class, boy. That's the ticket, see. You take those quarter mares and you breed right back to Thoroughbreds, racing stock, and you got yourself an all-purpose-type horse. You got refinement when you outcross like that. You take Three Bars. If it weren't for that damn stud horse the whole quarter horse breed would look like Angus steers by now. That's the truth. Refinement, that's what he brought to the breed. Look at the heads he threw. Anyway, the Appaloosa isn't hurtin' from Thoroughbred blood neither. What's that Indian Hemp stud they got now? Forget his name. Good blood. And that Sheljet horse outa' Colorado. Shit man, you never seen a pedigree like that. Jet Deck on the top side. Lady Bug Moon on the bottom. Bright red sorrel horse. Sure to throw colored foals. You take any Appaloosa mare to him and I guarantee you'd get a colored foal. Speed too. He's a flyin' machine. 'Course they all got speed outa' Colorado. It's that mountain air. Must be. Grass ain't bad either. Out here they got that all-purpose pasture. Ain't worth a damn. Too much blue alfalfa. Blows 'em up. Blow a horse inside out with that stuff. Gets inside there and ferments. I've seen it. Swells 'em up like a Goodyear blimp. That Colorado grass is the real stuff. Rocky Mountain. No wonder they got so many triple-A horses comin' outa' there. Out here they feed pellets and then wonder how come a horse don't put the flesh on. Can't beef a racin' horse up like that. Needs grain and good pasture. I'd send the whole string out there for the summer if I could afford it. I would. 'Course out here you got the money. You got the mares too. Never seen such mares. You take that T-Dok mare. I was ridin' her flat out the other day and I swear to God she wasn't even blowin' at the finish. Musta' done six furlongs at full tilt, and she had everything left. Took all I had to haul her in. We had that gelding out there with her and she left him standin'. Had six lengths on him. He's a tough horse too. Barrel racer. 'Course the shoer said he's got a slight touch a' ring bone. That shouldn't hurt him though if we keep him workin'. I noticed he was a little turned in on his front feet but I took him to be over-muscled. Shoer says he can compensate by filing down the outside horn. You know, that gelding was out to pasture for four months straight, never had a soul on his back, and I took him straight in and cut five calves with him. Right off the dime like that. Five calves. That's what I call cow sense. Too bad he ain't registered. We could make some money off that pony. Put him in the Snaffle Bit Futurity and clean up. I put a snaffle on him the other day and it made all the difference. That curb was puttin' too much pressure on his jaw. You could tell the way he was tossin' his head all the time. Skeeter told me to try a martingale on him but I could tell that wasn't it. It was that damn bit. Too much pressure. Soon's I put that snaffle in his mouth he turned as soft as butter. Just neck reinin' to beat all hell. Dandy horse.

(He stops suddenly and just sits silently, no movement, lasting for one full minute, then he begins again.)

MAZON: Dude says he can give me a deal on that blue truck. Almost four hundred off the list price. Smells good inside that thing. Sweet. Steers like a damn cat. Got that big eight-foot bed. No extras. Got those skinny bicycle tires on it. Comes stock like that. Put some big mags on there and she'll be tough. Should pull that two-horse trailer. Furthest I'd take it is down to L.A. Highway Five all the way. Right down through the center. Over the Grapevine. Bakersfield. Should pull that okay. That V-8 would do it better but I can't afford the gas. Damn thing only gets about twelve to the gallon. Ain't worth it in the long run. Only be makin' that long haul once a season. Just to hit that fair circuit. 'Couple a' auctions maybe. It's a full eight hours no matter how ya' cut it. Specially with a double rig. Full day's ride.

(He stops suddenly again and sits silently. The lights begin to dim very slowly and take a full minute to come to black. Just as the lights reach black the chair ignites with an electric charge that lights up MAZON's *entire body. He makes no sound. The electric charge is very short, just long enough to take in the illuminated body, then back to black.)*

CURTAIN

Grateful acknowledgement is made to the following for permission to reprint previously published material:

Screen Gems-EMI Music Ltd: excerpt from "Wrap Your Troubles in Dreams" words and music by Lou Reed. Copyright © 1966 by Oakfield Avenue Music Ltd/Screen Gems–EMI Music Inc., USA. Reproduced by permission of Screen Gems–EMI Music Ltd, London WC2H 0EA.

Lowery Music Co., Inc.: "Ahab the Arab" by Ray Stevens, copyright © 1962 by Lowery Music Co., Inc. Reprinted by permission of Lowery Music Co., Inc.

Myers Music and Capano Music: Excerpt from "Rock Around the Clock" by Max Freedman and Jimmy De Knight, copyright renewed 1982 by Myers Music and Capano Music. All rights reserved. Reprinted by permission of Myers Music and Capano Music.

Peermusic: Excerpts from "T. B. Blues" by Jimmie Rodgers and Raymond Hall, copyright © 1931 by Peer International Corporation USA, copyright renewed. International copyright secured. Reprinted by permission of Peermusic (UK) Ltd, 8–14 Verulam Street, London WC1.

Methuen World Classics *and*
Methuen Contemporary Dramatists

Aeschylus (two volumes)
Jean Anouilh
John Arden (two volumes)
Arden & D'Arcy
Aristophanes (two volumes)
Aristophanes & Menander
Peter Barnes (three volumes)
Brendan Behan
Aphra Behn
Edward Bond (four volumes)
Bertolt Brecht
(five volumes)
Howard Brenton
(two volumes)
Büchner
Bulgakov
Calderón
Jim Cartwright
Anton Chekhov
Caryl Churchill
(two volumes)
Noël Coward (five volumes)
Sarah Daniels (two volumes)
Eduardo De Filippo
David Edgar (three volumes)
Euripides (three volumes)
Dario Fo (two volumes)
Michael Frayn (two volumes)
Max Frisch
Gorky
Harley Granville Barker
(two volumes)
Henrik Ibsen (six volumes)
Terry Johnson

Lorca (three volumes)
David Mamet (three volumes)
Marivaux
Mustapha Matura
David Mercer (two volumes)
Arthur Miller
(five volumes)
Anthony Minghella
Molière
Tom Murphy
(three volumes)
Musset
Peter Nichols (two volumes)
Clifford Odets
Joe Orton
Louise Page
A. W. Pinero
Luigi Pirandello
Stephen Poliakoff
(two volumes)
Terence Rattigan
Willy Russell
Ntozake Shange
Sam Shepard (two volumes)
Sophocles (two volumes)
Wole Soyinka
David Storey (two volumes)
August Strindberg
(three volumes)
J. M. Synge
Sue Townsend
Ramón del Valle-Inclán
Frank Wedekind
Oscar Wilde

Methuen Modern Plays

include work by

Jean Anouilh	John McGrath
John Arden	David Mamet
Margaretta D'Arcy	Patrick Marber
Peter Barnes	Arthur Miller
Sebastian Barry	Mtwa, Ngema & Simon
Brendan Behan	Tom Murphy
Edward Bond	Phyllis Nagy
Bertolt Brecht	Peter Nichols
Howard Brenton	Joseph O'Connor
Simon Burke	Joe Orton
Jim Cartwright	Louise Page
Caryl Churchill	Joe Penhall
Noël Coward	Luigi Pirandello
Sarah Daniels	Stephen Poliakoff
Nick Dear	Franca Rame
Shelagh Delaney	Philip Ridley
David Edgar	Reginald Rose
Dario Fo	David Rudkin
Michael Frayn	Willy Russell
John Godber	Jean-Paul Sartre
Paul Godfrey	Sam Shepard
John Guare	Wole Soyinka
Peter Handke	C. P. Taylor
Jonathan Harvey	Theatre de Complicite
Iain Heggie	Theatre Workshop
Declan Hughes	Sue Townsend
Terry Johnson	Judy Upton
Barrie Keeffe	Timberlake Wertenbaker
Stephen Lowe	Victoria Wood
Doug Lucie	

For a Complete Catalogue of Methuen Drama titles
write to:

Methuen Drama
Michelin House
81 Fulham Road
London SW3 6RB